Cambridge English

SECOND EDITION

Complete
First

Student's Book **with** answers

Guy Brook-Hart

CAMBRIDGE
UNIVERSITY PRESS

University Printing House, Cambridge CB2 8BS, United Kingdom

One Liberty Plaza, 20th Floor, New York, NY 10006, USA

477 Williamstown Road, Port Melbourne, VIC 3207, Australia

4843/24, 2nd Floor, Ansari Road, Daryaganj, Delhi – 110002, India

79 Anson Road, #06–04/06, Singapore 079906

Cambridge University Press is part of the University of Cambridge.

It furthers the University's mission by disseminating knowledge in the pursuit of education, learning and research at the highest international levels of excellence.

www.cambridge.org
Information on this title: www.cambridge.org/9781107656178

First published 2008
20 19 18 17 16 15 14 13 12

Printed in Spain by GraphyCems

A catalogue record for this publication is available from the British Library

ISBN 978-1-107-63390-2 Student's Book without answers with CD-ROM
ISBN 978-1-107-65617-8 Student's Book with answers with CD-ROM
ISBN 978-1-107-64394-9 Teacher's Book with Teacher's Resources CD-ROM
ISBN 978-1-107-65220-0 Workbook without answers with Audio CD
ISBN 978-1-107-66339-8 Workbook with answers with Audio CD
ISBN 978-1-107-68734-9 Class Audio CDs (2)
ISBN 978-1-107-66666-5 Presentation Plus
ISBN 978-1-107-65186-9 Student's Pack (Student's Book without answers with CD-ROM, Workbook without answers with Audio CD)
ISBN 978-1-107-69835-2 Student's Book Pack (Student's Book with answers with CD-ROM with Class Audio CDs (2)

Contents

Unit title	Reading and Use of English	Writing	Listening
1 A family affair	Part 6: 'Surviving teenagers' Part 2: 'Doing the chores'	Part 1 An essay: Teenagers and young people should share housework equally with their parents. Do you agree? Expressing opinions Using *although, however, on the other hand* and *whereas*	Part 1: Young people talking about their families and activities
2 Leisure and pleasure	Part 5: 'My first bike' Part 4: Key word transformation	Part 2 An article: A leisure-time activity you really enjoy Writing compound and complex sentences	Part 2: A talk from a games developer
Vocabulary and grammar reviews Units 1 and 2			
3 Happy holidays?	Part 3: 'A bus journey' Part 7: 'My nightmare holiday!'	Part 2 A report: A one-day excursion	Part 3: Five young people talking about their holidays
4 Food, glorious food	Part 6: 'Learning about food' Part 1: 'Moso Moso' – a restaurant review	Part 2 A review: A local restaurant, café or snack bar	Part 4: A radio interview with the owner of a popular café
Vocabulary and grammar reviews Units 3 and 4			
5 Study time	Part 7: 'At school abroad' Part 3: 'Culture shock for international students'	Part 1 An essay: All young people who have the opportunity should study in a foreign school or college for a year. Do you agree? Writing opening paragraphs Using linking words and phrases	Part 1: People talking about studying and school
6 My first job	Part 5: 'Lucy's first job' Part 2: 'A new summer programme'	Part 2 A letter or email: Describe the jobs students do in your country Commonly misspelled words	Part 3: Five people talking about their first job
Vocabulary and grammar reviews Units 5 and 6			
7 High adventure	Part 6: 'Are you ready for an adventure race?' Part 4: Key word transformation	Part 2 An article: A great way to keep fit	Part 2: A talk about adventure racing Part 4: A radio interview with a paraglider
8 Dream of the stars	Part 7: 'Five young actors' Part 1: 'YouTube millionaire celebrities'	Part 1 An essay: There are both advantages and disadvantages to a career as a musician or an actor. Writing a balanced essay	Part 2: A talk about a television quiz show
Vocabulary and grammar reviews Units 7 and 8			
9 Secrets of the mind	Part 5: 'The secrets of happiness' Part 4: Key word transformation	Part 2 A report: The benefits of improving classrooms and students' social activities Making suggestions and recommendations	Part 1: People talking about different aspects of psychology
10 Spend, spend, spend?	Part 2: 'Shopping online versus shopping locally' Part 5: 'My greatest influence'	Part 2 A review: A place where people have a good time Words/Phrases to build up more complex sentences	Part 4: A student interview about a new shopping centre
Vocabulary and grammar reviews Units 9 and 10			
11 Medical matters	Part 6: 'What's it like to study medicine?' Part 3: 'Is there a doctor on board?'	Part 1 An essay: Modern lifestyles can seriously endanger our health. Do you agree? Writing concluding paragraphs An essay: Young people generally don't pay enough attention to their health and fitness. Do you agree?	Part 3: Five people talking about visits to the doctor
12 Animal kingdom	Part 1: 'My sister's circus' Part 7: 'Surviving an animal attack'	Part 2 A letter or email: Advice to a visitor to your country Giving advice	Part 1: People talking about animals in different situations
Vocabulary and grammar reviews Units 11 and 12			
13 House space	Part 5: 'My new home in Venice, 1733' Part 2: 'Living on a houseboat'	Part 2 An article: My ideal home	Part 2: A talk about a haunted house
14 Fiesta!	Part 6: 'The world's highest festival?' Part 3: 'My local festival'	Part 1 An essay: Is it better to watch films at the cinema or at home? *it, this, that* and *they* for reference	Part 4: A radio interview with a street performer
Vocabulary and grammar reviews Units 13 and 14			

Speaking	Pronunciation	Vocabulary	Grammar
Part 1: Talking about yourself, your home and your family Giving extended answers	Word stress (1): Stress in words with two or more syllables	Phrasal verbs: *get on with*, *do up*, etc. Collocations with *make* and *do*	Present perfect simple and continuous
Part 2: Comparing photos of free-time activities Using discourse markers to structure the answer	Sentence stress (1): Stress on words carrying the most meaning	Phrasal verbs and expressions: *take up*, *sum up*, etc.	Making comparisons Adjectives with *-ed* and *-ing*
Part 3: Discussing the benefits of different kinds of trip Phrases to involve partners in discussion Strategies for dealing with the second section of Part 3	Intonation (1): Indicating when you have/haven't finished speaking	*travel*, *journey*, *trip* and *way* Adjective suffixes	Past simple, past continuous and *used to* *at*, *in* or *on* in time phrases Past perfect simple and continuous
Part 4: Discussing diet, food and health Supporting opinions with reasons and examples	Grouping words and pausing (1)	*food*, *dish* and *meal* Adjectives to describe restaurants	*so* and *such* *too* and *enough*
Part 1: Talking about your studies Giving reasons, offering several possible ideas	Word stress (2): Shifting word stress	Phrasal verbs: *get over*, *live up to*, etc. *find out*, *get to know*, *know*, *learn*, *teach* and *study*; *attend*, *join*, *take part* and *assist* Forming nouns from verbs	Zero, first and second conditionals
Part 2: Comparing photos of different kinds of work Describing similarities and differences when comparing	Sentence stress (2): Contrastive sentence stress	*work/job*; *possibility/occasion/opportunity*; *fun/funny* Collocations with *work* and *job*	Countable and uncountable nouns Articles
Part 3: Discussing ways of encouraging people to do more sport Suggesting ideas, asking opinion, agreeing and disagreeing	Intonation (2): Showing attitude	Verb collocations with sporting activities *look*, *see*, *watch*, *listen* and *hear*	Infinitive and verb + *-ing*
Part 4: Discussing different aspects of media and celebrity Giving balanced, general answers Expressing agreement/disagreement	Grouping words and pausing (2)	Verb collocations with *ambition*, *career*, *experience* and *job* *play*, *performance* and *acting*; *audience*, *(the) public* and *spectators*; *scene* and *stage*	*at*, *in* and *on* in phrases expressing location Reported speech
Part 2: Comparing photos of different kinds of feeling and emotion Speculating about photos using *look*, *seem* and *appear*	Sentence stress (3): Using sentence stress for emphasis	*achieve*, *carry out* and *devote* *stay*, *spend* and *pass*; *make*, *cause* and *have*	Modal verbs to express certainty and possibility
Part 1: Talking about how you spend your money Strategies for answering Part 1 questions	Linking (1): Linking to increase fluency	*arrive*, *get* and *reach* Phrasal verbs: *come up with*, *pull in*, etc.	*as* and *like* Modals expressing ability
Part 2: Comparing photos of situations related to health Strategies for dealing with difficulties: finding the right word	Intonation (3): Showing certainty/uncertainty	Idiomatic expressions: *taken aback*, etc. Health vocabulary: *illness*, *infection*, etc.	Relative pronouns and relative clauses
Parts 3 and 4: Discussing topics related to animals Commenting on the question Expressing other people's opinions Expressing agreement/disagreement	Word stress (3): Strong and weak forms	*avoid*, *prevent* and *protect*; *check*, *control*, *keep an eye on* and *supervise* Negative prefixes	Third conditional and mixed conditionals *wish*, *if only* and *hope*
Part 2: Comparing photos of people in different locations	Linking (2): Linking with consonant sounds	*space*, *place*, *room*, *area*, *location* and *square*	Causative *have* and *get* Expressing obligation and permission
Parts 3 and 4: Discussing different topics related to festivals and celebrations	Improving fluency	Vocabulary for festivals: *celebrate*, *commemorate*, etc. Suffixes to form personal nouns	The passive

Introduction

Who this book is for

Complete First Second Edition is a stimulating and thorough preparation course for students wishing to take the revised **Cambridge English: First** exam from 2015. It teaches you the reading, writing, listening and speaking skills which are necessary for the exam, how to approach each exam task, as well as essential grammar and vocabulary. The book also teaches you the language knowledge and develops the skills you need to reach an upper-intermediate B2 level in the Common European Framework of Reference. *Complete First Second Edition* is official Cambridge English preparation material for the exam.

What the book contains

In the **Student's Book** there are:

- 14 units for classroom study. Each unit contains:
  - at least one part of each of the Writing, Speaking and Listening papers and two parts of the Reading and Use of English Paper in the Cambridge English: First exam. The units provide language input, skills practice and exam technique to help you to deal successfully with each of the tasks in the exam.
  - essential information and advice on what each part of the exam involves and the best way to approach each task.
  - a wide range of enjoyable and stimulating speaking activities designed to increase your fluency and your ability to express yourself.
  - detailed advice and practice of strategies to perfect your performance in the Speaking paper.
  - a pronunciation section working on stress, intonation, pausing, linking and fluency.
  - a step-by-step approach to doing Cambridge English: First writing tasks.
  - grammar activities and exercises with the grammar you need to know for the exam. When you are doing grammar exercises you will sometimes see this symbol: ⊙. These are exercises which are based on research from the Cambridge English Corpus and they deal with areas which cause problems for many candidates in the exam.

- vocabulary input needed for success at Cambridge English: First based on the English Vocabulary Profile (EVP) at B2 level. When you see this symbol: **EP**, the exercise is based on EVP research. When you see this symbol ⊙ next to a vocabulary exercise, the exercise is based on research from the Cambridge English Corpus and focuses on words which candidates often confuse or use wrongly in the exam.

- 14 Vocabulary and Grammar reviews. These contain exercises which revise the grammar and vocabulary that you have studied during the unit.

- A **Language reference section** which clearly explains all the main areas of language, including grammar, word formation, spelling and punctuation, which you need to know for the Cambridge English: First exam.

- **Writing and Speaking reference sections**. These explain the possible tasks you may have to do in the Speaking and Writing papers, and they give you examples, language and advice on how best to approach them.

- A **CD-ROM** provides extra practice, with all activities linked to the topics in the Student's Book.

Also available are:

- **two audio CDs** containing listening material for the 14 units. The listening material is indicated by different-coloured icons in the Student's Book as follows: ▶02. ▷02.

- a **Workbook** to accompany the Student's Book, with four pages of exercises for each unit. The Workbook is also accompanied by an **audio CD**.

Cambridge English: First content and overview

Part / timing	Content	Test focus
Reading and Use of English 1 hour 15 minutes	**Part 1** A modified cloze text containing eight gaps and followed by eight multiple-choice items **Part 2** A modified open cloze text containing eight gaps **Part 3** A text containing eight gaps. Each gap corresponds to a word. The stems of the missing words are given beside the text and must be changed to form the missing word. **Part 4** Six separate questions, each with a lead-in sentence and a gapped second sentence to be completed in two to five words, one of which is given as a 'key word' **Part 5** A text followed by six multiple-choice questions **Part 6** A text from which six sentences have been removed and placed in a jumbled order after the text. A seventh sentence, which does not need to be used, is also included. **Part 7** A text, or several short texts preceded by ten multiple-matching questions	Candidates are expected to demonstrate the ability to apply their knowledge of the language system by completing the first four tasks; candidates are also expected to show understanding of specific information, text organisation features, tone and text structure.
Writing 1 hour 20 minutes	**Part 1** One compulsory essay question presented through a rubric and short notes **Part 2** Candidates choose one task from a choice of three task types. The tasks are situationally based and presented through a rubric and possibly a short input text. The task types are: • an article • a letter or email • a review • a report	Candidates are expected to be able to write using different degrees of formailty and diffferent functions: advising, comparing, describing, explaining, expressing opinions, justifying, persuading, recommending and suggesting.
Listening Approximately 40 minutes	**Part 1** A series of eight short unrelated extracts from monologues or exchanges between interacting speakers. There is one three-option multiple-choice question per extract. **Part 2** A short talk or lecture on a topic, with a sentence-completion task which has ten items **Part 3** Five short related monologues, with five multiple-matching questions **Part 4** An interview or conversation, with seven multiple-choice questions	Candidates are expected to be able to show understanding of attitude, detail, function, genre, gist, main idea, opinion, place, purpose, situation, specific information, relationship, topic, agreement, etc.
Speaking 14 minutes	**Part 1** A conversation between the examiner (the 'interlocutor') and each candidate (spoken questions) **Part 2** An individual 'long turn' for each candidate, with a brief response from the second candidate (visual and written stimuli, with spoken instructions) **Part 3** A discussion question with five written prompts **Part 4** A discussion on topics related to Part 3 (spoken questions)	

Starting off

Work in pairs.

- What aspects of family life does each of the photos show?
- Which of these activities do you most enjoy doing with members of your family? Which do you prefer to do with friends? Why?
- What other activities do you enjoy doing with members of your family? Why?
- How important is it for families to spend time together? Why?

Listening | Part 1

Exam information

In Listening Part 1, you:

- listen to people talking in eight different situations which may be either a conversation between two or more people, or just one person speaking;
- answer one question for each situation by choosing A, B or C;
- hear each piece twice.

This part tests your ability to understand a variety of things, including the general idea being expressed, a detail, a reason or a purpose.

1 Work in pairs. You will hear people talking in eight different situations. Before you listen, read questions 1–8 and underline the main idea in each. An example has been done for you.

1 You hear part of a conversation with a boy called Patrick. He thinks his <u>mother helps</u> him <u>because</u>
A she enjoys it.
B she worries about him.
C she has plenty of time.

2 You hear a girl called Tracey talking to a friend. What is her family doing to the house at the moment?
A extending it
B painting it
C cleaning it

3 You hear a girl called Vicky taking part in a class discussion. How often does she do sporting activities with her father?
A more often than before
B the same as before
C less often than before

4 You hear a boy called Kostas talking about family celebrations. How does he feel about them?
A bored
B embarrassed
C amused

5 You hear a boy called Rajiv talking to his sister on the phone. He is annoyed with her because
   A she has taken something without permission.
   B she has gone out without telling him.
   C she has lost something he needs.

6 You hear a boy called Marco talking to a friend. He is tired because he has done too much
   A studying.
   B exercise.
   C travelling.

7 You hear a girl called Samin leaving a telephone message for her mother. She is phoning to
   A explain something.
   B complain about something.
   C ask permission for something.

8 You hear an interview with a young musician called Pau. Why does he say he chose to play the trumpet?
   A It was the only instrument available.
   B It was his favourite instrument.
   C It was a family tradition.

2 ▶02 Listen and choose the best answer (A, B or C).

3 Work in pairs. Correct the mistakes in questions 1–6 on the tablet.

1 How much you help around the house?
  How much do you help around the house?
2 How often you all doing things together as a family?
3 You ever do sports with other people in your family?
4 Are you enjoy family celebrations?
5 How other members of the family annoy you?
6 You have any family traditions?

4 Now take turns to ask and answer questions 1–6 in Exercise 3.

Vocabulary
Phrasal verbs

1 **EP** Match these phrasal verbs from Listening Part 1 with their definitions.

1 get on with	a collect (or go and get) someone or something
2 do up	b continue
3 clear up	c continue doing something, especially work
4 go on	d make a place tidy by removing things from it or putting them where they should be
5 wear out	e make someone extremely tired
6 pick up	f repair or decorate a building so that it looks attractive

2 Complete these sentences by writing a phrasal verb from Exercise 1 in the correct form in each of the gaps.

1 I need to .get on with. my homework project, otherwise I won't finish it for tomorrow.
2 Mati had a little sleep because she felt .... after spending all morning .... the mess in her room.

3 I got bored with the film because it .... for too long.
4 We'll need to .... some more pots of paint if we're going to .... your room this weekend.

Reading and Use of English | Part 6

1 **EP** Work in pairs. You are going to read an article giving advice to parents. Before you read, write these adjectives in the most appropriate column below.

aggressive anxious bad-tempered concerned critical enthusiastic hard-working impatient impolite mature organised reasonable responsible self-confident sensitive strict understanding unreliable

usually positive	usually negative	could be either
	aggressive	

2 Add one of these prefixes *dis-*, *un-*, *im-*, *ir-*, *in-* to each of these words to make opposites.

critical uncritical concerned enthusiastic mature organised reasonable responsible sensitive

➡ page 181 Language reference: Word formation – adding prefixes

3 Work in pairs. Which of the adjectives in Exercise 2 describe typical attitudes of parents to teenagers? Why? Which describe typical attitudes of teenagers to parents? Why?

4 Work in groups.

- Make a list of things that parents sometimes say about their teenage children.
  He's so bad-tempered! He gets angry whenever I ask him to tidy his room!
  She's very hard-working. She spends hours studying in her room.
- What do you think parents can do to live happily with their teenage children?
  Listen to what their children say.

5 Read the article carefully, ignoring the gaps, and make a note of the main idea of each paragraph. An example has been done for you.

SURVIVING TEENAGERS

It might be difficult to accept, but a new approach to living happily with teenagers is for parents to look at their own behaviour.

"The key to getting teenagers to respect you is to respect them first," says Penny Palmano, who has written a best-selling book on teenagers. "You can't continue to treat them the same way that you have been treating them for the previous 12 years; they have opinions that count. **1** ☐ You'd be very upset. You'd never say that to an adult, because it shows a total lack of respect."

treat teenagers differently from before

Palmano, who has a daughter aged 19 and a 16-year-old stepdaughter, has even allowed the children to hold several teenage parties at her home. They passed without problems. "I've found that if you have brought them up to do the right thing, and then trust them to do it, usually they'll behave well," she says. "I make them sandwiches and leave them alone. But I make it clear that they have to clear up any mess. **2** ☐ "

She agrees that teenagers can be irritating: enjoying a world that is free of responsibility, yet desperate for independence. She doesn't think, however, that they are trying to annoy you. Until recently, scientists assumed that the brain finished growing at about the age of 13 and that teenage problems were a result of rising hormones and a desire for independence. **3** ☐

"This would explain why <u>many teenagers can't make good decisions, control their emotions, prioritise or concentrate on several different things at the same time.</u> **4** [ ] It means that they do not intentionally do the wrong thing just to annoy their parents," says Palmano.

The key to happiness for all, Palmano believes, is calm negotiation and compromise. If you want your teenagers to be home by 11 pm, explain why, but listen to their counter-arguments. If it's a Saturday, <u>you might consider agreeing to midnight</u> (rather than 1 am, which is what they had in mind). **5** [ ] <u>Instead, ask if they've had a problem with public transport and let it pass;</u> they've almost managed what you asked. She urges a bit of perspective about other things, too. "There have been times when my daughter's room has not been as tidy as I expected, but as she said once, 'I'm a teenager – what do you expect? I'm not turning into a criminal, it's just clothes on the floor.'"

"It's vital to choose your battles carefully: don't criticise teenagers for having an untidy room, then suddenly <u>criticise them for other things.</u> **6** [ ] One minute, it's about an untidy room and the next, you're saying, 'And another thing …' and <u>criticising them for everything.</u>"

Adapted from *The Daily Telegraph*

6 Six sentences have been removed from the article. Choose the correct sentence from A–G which fits each gap (1–6). There is one extra sentence which you do not need. Use the <u>underlined</u> words and phrases in the sentences and in the text to help you.

A <u>But it turns out that the region of the brain</u> that controls common sense and emotions <u>is not fully mature until the early twenties</u>.

B <u>If they are up to 20 minutes late, don't react angrily</u>.

C <u>For example, they may find it difficult to make the right decision</u> between watching television, ringing a friend, or finishing their homework.

D <u>Parents often complain that teenagers</u> can be charming to people outside the home but <u>irritating</u> to their family.

E I've never had a problem; in fact, <u>the kitchen was sometimes cleaner than I'd left it</u>.

F <u>On these occasions</u>, parents tend to mention <u>all the other things</u> that they may or may not have done wrong.

G Imagine if you'd spent two hours getting ready to go out for the evening and someone said, '<u>You're not going out looking like that, are you</u>?'

7 Work in groups of four. Two students should take the role of parents and two students should take the role of teenagers.

- Work with the student who has the same role as you. Read your role and prepare what you are going to say.
- When you are ready, change partners and have your conversations.

> **Parents**
> It is Saturday night and your teenage son/daughter has gone out with friends. You are annoyed because
> - you asked them to be back by midnight and they came home half an hour late
> - you phoned their mobile but they did not answer
> - this has already happened once before this month.
>
> Have a conversation with your teenage son/daughter. Find out what happened and decide how to avoid this situation in the future.

> **Teenage son/daughter**
> It is Saturday night. You went out with your friends, but you promised your parent(s) you would be back by midnight. However, you got home half an hour late.
>
> Have a conversation with your parents. Explain what happened and discuss how to avoid this situation in the future.

Grammar
Present perfect simple and continuous

1 Look at each of the pairs of sentences in *italics* and answer the questions that follow.

1   a   *Penny Palmano has written a best-selling book on teenagers.*
    b   *She's been writing books for more than 20 years.*

   Which sentence (a or b) talks about ...
   1   the result of an activity?
   2   the length of an activity?

2   a   *I've been learning how to do things like carpentry and so on.*
    b   *I've phoned her more than six times, but she never answers the phone.*

   Which sentence (a or b) talks about ...
   1   how many times something has been repeated?
   2   changes or developments which are not finished?

3   a   *I've been helping my mum while her assistant is on holiday.*
    b   *We've lived in this house since I was a small child.*

   Which sentence (a or b) talks about something which is ...
   1   temporary?
   2   permanent?

→ page 178 Language reference: Verb tenses – present perfect simple and continuous

2 Complete these sentences by writing the verbs in brackets in the correct form (present perfect simple or continuous) in the gaps.

1   I .....'ve been visiting..... (*visit*) friends, so I haven't spoken to my parents yet today.
2   I .... (*ask*) him to tidy his room several times.
3   I .... (*clean*) the kitchen, so what would you like me to do next?
4   My neighbour .... (*play*) the violin for the last three hours and it's driving me mad!
5   Congratulations! You .... (*pass*) the exam with really high marks!
6   We can't leave Adrianna to run the shop. She .... (*only work*) here for a few days.
7   We .... (*spend*) every summer in Crete since I was a child, so it'll be sad if we don't go there this year.
8   I'm really tired because I .... (*cook*) all day!

3 👁 Candidates often make mistakes with the present perfect simple and continuous. Correct one mistake with a verb tense in each of these sentences.

1 I ~~was~~ interested in it since I was a child.   *have been*
2 In the last three weeks, I learned so many interesting things which I didn't know how to do before.
3 This isn't the first time I work at a camp.
4 My name is Sarah Beauland, I'm 25 years old and I play tennis since 1996.
5 Since I started the project, I had been doing research on someone famous from my country.
6 Vicky and Kostas are friends for many years. They actually met at primary school.
7 They had been talking about it for years, but nothing has been done up to now.
8 I dance since I was very young and now I'm working very hard to fulfil my dream of becoming a famous dancer.

Reading and Use of English | Part 2

1 Work in pairs. You will read an article about housework. Before you read, match the verbs (1–8) with the nouns (a–h) to make phrases for common household chores.

1 do	a the beds
2 do	b the dinner ready
3 dust	c the floor
4 get	d the furniture
5 hang	e the ironing
6 lay	f the table
7 make	g the washing out to dry
8 sweep	h the washing-up

2 Work in groups.

* Who does each of the chores in Exercise 1 in your family, and why?
  We all do our own ironing because we're all very busy. My dad gets the dinner ready because he says it helps him relax.
* Which of the chores do you not mind doing? Which would you prefer to avoid?

3 Read the text quickly. Why do teenagers do housework?

4 Complete the text by writing one word in each gap. Make sure that you spell the word correctly.

Doing the chores

According to a recent study of teenagers, most of them do not do housework just **(0)** ....*for*........ pocket money. While many do household chores because they see it **(1)** .... a way of getting ready for adult life, others feel they have a duty to help their parents because it is fair, especially if their parents work.

More than two-thirds of the young people who were surveyed clean floors **(2)** .... least once a week and more than 80% regularly set the table for meals or **(3)** .... the washing-up. Girls are more likely than boys to wash **(4)** .... own clothes.

(5) .... are, however, a few teens who only do the housework because they are made **(6)** .... by their parents. They argue that they should **(7)** .... be expected to help out at home because in their view, their teenage years are a period which should be enjoyed **(8)** .... than interrupted with household responsibilities.

5 Now check or complete your answers by using these clues.

1 This preposition is used with *see* to mean *believe it is (that thing)*. Other verbs which are followed by this preposition are *consider* and *regard*.

2 In other words, they clean floors a minimum of once a week.

3 Which verb do we use with *washing-up*?

4 Whose clothes do they wash?

5 This word is often used to introduce a sentence before the verb *be*.

6 *Their parents make them do the housework* = They are made .... do the housework by their parents.

7 Do you understand that a *minority of teens* mentioned in this paragraph believe they should help?

8 This word is part of a two-word phrase which means *instead of*.

Exam information

In Reading and Use of English Part 2, you read a text of 150–160 words with eight gaps where words have been removed. You write one word in each gap. You are given an example (0).

This part tests your knowledge of grammar, e.g. articles (*a*, *the*, *an*), prepositions (*to*, *with*, *by*, etc.), modal verbs (*can*, *must*, *should*, etc.) auxiliary verbs (*do*, *did*, *have*, etc.), pronouns (*it*, *them*, *which*, etc.), conjunctions (*and*, *although*, *but*, etc.), quantifiers (*much*, *few*, *a little*, etc.).

6 Work in pairs. Do you think what the text says about teenagers and household chores is true in your country as well?

Vocabulary
Collocations with *make* and *do*

1 **EP** Complete the third column of the table below by writing these words and phrases in the correct row.

~~an activity~~ ~~an appointment~~ an arrangement the bed business a change a choice the cleaning a course a decision an effort an excuse (an) exercise a favour friends homework housework an impression a job a mistake money a noise a phone call a plan progress a promise the shopping (a) sport work

verb	definition	common collocation
make	to create or produce something	make an appointment
do	to perform an activity or job	do an activity

2 **⊙** Candidates often confuse *make* and *do*. Complete these sentences by writing *make* or *do* in the correct form in the gaps.

1 According to a recent study of teenagers, most of them .... not do housework just for pocket money.

2 I always .... my own bed in the morning, but I don't .... any cleaning.

3 He had to .... a phone call in order to .... the arrangements.

4 Essential changes should be .... so that we avoid .... the same mistake in the future.

5 People who .... language courses tend to .... a lot of friends at the same time.

6 This weekend, as well as .... the shopping, I'm hoping to .... some outdoor activities as well.

3 Work in pairs. Each choose five words/phrases from the box in Exercise 1 and think about when you did or made each of these things. Then take turns to tell your partner about each of them.

I had to make a choice between going away with my family, or doing a language course during the summer. Although it was a difficult choice to make, I decided to do the language course and miss my holiday.

Speaking | Part 1

1 Look at these two questions, which the examiner may ask you in Speaking Part 1.

- Where are you from?
- What do you like about the place where you live?

1 Which question asks you to give your personal opinion? Which asks you for personal information?

2 Which question can be answered with quite a short phrase? Which question needs a longer answer?

2 ▶03 Listen to two candidates, Irene and Peter, answering the questions above. Who do you think gives the best answers? Why?

3 In the exam, you will get higher marks if you use a range of appropriate vocabulary. Work in pairs. Which of these phrases can you use to describe the place where you live?

a a large industrial city
b a relaxed atmosphere
c a busy tourist resort
d in the middle of some great countryside
e a pleasant residential district
f an important business centre
g some impressive architecture
h a lot of historic buildings
i a lot of attractive buildings
j some pretty good shopping
k a busy city centre
l wonderful beaches nearby

4 Which of the phrases (a–l) can you use with … ?

It is … a large industrial city
It has …

(In some cases, both are correct.)

5 **Pronunciation:** word stress

In the Speaking paper, you will get higher marks if your pronunciation is clear. In words of more than one syllable, one syllable is stressed more than the others. If you stress the wrong syllable, the word becomes difficult to understand. In dictionaries the stressed syllable is marked like this: in'dustrial.

1 <u>Underline</u> the stressed syllable in each of these words and phrases.

> industrial   relaxed atmosphere   wonderful
> important business   impressive   historic
> attractive   residential

2 ▶04 Listen and check your answers. Then work in pairs and take turns to read the words aloud.

6 How can you extend your answers to these two questions? Think about Irene's extended answers you heard in (Speaking) Exercise 2, and use the frameworks given to help you.

Examiner: Where are you from?
Student: I'm from … It's a … which …

Examiner: What do you like about the place where you live?
Student: Well, it's … , so … , but … and … Also …

7 Work in pairs. Take turns to ask and answer the questions in Exercise 6. Use some of the vocabulary from (Speaking) Exercise 3.

8 Read questions 1–8.

- Spend a little time thinking about how you can give extended answers.
- Work in pairs and take turns to ask and answer the questions.

1 Do you come from a large family?
2 What do you like about being part of a large/small family?
3 Who does the housework in your family?
4 What things do you enjoy doing with your family?
5 Tell me about your friends.
6 What things do you enjoy doing with your friends?
7 Which are more important to you: your family or your friends?
8 Do you have similar interests to your parents?

➡ page 194 Speaking reference: Speaking Part 1

Writing | Part 1 An essay

Exam information

In Writing Part 1, you:
- write an essay in which you discuss a question or topic. After the essay title, there are some notes which you must use.
- must also include your own ideas.
- must write between 140 and 190 words.

This part tests your ability to develop an argument or discussion on a topic, express your opinion on the topic clearly and support your ideas with reasons and examples.

1 Read this writing task and <u>underline</u> the points you must deal with.

In your English class, you have been talking about how much teenagers and young people should help with the housework.

Now your English teacher has asked you to write an essay.

Write an essay using **all** the notes and give reasons for your point of view.

Essay question
Teenagers and young people should share housework equally with their parents. Do you agree?

Notes
Write about:

1. who has more time for housework
2. who does housework better
3. ……… (your own idea)

Write your **essay**.

2 Work in groups. Discuss the task and try to find two or three things you can say about each of the notes 1–3.

3 Read Violetta's answer to the task, ignoring the gaps. Which of her ideas do you agree with and which do you disagree with?

> **(1)** .... it is fashionable to say that everyone should share the housework equally, in many homes parents do most of it. **(2)** .... , I believe people of all ages should do their fair share.
>
> It is true that young people spend most of the day at school or college and they also have large amounts of homework to do when they come home. **(3)** .... , parents go out to work and come home tired. In my view, family life is more pleasant when everyone shares the responsibility for cleaning and tidying because it takes less time.
>
> People often argue that parents do the cooking and ironing better. **(4)** .... in my opinion, young people should learn to do them as preparation for the future.
>
> Finally, housework is boring if you do it alone **(5)** .... when families do it together, it gives parents and children a chance to talk to each other about the things that matter to them. This greatly improves family life and makes young people more cooperative and responsible.
>
> For all these reasons, I think that family life is more pleasant when everyone shares the chores.

4 Complete this plan for Violetta's essay by matching the notes (a–e) with the paragraphs (1–5).

> Para. 1: intro: ....
> Para. 2: ....
> Para. 3: ....
> Para. 4: ....
> Para. 5: conclusion: ....

a life more enjoyable doing things together

b time: young people studying, parents working, chores finished more quickly

c get practice – you improve

d sharing work together – better family life

e parents do most of it + my opinion

5 It is important to express your opinions in an essay. Find four phrases which Violetta uses to introduce her personal opinions.

6 When you write an essay, you should try to present contrasting points of view. Complete Violetta's essay by writing *although, however, on the other hand* or *whereas* in each of the gaps 1–5. Then check your answers by reading the Language reference.

⮕ page 168 Language reference: Linking words for contrast

7 Complete these sentences by writing *although, however, on the other hand* or *whereas* in the gaps. In some cases, more than one answer may be possible.

1 Adults tend to worry more about their health, ... young people are more concerned about money.

2 .... I am happy to do some of the cooking, I don't want to do it all.

3 My mum and dad have similar tastes. .... , mine are completely different.

4 .... my parents give me a lot of freedom, I would prefer to have even more independence.

5 Young people often spend many hours a week on their social life. .... , older people are often too busy.

6 I enjoy making beds. .... , I'm not at all keen on doing the ironing.

8 Write your own answer to the writing task in Exercise 1. Before you write, use the notes you made in Exercise 2 to write a plan. Write between 140 and 190 words.

- Use Violetta's answer in Exercise 3 as a model, but express your own ideas and the ideas which came up during your discussion.

⮕ page 186 Writing reference: Part 1 Essays

Starting off

Work in pairs.

1 Which of the activities in the photos have you done?
2 Which do you think is ...
  A the most enjoyable?
  B the cheapest?
  C the healthiest?
  D the most relaxing?
  E the least active?
  F the best one to do with friends?
  G the most popular among young people?
3 Which would you like to try? Why?

Listening | Part 2

1 Work in groups. You are going to hear a games developer talking about his life and work. Before you listen, complete the advantages and disadvantages of video or computer games by writing a word from the box in the gaps.

> concentrate   contribute   develop   distract
> encourage   make   require   solve   waste

Advantages

1 They .... people to be more creative.
2 They can .... you from your problems.
3 People learn to .... on complicated tasks.
4 They .... many skills, such as hand and eye coordination.
5 They teach people how to .... problems.

Disadvantages

6 People .... little imagination to play them.
7 They .... people less sociable.
8 They .... to violence in society.
9 People .... time doing something which is not very useful.

2 Which sentences do you agree with? Why?

Exam information

In Listening Part 2, you hear a talk or lecture by one speaker. You:

- listen and complete ten sentences with between one and three words.
- write words you actually hear and try to spell them correctly.
- hear the recording twice.

This part tests your ability to pick out and write down details, specific information and opinions.

For questions 1–6, complete the second sentence so that it has a similar meaning to the first sentence, using the word given. Do not change the word given. You must use between two and five words, including the word given.

4 ▶06 You will hear a girl talking about one of these experiences (a–g). Listen and decide which experience she is talking about.

a She rode a motorbike for the first time.
b She was punished for something she didn't do.
c She had to study all weekend for an exam.
d She broke a bone.
e She was trapped in a lift.
f She won a competition.
g She did a parachute jump.

5 Listen again. Which adjectives did she use to describe how she felt …

1 about the whole experience: …amazing….
2 after studying: …………… and ……………
3 about her boyfriend's suggestion: ……………
4 about the thought of breaking a bone: ……………
5 in the plane: …………… and ……………
6 about the jump itself: ……………

6 Work in pairs. Look at the experiences a–g in Exercise 4. Have you done any of these or have any of them happened to you? How did you feel about them? Take turns to describe your experience.

Reading and Use of English | Part 4

Exam information

In Reading and Use of English Part 4, you:

- complete six sentences with between two and five words so that they mean the same as the sentences printed before them
- use a word given in CAPITALS without changing it in any way.

This part tests your ability to manage different grammar, vocabulary and collocations.

0 He doesn't enjoy running as much as cycling.
MORE
He likes …cycling more than… running.
1 It is easier to learn the guitar than most other musical instruments.
ONE
The guitar is …………………………… musical instruments to learn.
2 Olivia finds watching TV more boring than reading.
NOT
For Olivia, watching TV is …………………………… reading.
3 Maria's brothers are better tennis players than her.
AS
Maria doesn't …………………………… her brothers.
4 No one in the class makes as much noise as Peter.
PERSON
Peter …………………………… the class.
5 In general, cars are more expensive than motorbikes.
NOT
In general, cars are …………………………… motorbikes.
6 It took Janusz longer to finish the game than Sarah.
MORE
Sarah finished the game …………………………… Janusz.

Speaking | Part 2

In Speaking Part 2, you and the other candidate take turns to speak on your own for a minute during which you:

- compare two photos which the examiner gives you.
- answer a question connected with both photos.
- answer a question quite briefly about your partner's photos.

This part tests your ability to speak at length, organise your ideas, compare, describe and express opinions.

1 Work in pairs. Look at the examiner's instructions and the question and photos below. Then discuss what you can say to compare them.

Here are your photographs. They show people doing different activities in their free time. I'd like you to compare the photographs, and say how you think the people can benefit from spending their free time doing these different activities.

How can the people benefit from spending their free time doing these different activities?

2 ▶07 Listen to an examiner giving this task to a candidate called Martyna. According to Martyna, how can people benefit from each activity?

3 Listen again and tick ✓ this checklist.

Martyna	Yes	No
1 introduces her talk.		✓
2 describes each photo in detail.		
3 deals with each photo in turn.		
4 spends most of the time answering the printed question.		
5 refers to the first photo when talking about the second photo.		
6 talks about things not connected with the question.		
7 speaks until the examiner says 'Thank you'.		

4 Work in pairs. Complete the sentences from Martyna's answer which begin with these words and phrases.

1 I think they benefit from …
2 Firstly …
3 At the same time …
4 Also …
5 I think they also benefit because …

5 Which word(s)/phrase(s) (1–5) in Exercise 4 does Martyna use to:

a introduce her answer to the examiner's question?
b introduce the first point she wants to make?
c add additional points?

6 Which of these words/phrases could also be used for b and c in Exercise 5?

Besides   First of all   In addition
To start with   What is more

7 Pronunciation: sentence stress (1)

We stress the words in sentences that we particularly want our listeners to hear, the words which carry the most meaning. These are usually nouns, verbs or adjectives, not small grammar words like articles or prepositions.

1 08 <u>Underline</u> the words you think are stressed in these sentences. Then listen to check your answer.

1 <u>Firstly</u>, they're getting some <u>exercise</u>, which is always <u>good</u> for you.
2 It's great for your health and helps you to relax.
3 At the same time, they're having fun together…
4 … which is important because it builds up their social relationships and their friendships.
5 Also, it's good to see boys and girls doing a bit of sport together instead of separately.
6 I think it helps break down social boundaries between boys and girls.

2 Work in pairs. Take turns to read the sentences aloud using the same sentence stress.

3 Work in pairs. Take turns to read these extracts.

• Firstly, they're getting some exercise, which is always good for you because it's great for your health and helps you to relax.
• At the same time, they're having fun together, which is important because it builds up their social relationships and their friendships. Also, it's good to see boys and girls doing a bit of sport together instead of separately because I think it helps to break down social boundaries between boys and girls.

8 Change partners and take turns to do the Speaking Part 2 task in (Speaking) Exercise 1.

• Try to speak for a minute.
• Try to use some of the words and phrases from (Speaking) Exercise 4.
• Use your own ideas and Martyna's ideas.
• While you are listening to your partner, use the checklist in (Speaking) Exercise 3 and give feedback when your partner has finished.

9 Work in pairs and take turns to do this Speaking Part 2 task.

The photographs show people doing different free-time activities.

Compare the photographs, and say what you think the people enjoy about doing these different activities.

What do the people enjoy about doing these different activities?

page 195 Speaking reference: Speaking Part 2

25

Writing | Part 2 An article

1 Look at this writing task and <u>underline</u> the points you must write about.

> You see this announcement in an English-language magazine for teenagers.
>
> ### A great way to spend your free time!
> Tell us about a leisure-time activity you really enjoy.
> - How did you get started?
> - Why do you enjoy it so much?
>
> We will publish the most interesting articles in next month's issue.
>
> Write your **article**.

2 Work in pairs. Tell your partner about one of your free-time activities. While speaking, answer the questions in the writing task above.

3 Work in pairs. The article in the next column would lose marks in the exam because it is not divided into paragraphs.

1 Divide it into four paragraphs.
2 Say what the main idea is in each paragraph.

Cooking – it's creative and fun!

I first got interested in cookery one summer holiday when I was about 12. I was staying with my aunt, who is a keen cook, and I wanted to try cooking for myself. She started by teaching me how to do fairly simple dishes at first. I found I really enjoyed cooking and I was soon doing things which were more complicated. Not everything I cooked was as successful as my aunt's cooking. My younger brother and sister complained about some of my dishes, but they usually ate the food quite happily. When I went back to school after the summer, I decided to do cookery lessons and now I think I'm quite a competent cook. When friends come round to my house, I often cook them something because I find it really satisfying and relaxing. I find creating new dishes fascinating and it's wonderful to see my family and friends enjoying a meal I've cooked. I'd recommend it as a hobby because for me it's one of the most creative and useful free-time activities that anyone can do.

→ page 193 Writing reference: Writing Part 2 Articles

4 You can write compound sentences by joining two sentences with *and, but* and *because*. Which two sentences are joined in these compound sentences?

1 I found I really enjoyed cooking and I was soon doing things which were more complicated.
2 My younger brother and sister complained about some of my dishes, but they usually ate the food quite happily.
3 When friends come round to my house, I often cook them something because I find it really satisfying and relaxing.
4 I'd recommend it as a hobby because for me it's one of the most creative and useful free-time activities that anyone can do.
5 When I went back to school after the summer, I decided to do cookery lessons and now I think I'm quite a competent cook.

5 Write compound sentences by joining these sentences with *and, but* and *because*. Use pronouns (*he, she, it*, etc.) to avoid repetition.

1 I'd like to learn to fly. I think learning to fly is too expensive. *I'd like to learn to fly, but I think it's too expensive.*
2 I got interested in flying when I was about 14. My father took me to an airshow.
3 My parents don't want me to fly. They think flying is dangerous.
4 One of my friends is learning to fly. My friend has asked me to come with him. My friend thinks I'd like flying.

6 You can write complex sentences by joining two sentences with words such as *when, who, which* and *that*. Write these complex sentences as two separate sentences.

1 I first got interested in cookery one summer holiday when I was about 12.
I first got interested in cookery one summer holiday. I was about 12.
2 I was staying with my aunt, who is a keen cook.
3 I was soon doing things which were more complicated.
4 When I went back to school after the summer, I decided to do cookery lessons.
5 When friends come round to my house, I often cook them something.
6 For me, cooking is one of the most creative and useful free-time activities that anyone can do.

7 Join these sentences using *when, who, which* and *that*.

1 I was 13. I started running seriously.
2 My aunt encouraged me. My aunt's a keen athlete.
3 I go running most days. I've finished school and done my homework.
4 Running is a sport. Running gets you really fit.

8 Join these sentences using *and, because, but, when, which* and *who*. Use pronouns (*he, she, it*, etc.) to avoid repetition.

1 I started windsurfing. I was 13. I was staying with friends by the sea.

2 One of my friends is a keen windsurfer. She encouraged me to start. She thought I would enjoy it.
3 I kept falling into the sea to start with. It was a fairly windy day. There were a lot of waves.
4 I didn't enjoy it at first. I had to concentrate quite hard. I carried on trying.
5 I started to windsurf quite fast. It was exciting. I started to find it quite enjoyable.

9 Find adjectives in the article which describe the following.

1 the writer's feelings about cooking:
.... , ... , ... , ...
2 cooking as a leisure-time activity:
.... , ...
3 the writer's ability to cook: ....

10 (EP) Complete the table below by writing these words and phrases in the correct column.

astonishing competitive delightful demanding
depressing dreadful economical entertaining
exhausting incredible irritating popular
superb time-consuming tremendous unbelievable

feelings about an activity	the type of activity

11 You are going to write your own article to answer the writing task in Exercise 1. Before you write,
- decide on a title for your article which will encourage people to read it.
- decide how many paragraphs you need, the subject of each paragraph and write a short plan.
- think about some of the vocabulary you can use.

12 When you are ready, write your article using between 140 and 190 words.

Exam information

In Writing Part 2:
- you do one writing task from a choice of three.
- the possible tasks are an article, a letter or email, a review or a report.
- you must write between 140 and 190 words.

This part tests your ability to write effectively for a range of different purposes.

Vocabulary and grammar review Unit 1

Vocabulary

1 **EP** Complete each of these sentences by writing an adjective in the gap. Choose from the adjectives or their opposites in the exercises in Reading and Use of English Part 6 on page 10. In some cases, more than one answer may be possible.

1 Juan's parents are very ...strict... and don't allow him to do everything he wants.
2 You need to be careful what you say to my brother, as he can be rather .... in the morning.
3 Pascale is very .... , so she's bound to finish her part of the project on time.
4 David is so .... that you can never trust him to do what he says he's going to do.
5 Melanie tries to act confidently even when she's feeling very .... about things.
6 I wouldn't have criticised you if I had known how .... you were!
7 Helen is very young, but she behaves in a .... and responsible way.
8 We're all feeling rather .... about Luis, because he's been looking rather depressed recently.

2 Complete these sentences with a phrasal verb in the correct form.

1 Your room is such a mess! Could you .... it .... before you go out?
2 Dad will .... you .... from the station when you arrive.
3 I must .... the housework, otherwise I'll never finish it.
4 I need a rest – all this shopping has .... me ....
5 We'll need to .... the flat before we move in – the paintwork is very old.
6 The game .... for about two hours, but I won in the end.

3 Complete these sentences with the correct form of *make* or *do*.

1 Could you .... me a favour and let me copy your notes from the last class?
2 Do you mind if I use your phone? I've got to ....
an urgent phone call.

3 I'll .... the shopping on my way home this evening.
4 I'm .... this English course because I'm hoping to study in the USA next year.
5 I've got so much homework to .... that I can't come out with you tonight.
6 Marco has .... a big effort with his students, so I'm afraid he's a bit disappointed with their results.
7 Sarah wasn't enjoying the party, so she .... an excuse and left.
8 We phoned the police because our neighbours were .... too much noise.

Grammar

4 Complete these sentences by writing the verbs in brackets in the correct form (present perfect simple or continuous). In some cases, both forms are possible.

1 I'm celebrating because my team has .... (*win*) the league!
2 At last you .... (*arrive*) – we .... (*expect*) you for ages.
3 Of course I'm annoyed. I .... (*spend*) ages preparing for this party and no one .... (*turn up*) yet.
4 We .... (*have*) a really interesting time. Gavin .... (*tell*) us about his trip round the world. There are a few countries he still .... (*not tell*) us about, but I get the impression he .... (*see*) almost everything!
5 Kate .... (*lose*) weight recently because she .... (*get*) more exercise.
6 I wonder if Irina .... (*finish*) reading that book yet. I .... (*wait*) to read it for ages.
7 Tatiana is so greedy! She .... (*eat*) all the cakes and she .... (*not leave*) any for us.
8 Paolo .... (*look*) very tired recently. I think it's because he .... (*study*) too hard.

Vocabulary and grammar review Unit 2

Vocabulary

1 Complete these sentences by writing a phrasal verb or expression from the Vocabulary section on page 21 in the correct form in the gaps.

1 If you can't .... , no one will ever trust you.
2 I just don't like .... , so I'd never get a motorbike.
3 Mario is thinking of .... jogging, as he doesn't feel he's getting enough exercise.
4 Instead of reading to the children, I think I'll just .... a story for their bedtime.
5 I'll .... all our ideas in just a few words to save time.
6 I .... how to solve this maths problem; would you like to .... and see if you can do it?

Grammar

2 Join these sentences to form compound and complex sentences. More than one answer may be possible.

1 Katya took up karate. She was seven years old. She was interested in karate.
2 Her father is a professional karate instructor. He taught her karate. She progressed quickly. She soon became junior regional champion.
3 She did karate with other children. The other children were the same age as her. None of them was as good as her. She felt dissatisfied.
4 Last year, she participated in the national championship. She did not win. She was injured during one of the matches.
5 She hopes to become a professional karate instructor. She hopes to work in the same sports centre as her father. Her father has too many students.
6 Some of her father's students have been studying karate for several years. Her father thinks they would benefit from a different teacher. They are too familiar with his style of karate.

3 For questions 1–6, complete the second sentence so that it has a similar meaning to the first sentence, using the word given in capitals. Do not change the word given. You must use between two and five words, including the word given.

1 This motorbike is not as noisy as my previous one.
MADE
My previous .... this one.

2 Small towns are safer than large cities.
NOT
Small towns .... as large cities.

3 No one in the team plays better than Gemma.
PLAYER
Gemma .... in the team.

4 She looks more relaxed than she did before the exam.
STRESSED
She does not look .... she did before the exam.

5 Tatiana does not speak nearly as clearly as Irina.
MUCH
Irina speaks .... Tatiana.

6 None of the other sofas in the shop are as comfortable as this one.
ANY
This sofa is .... the others in the shop.

Word formation

4 EP Use the word given in capitals at the end of each sentence to form a word that fits in the gap.

1 What an .... band! I never expected they'd be that good. **AMAZE**
2 They found the journey so .... that they fell asleep as soon as they arrived. **EXHAUST**
3 It's a .... problem – I don't really know what to do about it. **PUZZLE**
4 Jake felt .... with his exam results. He had hoped to do better. **DISAPPOINT**
5 You can't expect children to work hard if they don't feel .... **MOTIVATE**
6 We were .... by the way they shouted at us. **ASTONISH**

3 Happy holidays?

Starting off

1 Work in pairs. Complete the table below by writing the words and phrases from the box in the most appropriate column.

camping holiday   at a campsite   walking and climbing
at a luxury hotel   a beach holiday   on a cruise ship
meeting new people   sunbathing   a sightseeing tour
relaxing   a cruise   at a youth hostel   backpacking
visiting monuments   in the city centre   at the seaside
seeing new places

types of holiday	holiday locations and places to stay	holiday activities

2 Now look at the photos and answer these questions using words and phrases from the table.

1 What type of holiday does each photo show?
2 What do people do on these types of holiday?
3 Why do people choose these types of holiday?
4 Which types of holiday would you enjoy most? Which would you enjoy least? Why?

Listening | Part 3

1   You are going to hear five people talking about the holiday they took last year. Before you listen, underline the main idea in each statement A–H.

   A   I didn't enjoy it much at first.
   B   I didn't mind the discomfort.
   C   I got to know lots of people.
   D   I'd done something similar before.
   E   I wanted a low-cost holiday.
   F   I didn't do much during the day.
   G   I wasn't in as much danger as some people imagined.
   H   I went on the trip as a break from my parents.

2   ▶09 Now listen and, for questions 1–5, choose from the list (A–H) in Exercise 1 what each speaker says about their holiday. Use the letters only once. There are three extra letters which you do not need to use.

Francesca	1
Mike	2
Sally	3
Paul	4
Katie	5

3   Work in groups.

   What do you like about holidays with your:
   - family?
   - friends?

Grammar

Past simple, past continuous and *used to*

1   ▶09 Complete these extracts from Listening Part 3 by writing the verbs in brackets in the correct form in the gaps. Then listen again to check your answers.

   - ... on family holidays we always (1) .... (*go*) to the same campsite and lie on the same beach ...
   - My dad (2) .... (*be*) a climber when he (3) .... (*be*) younger ...
   - Still, there was an upside because while we (4) .... (*go*) round yet another museum, I (5) .... (*get*) to meet this Polish girl called Jolanta.
   - ... so we just (6) .... (*dump*) our parents and (7) .... (*go*) off for the day together. We (8) .... (*have*) a really great time ...
   - ... we (9) .... (*stay*) in youth hostels, which saved us a bit of money. There were lots of other people like us from all over the world who (10) .... (*do*) the same sort of thing.

➡ page 179 Language reference: Verb tenses – past simple, past continuous and *used to*

2   Circle the correct form of the verb in *italics* in each of these sentences.

   1   When he *walked / was walking* home, he found a wallet with a huge amount of money in it!
   2   When I was at primary school, I *was doing / used to do* about one hour's homework a day.
   3   As soon as Mandy *was getting / got* Simon's text, she *was jumping / jumped* on her bike and *was riding / rode* round to his house to speak to him.
   4   When I was younger, we *used to spend / were spending* our holidays in my grandparents' village.
   5   Luckily, we *walked / were walking* past a shopping centre when the storm *began / was beginning*.
   6   My mum *used to visit / was visiting* lots of exotic places when she *was / was being* a tour guide.

3   ◉ Candidates often make spelling mistakes when adding -*ed* to past tense verbs. Add -*ed* to each of these words.

   develop   enjoy   happen   mention   occur   open
   plan   prefer   stop   study   travel   try

➡ page 176 Language reference: Spelling

Vocabulary
travel, journey, trip and way

1 ◉ Candidates often confuse the following nouns: *travel, journey, trip* and *way*. Look at these sentences from the recording script in Listening Part 3 and complete the extract below by writing *travel, journey, trip* or *way* in the gaps.

- I went on one of those **journeys** overland to Kenya …
- … we made a **trip** to the beach, which was only about 20 minutes away by bus.
- We were on our **way** back down the mountain when we got caught in this really big storm.
- I really like that sort of mixing of cultures – it's one of the best things about foreign **travel** …

travel, journey, trip or *way*?

- ❯ A **(1)** .... is a journey in which you visit a place for a short time and come back again.
- ❯ '**(2)** ....' refers only to the route that you take to get from one place to another.
- ❯ The noun '**(3)** ....' is a general word which means the activity of travelling.
- ❯ Use '**(4)** ....' to talk about when you travel from one place to another.

2 ◉ Circle the correct word in *italics* in each of these sentences.

1 She met plenty of interesting people during her weekend *travel / trip* to Montreal.
2 We stopped at the supermarket on the *way / trip* to the beach to pick up some cold drinks.
3 My mum and dad have booked a *journey / trip* to Greece for our holidays this August.
4 My mum is away on a business *journey / trip*, so the house is really quiet at the moment.
5 People spend far more on foreign *travel / journeys* than they did 50 years ago.
6 The *travel / journey* to my village will take about three hours.
7 'Have a good *travel / trip* to Budapest!' 'Thanks! See you next week when I get back!'
8 You can't get to school by bicycle if the *journey / way* is too long – over 30 kilometres, for example.
9 Excuse me, I'm a bit lost. Can you tell me the best *journey / way* to the bus station?

3 Complete each of the sentences by writing an adjective from the box. In some cases, more than one answer may be possible.

a(n) homeward/outward/hard/dangerous **journey**
a business/sightseeing/shopping/day/forthcoming/ round **trip**
a(n) outward/pleasant/successful/safe/extended/ overnight **journey/trip**

1 I hope you have a(n) .... journey.
2 I'm going on a(n) .... trip to Zurich, so I won't be back till tomorrow.
3 The .... journey wasn't nearly as hard as the homeward one.
4 They've gone on a(n) .... trip, so I guess they'll come home with lots of new clothes.
5 What are you going to do on your .... trip to New York? Is it for business or pleasure?
6 Have a(n) .... journey and don't drive too fast!

4 Work in groups. Imagine you are planning a trip together this weekend. Decide:

- where to go
- how to get there
- what to do when you arrive.

Reading and Use of English | Part 3

1 (EP) Form adjectives from these nouns and verbs by adding a suffix.

	noun (n) or verb (v)	adjective
1	nature (n)	natural
2	adventure (n)	
3	friend (n)	
4	memory (n)	
5	mystery (n)	
6	risk (n + v)	
7	crowd (n + v)	
8	thrill (n + v)	
9	doubt (n + v)	
10	success (n)	
11	remark (n + v)	
12	access (n + v)	

➡ page 181 **Language reference:** Word formation – adding suffixes

2 (EP) Form adjectives from the nouns and verbs in the box. In some cases, more than one answer may be possible. When you have finished, use your dictionary to check your answers.

artist caution colour educate emotion energy mass
predict reason respond storm thought wealth

Exam information

In Reading and Use of English Part 3, you read a text of 150–160 words with eight gaps and one example (0). You write the correct form of the word given in **CAPITALS** at the end of the line in each gap.

This part tests your knowledge of vocabulary and your ability to form words by adding prefixes and suffixes and making other changes.

In the test, the words will be a mix of nouns, adjectives, adverbs and verbs.

3 (EP) Read the text on the right. Use the word given in capitals at the end of some of the lines to form a word that fits in the gap in the same line. When you have finished, use your dictionary to check your answers.

A bus journey

Tasha climbed onto a (0) ....*crowded*........ CROWD
bus which was going to take her to
a nearby village. The wooden seats
looked quite (1) .... , so COMFORT
she decided to stand, even though a
(2) .... passenger offered THOUGHT
her a seat. As the bus moved through the
countryside, it filled with women dressed
in bright, (3) .... clothes COLOUR
on their way to market to do their weekly
shopping. 'This is an (4) .... FORGET
experience,' thought Tasha, who was
beginning to feel (5) .... OPTIMIST
about her journey.
More passengers climbed aboard laughing
and chatting, and the noise became
(6) .... Gradually, the bus CONSIDER
grew hotter and Tasha began to feel a little
(7) .... that she might not get ANXIETY
to the door when the bus reached her stop.
Fortunately, though, a (8) .... SYMPATHY
passenger saw her problem and shouted
to the other passengers to let her pass and
suddenly everyone made room for her to
get off.

4 Work in groups. What things make you nervous or anxious when you're travelling?

Grammar

at, *in* or *on* in time phrases

1 Complete these sentences from Listening Part 3 by writing *at, in* or *on* in the gaps.

1 We got up late .... the morning or even .... the afternoon …

2 Except of course .... days when it was cloudy.

3 But .... night, we were down at the clubs, partying to the small hours, getting back to the hotel .... two or three in the morning.

4 I went off with a couple of my friends .... March.

➡ page 172 Language reference: Prepositions – *at, in* and *on* in time expressions

2 👁 Candidates often make mistakes with *at, in* and *on* in time phrases. Some of these sentences are correct. Find and correct the mistakes.

1 I would like to travel on July because it is the perfect time to go to the camp.

2 In the weekends, he only stays at home on Sunday on the afternoon, because in the mornings he goes to see football games.

3 At weekends, everything opens in 11.00 a.m.

4 I would advise you to come in summer because the weather is great and there are many islands with great beaches.

5 She graduated from Cambridge University at 2008.

6 So I prefer shopping on weekdays unless I am busy or have an appointment.

7 The traffic makes us nervous, particularly in certain times of the day when the roads are busy.

8 We used to go to the beach at the morning in a normal day, and clubbing every night.

Reading and Use of English | Part 7

In Reading and Use of English Part 7, you will read either one long text divided into four to six sections, or four to six separate short texts. The total length will be 500–600 words. There are ten questions which you must match with the different texts or sections.

This part tests your ability to understand specific information, detail and opinion.

1 Work in groups. You are going to read about four people's nightmare holidays. Before you read, discuss what things sometimes spoil people's holidays.

2 Read questions 1–10 carefully and underline the key words in each question.

Which person

had to hide from danger?	1
found an employee intimidating?	2
was not pleased to spend so long somewhere?	3
had visited the country on a previous occasion?	4
worried about how strong something was?	5
missed speaking to people?	6
had a painful experience?	7
travelled with an ex-criminal?	8
was unaware of the danger in what they were doing?	9
realised the holiday might be a mistake before arriving?	10

3 For questions 1–10, choose from the people (A–D). Each person may be chosen more than once.

4 Work in groups. Which of the holidays sounds the worst to you? Take turns to tell each other about a memorable holiday you have had. Then decide which of you had the most interesting holiday.

2 Complete these sentences by writing *too, too many, too much* or *enough* in the gaps.

1 I really enjoyed the meal, although I thought there were .... chips and not .... fresh vegetables.
2 Few schools spend .... time teaching students about nutrition.
3 A lot of people eat .... quickly to enjoy their food properly.
4 The school canteen is .... small for everyone to eat lunch at the same time.
5 Students don't take .... interest in their diets.

3 ⊙ Candidates often make mistakes with *too, too many, too much, enough* and *very*. Rewrite these sentences correctly. More than one answer may be possible.

1 I liked the restaurant but the food wasn't enough.
2 Experts say that fast food is not too much good for you.
3 I don't have money enough to pay for your dinner.
4 We didn't like the hotel because it wasn't enough comfortable.
5 The food takes too much long to prepare, so customers become impatient.
6 Some people suffer from doing too hard work.
7 The food was not too much tasty.
8 I'm afraid the meal was too much expensive.

4 For questions 1–4, complete the second sentence so that it has a similar meaning to the first sentence, using the word given. Do not change the word given. You must use between two and five words, including the word given.

1 Few people can afford to eat in that restaurant.
   TOO
   That restaurant .... most people.
2 We ran out of petrol before we reached our destination.
   ENOUGH
   We did not have .... to our destination.
3 The news surprised her so much that she couldn't speak.
   ASTONISHED
   She .... the news to speak.
4 We did not go swimming because of the cold weather.
   WARM
   The weather .... us to go swimming.

5 Work in pairs. Imagine you have both been to a birthday party at a friend's house, but you didn't really enjoy yourselves. Discuss what was wrong with the party, e.g. *The house was too cold, so we were shivering to start with. There wasn't enough food, so we had to go out and get some more.*

You can talk about:

- the food
- the place
- the other guests
- the music
- how you felt.

Speaking | Part 4

1 Martyna and Miguel are answering an examiner's question in Speaking Part 4. Read their answers, ignoring the gaps, and match the words and phrases in bold with the definitions a–g below.

Examiner: Do you think fast food is bad for you?

Martyna: I think it depends. I think the most important thing is to have **a balanced diet**, (1) .... you eat a variety of vegetables, meat, cereals and so on. I'm not sure it matters so much how long it takes to prepare, (2) .... I think fast food is just food which is prepared quickly. (3) .... , if you just **live on**, what's it called, **junk food**, for instance hamburgers and pizzas and things like that, (4) .... you probably need to **cut down** and have a more balanced diet.

Examiner: And Miguel, what do you think?

Miguel: I agree with Martyna. I think it's fine to eat fast food occasionally, (5) .... you have to balance it with other things like fresh fruit and vegetables (6) .... are in season and cut down on **dairy products** and **fat**. Also, I think that (7) .... you eat is only one part of a healthy **lifestyle**.

a solid or liquid substance obtained from animals or plants and used especially in cooking   fat
b combination of the correct types and amounts of food
c do less of something
d food that is unhealthy but is quick and easy to eat
e foods made from milk, such as cream, butter and cheese
f only eat a particular type of food
g someone's way of living; the things that a person or particular group of people usually do

2 ▶14 Complete Martyna's and Miguel's answers by writing a word or phrase from this box in the gaps. Then listen to check your answers.

> because   but   in other words   on the other hand   then   what   which

3 Find words or phrases in Martyna's and Miguel's answers where they:
1 explain what they mean using different words
2 give a reason
3 give examples
4 balance one idea or opinion with another.

4 **Pronunciation:** grouping words and pausing (1)

When we speak, we say words in groups which form a meaning together, almost like one word, and we pause slightly between these groups of words.

1 ▶15 Listen to Miguel and Martyna answering the examiner's next question and use a (/) to mark where they pause.

Examiner: How can families benefit from eating together?

Miguel: Well, / the important thing is not eating, / it's spending time together / so that they can talk about what they have been doing during the day. They get the chance to exchange opinions and make plans as well, because everyone can contribute and that's what makes a rich, meaningful family life. Children learn ideas and attitudes from their parents, while parents keep up to date with their children and what they are thinking and doing.

Examiner: And Martyna, do you agree?

Martyna: Yes, I do. And also I think people cook better when they are cooking for several people than when they are just cooking for themselves, so that as a result, people who eat together eat more healthily.

2 Work in pairs. Read Miguel's and Martyna's answers aloud. While your partner is speaking, check where they pause and if the pause sounds natural.

3 Look at Martyna's and Miguel's answers in Exercise 1 and use a (/) to mark where you think they pause. Then listen again to check your answers.

4 Work in pairs. Read Martyna's and Miguel's answers aloud.

5 Write your answer to the question in the box in three or four sentences. Where necessary, use phrases to explain what you mean, give examples and reasons, and balance one opinion or idea against another.

> How can children and young people be encouraged to eat healthily?

When you have finished, mark where you think you need to pause when you speak.

6 Work in pairs and take turns to ask and answer the question in Exercise 5.

7 Think about how you can answer each of these questions. Then work in pairs and take turns to ask and answer the questions.

1 How important is it for people to be interested in the food they eat?
2 What, for you, is a healthy diet?
3 How are the things we eat nowadays different from the things our grandparents used to eat when they were young?
4 Do you think young people should learn to cook at school? Why? / Why not?

➡ page 198 Speaking reference: Speaking Part 4

Reading and Use of English | Part 1

1 You are going to read a short review of a restaurant in Manchester. Read the review quickly to find out what the writer liked about the restaurant, e.g. *the price*.

MosoMoso

I **(0)** ..tried.. Moso Moso for the first time this month, and **(1)** .... that it was easily the best Chinese restaurant I've eaten in.

The surroundings were modern, yet it still felt airy and cosy. The waiters were very welcoming and informative, and not too rushed, as is often the **(2)** .... in some of the city's more popular restaurants.

As I was eating with a party of eight, we **(3)** .... to sample a good range of items on the menu, and between us couldn't find a single item that wasn't satisfying and delicious. Every **(4)** .... featured wonderful combinations of flavours.

All the ingredients were clearly fresh and of the highest **(5)** .... and in my opinion, the seafood was particularly tasty. We felt that we were given very good **(6)** .... for money, because the meal **(7)** .... to about £15 per person which we thought was very reasonable.

All of us would highly **(8)** .... this restaurant and, as it is located just a short walk from our workplace, we will no doubt be back for many more lunches!

Adapted from the *Manchester Evening News*

2 For questions 1–8, read the review again and decide which answer (A, B, C or D) best fits each gap. There is an example at the beginning (0).

	A	B	C	D
0	checked	(B tried)	tested	proved
1	revealed	noticed	found	knew
2	reality	case	situation	fact
3	achieved	succeeded	managed	reached
4	plate	dish	food	meal
5	quality	level	condition	choice
6	price	worth	cost	value
7	arrived	reached	came	rose
8	recommend	propose	suggest	advise

3 Work in groups. Where is the best place in your town for:

- a night out with your friends?
- a big family celebration?

Writing | Part 2 A review

1 Work in pairs. Read the Exam information and advice box on page 49, then read the writing task below and <u>underline</u> the points you must deal with.

> You see this announcement in your local English-language newspaper.
>
> Can you recommend a local restaurant, café or snack bar? If so, why not write a review for our Food section? Tell our readers what the place and the food are like, and say why you think everyone in the family would enjoy eating there.
>
> All reviews published will receive vouchers for a free meal.
>
> Write your **review**.

2 Answer these questions with a partner.

1 Which features below (a–j) do you think a review of a restaurant or snack bar should cover?
2 Which features does the review in Reading and Use of English Part 1 cover?

a The type of restaurant, café or snack bar
b The writer's general opinion of the restaurant, café or snack bar
c A description of its design and surroundings
d A description of the food
e A description of the other customers
f A description of the service
g An explanation of how to get there
h A recommendation
i An indication of the price
j The location

4 **EP** Now add these adjectives to the table. You can add some of them to more than one row.

> attractive   cheerful   colourful   competitive   delightful
> elegant   exceptional   exclusive   original   raw
> satisfactory   superb   well-balanced

5 Read this writing task and <u>underline</u> the points you must deal with.

> You see this announcement in your college magazine.
>
> > Do you have a favourite restaurant, café or snack bar in town? If so, why not write a review for our 'Free Time' section, telling us what your favourite place is like and why you would recommend it to our students.
> >
> > The three best reviews will receive a prize of €50.
>
> Write your **review**.

6 Write a plan for your review and make notes on what you will put in each paragraph. Here are some things you can cover:

- Introduction: the name and type of place and where it is situated
- Your overall opinion of the place
- Particular dishes the place serves (and your opinion of them)
- The décor, the service, etc.
- Things you particularly like, such as the price
- A general recommendation

7 Work in pairs. Compare your plans.

8 Write your review. Write 140–190 words.

➡ page 192 Writing reference: Writing Part 2 Reviews

3 A review is a good opportunity to show your range of vocabulary. Complete the table below by writing each of the adjectives in the box from the review in Reading and Use of English Part 1 in the appropriate row. You can write some adjectives in more than one row.

> airy   cosy   delicious   fresh   informative   modern
> reasonable   rushed   satisfying   tasty   wonderful
> welcoming

the waiters / the service	
the interior	
the food and menu	
the price	
the restaurant in general	

Exam information and advice

- Writing a review tests your ability to describe and give your opinion about something you have experienced (e.g. a restaurant or a concert) and to make a recommendation to the reader.

When writing a review, you should think about what people want to know when they read the review, e.g. what sort of restaurant is it? What is the food like? Is it expensive?

Vocabulary and grammar review Unit 3

Vocabulary

1 Circle the correct word in *italics* in these sentences.

1 Welcome to the Intercity Hotel. I hope you had a pleasant *travel / journey.*
2 Sarah came back from her shopping *trip / journey* with lots of new clothes.
3 Among Brian's many interests, he lists foreign *journeys / travel* and climbing.
4 Do you know the *way / journey* to the cathedral?
5 It was a long, dangerous *trip / journey* to the South Pole.
6 I always stop for coffee at a café on my *journey / way* to work.
7 Are you all prepared for your forthcoming *trip / travel* to Egypt?
8 Many of our students have quite a long *travel / journey* to college each morning.

Grammar

2 For questions 1–6, complete the second sentence so that it has a similar meaning to the first sentence, using the word given. Do not change the word given. You must use between two and five words, including the word given.

1 During my visit to London, I took hundreds of photos.
   WHILE
   I took hundreds of photos .... London.
2 I didn't notice that my passport was missing until I reached the immigration desk.
   LOST
   When I reached the immigration desk, I noticed that .... my passport.
3 I've given up using the bus to go to school.
   USED
   I .... by bus, but I've given it up.
4 She was still at school when she passed her driving test.
   GOING
   She passed her driving test when .... school.

5 Paola and Antonio met for the first time at yesterday's party.
   NEVER
   Paola and Antonio .... before yesterday's party.
6 Pablo is no longer as frightened of spiders as in the past.
   USED
   Pablo .... frightened of spiders than he is now.

Word formation

3 **EP** Read this text. Use the word given in capitals at the end of some of the lines to form a word that fits in the gap in the same line.

Paradise Hotel

We had been promised an **(0)** ......*exceptional*...... holiday in a three-star hotel, so we made	**EXCEPT**
our reservation despite the **(1)**	**CONSIDER**
expense this involved. The website said it was an **(2)** .... three-star	**EXCLUDE**
hotel which promised outstanding views of **(3)** .... mountain scenery.	**DRAMA**
Imagine how disappointed we felt when we found that we had been given a room with a view over the kitchens, which was completely **(4)** .... When we went down	**ACCEPT**
for dinner the first evening, we found that the restaurant was so **(5)** .... that we	**ORGANISE**
had to wait for our table even though we had booked it in advance.	
When we finally sat down for dinner, the waitress was tired, irritable and generally **(6)** .... So we decided to spend	**HELP**
the **(7)** .... days of our holiday in a	**REMAIN**
quieter hotel nearby. It wasn't as luxurious as our first hotel, but the view of the mountains and river was certainly **(8)** .... to a view of the kitchens!	**PREFER**

Vocabulary and grammar review Unit 4

Vocabulary

1 Complete this text by writing *food, dish* or *meal* in the correct form in the gaps. In some gaps, more than one answer is possible.

Last week, my boyfriend, Nigel, invited me out for a
(1) .... in a restaurant. The **(2)** .... was not very
good though. For my first course, I chose a **(3)** ....
called 'Chef's special', which turned out to be a kind of
pizza. Generally, I'm not very keen on fast **(4)** .... , and
this **(5)** .... was quite disappointing because it wasn't
very special. Nigel didn't enjoy his **(6)** .... very much
either. Personally, I think we would have enjoyed ourselves
more if I'd cooked a **(7)** .... at home – after all, I had
plenty of **(8)** .... in the fridge.

Grammar

2 For questions 1–6, complete the second sentence so that it has a similar meaning to the first sentence, using the word given. Do not change the word given. You must use between two and five words, including the word given.

1 The food was so hot that we didn't really enjoy it.
TOO
The food was .... really enjoy.

2 The waitress spoke so quickly that we had difficulty understanding her.
ENOUGH
The waitress didn't speak ....
understand her easily.

3 We didn't get a table at the restaurant because it was too full.
SO
The restaurant .... we couldn't get a table.

4 I asked for a second helping because the food was so delicious.
SUCH
It was .... I asked for a second helping.

5 Julio is not a very good cook, so he won't get a job in that restaurant.
ENOUGH
Julio doesn't .... to get a job in that restaurant.

6 We ate very late because Phil spent too much time preparing the meal.
TIME
Phil spent .... preparing the meal that we ate very late.

Word formation

3 **EP** Read this text. Use the word given in capitals at the end of some of the lines to form a word that fits in the gap in the same line.

Changing diets

Even in quite **(0)** ....traditional...... societies, eating habits are changing. In the past, people used to prepare good **(1)** .... meals from fresh ingredients and what was readily available in markets, but now **(2)** .... food is becoming **(3)** .... popular. Research shows that eating some types of food too often may cause health problems, so governments and other **(4)** .... now offer information about diet and nutrition in the hope that it will **(5)** .... people from eating too much of the same thing and have a generally more **(6)** .... diet.

On the other hand, some people argue that despite the **(7)** .... of many traditional dishes from our menus, in general our diets are not as repetitive as they used to be. There is a much wider **(8)** .... of products available in supermarkets and other shops than there was 20 years ago.

	TRADITION
	FILL
	CONVENIENT
	INCREASE
	ORGANISE
	COURAGE
	BALANCE
	APPEAR
	CHOOSE

Starting off

Work in groups.

What aspects of school life do these photos show?
How can students benefit from these activities?
Which of these activities have you done?
Which did you enjoy most?

Listening | Part 1

1 **EP** You are going to hear people talking in eight different situations connected with studying. Before you listen, match these words or phrases (1–9) with their definitions (a–i).

1 tutor
2 research (verb)
3 learner
4 mark (verb)
5 admission
6 pass (noun)
7 sit (an exam)
8 course requirement
9 job prospects

a check a piece of work or an exam, showing mistakes and giving a number or a letter to say how good it is
b someone who is getting knowledge or a new skill
c something that is needed or demanded for a course
d study a subject in detail in order to discover new information about it
e successful result in a test or course
f take a test or exam
g the possibility of being successful at finding work
h university teacher who teaches a small group of students
i when someone is given permission to become a member of a club, university, etc.

2 Now read these questions and <u>underline</u> the main idea in each question (but not the options A, B or C).

1 You overhear a student talking about a course he has been doing. How does he feel about the course now?
   A discouraged
   B nervous
   C satisfied

2 You hear a student complaining about a problem she has had. What was the problem with her essay?
   A It had to be rewritten.
   B It was similar to another essay.
   C It was given a low mark.

3 You hear a student at a language school in Japan. What does she like most about the experience?
   A attending language classes
   B doing other activities after class
   C meeting other language students

4 You hear an interview with a student who is thinking of studying abroad. What does she think will be the main benefit?
   A living in a different culture
   B becoming more independent
   C getting a better qualification

5 You overhear the director of a school talking to students. Why is he talking to them?
   A to explain something
   B to remind them of something
   C to cancel something

6 You hear a girl leaving a message about her first day at a new school. What surprised her about the school?
   A the other students
   B the teachers
   C the classrooms

7 You hear two students talking about a lesson. What does the boy think about the lesson?
   A It was too advanced.
   B It was too long.
   C It was too disorganised.

8 You hear a teacher talking to a student. What is he giving her advice about?
   A sitting university exams
   B choosing a university course
   C paying for university fees

3 ▶16 Listen and, for questions 1–8, choose the best answer (A, B or C).

Exam advice

- Read the questions carefully, <u>underlining</u> the main ideas in the question as you read. This helps you to focus on what is being asked. In some cases, you may have to <u>underline</u> the whole question.
- The words you hear will usually be different from the words in the question; listen for the meaning rather than actual words.

Vocabulary
Phrasal verbs

1 (EP) Match these phrasal verbs from Listening Part 1 (1–8) with their definitions (a–h).

1 get over	a be as good as something
2 live up to	b decide or arrange to delay an event or activity until a later time or date
3 hand back	
4 get away with	c feel better after something or someone has made you unhappy, or get better after an illness
5 point out	
6 put off	
7 turn out	d be known or discovered finally and surprisingly
8 look back	
	e return something to the person who gave it to you
	f to think about something that happened in the past
	g succeed in avoiding punishment for something
	h tell someone about some information, often because you believe they are not aware of it or have forgotten it

2 Complete these sentences by writing a phrasal verb from Exercise 1 in the correct form in the gaps.

1 Franz hates writing essays and tries to .... writing them till the last moment.

2 I don't know how Charo .... copying her essays from the Internet, but the teacher never seems to notice.

3 Julia worked really hard for the test, but when the teacher .... it .... she found she'd got a very low mark. I hope she .... the disappointment soon because she's looking really depressed.

4 My mum is very ambitious for me and it's difficult to .... her expectations. I think when she .... at her youth, she feels she didn't study hard enough herself.

5 The exam .... to be easier than I expected and, just as you .... , it was all things we'd studied before.

find out, get to know, know, learn, teach and study; attend, join, take part and assist

3 ⊙ Candidates often confuse the following words: *find out, get to know, know, learn, teach* and *study; attend, join, take part* and *assist.* Circle the correct word in *italics* in these sentences, then check your answers by reading the definitions on page 183.

1 I've been thinking of going to an Italian university and *learning / studying* international business for a year.

2 I only *found out / knew* in my tutorial just now when the tutor handed my essay back to me.

3 ... the opportunity to live abroad would be extremely educational because I'd *learn / study* about the Italian way of life and way of thinking.

4 I *learn / know* Japanese from Japanese teachers.

5 I'm doing a karate course *learned / taught* in Japanese.

6 ... I'm *knowing / getting to know* lots of local people.

7 They also organise lots of other things for us learners to *assist / take part* in after school.

8 There are clubs we can *assist / join* if we're interested ...

9 You're expected to *join / attend* all your lessons ...

4 Complete these sentences by writing the words from Exercise 3 in the correct form in the gaps.

1 Dimitri has been .... Spanish because he hopes to study in Seville next year.

2 I've .... a lot of interesting people from different countries while doing this course.

3 Maria hopes to .... chemistry when she goes to university.

4 While Karen was at summer camp, she .... how to windsurf.

5 The best way to .... the answer to this question is to look on the Internet.

6 I'd like to ring Kevin, but I don't .... his phone number.

7 I had a wonderful course tutor who .... me to speak Spanish really well.

8 The university has an accommodation officer who will .... students with finding somewhere to live.

9 Kostas .... a youth club because he wanted to meet people.

10 It was the first time he had .... in a marathon, so people were surprised when he won.

Grammar
Zero, first and second conditionals

1 Read the sentences (1–6) below. Which ...

a refer to something which the speaker thinks is possible?

b refer to something which the speaker is imagining, thinks is improbable, or thinks is impossible?

c refer to something which is generally true?

1 If you speak a bit of the language, it's much easier to make friends.

2 If I went, it might make it more difficult for me to get a good degree.

3 If for any reason you can't make it to a tutorial, try to let your tutor know.

4 If I lived in Italy, I'd learn about how Italians live and think.

5 If your tutor has to cancel a tutorial or put it off, he or she'll try to tell you the week beforehand.

6 Your tutors will organise you into groups and suggest research unless you prefer working alone.

➡ **page 164 Language reference:** Conditionals

2 Match the beginning of each sentence (1–10) with its ending (a–j).

1 I won't mention your name

2 I'd travel round the world

3 We don't allow people to do the course

4 I'll have to buy the book

5 If I decide to study abroad,

6 If I see her,

7 If I wasn't so busy,

8 If I went to study in Australia,

9 I'd take a taxi

10 If students come to class regularly,

a I won't see my girlfriend for several months.

b they usually get good results.

c I'd go to the cinema with you.

d I wouldn't come back.

e I'll tell her you called.

f if I had the money.

g unless I can find it in the library.

h unless you want me to.

i if I could afford one.

j unless they have the right qualifications.

3 ⊙ Candidates often make mistakes with first and second conditionals. Find and correct one mistake in each of these sentences. There may be more than one way to correct some sentences.

1 If I say that technology has not changed the way we study, I would be lying.
2 If I live near my school, I would go there by bicycle or even on foot.
3 If we study together, I think we would be able to test each other at the same time.
4 If we'll have any free time during the term, we can organise a school excursion.
5 If you'll have any problems on your course, please contact your tutor, who will sort them out.
6 If there will be something that interests you, do write back, and I'll do my best to tell you.
7 If I buy a computer, I would have to spend all day in front of it.
8 If we take a good rest, we would be full of energy and we could do everything better.
9 If you'll decide to stay until Christmas, you'll find Athens very exciting.
10 I'd like to say that if more people travelled by bicycle, the atmosphere will be better.

4 Complete the second sentence so that it has a similar meaning to the first sentence, using the word given. Do not change the word given. You must use between two and five words, including the word given.

1 We will not be able to finish the project without your help.
   ASSIST
   Unless .... project, we will not be able to finish it.

2 You cannot use the swimming pool unless you become a member of the sports club.
   JOIN
   You can only use the swimming pool .... the sports club.
3 Stella will not participate in the concert because she is feeling ill.
   PART
   If Stella was not feeling ill, she .... the concert.
4 It will be necessary for us to postpone the match if the weather does not improve.
   PUT
   Unless the weather gets better, we .... the match.
5 Your English improves because your teacher shows you your mistakes.
   UNLESS
   Your English would not get .... out your mistakes.
6 I will only play in the basketball match if I recover from my cold.
   GET
   Unless .... , I will not play in the basketball match.

5 Work in pairs. Take turns to ask each other these questions.

- If you could study anywhere in the world, where would you go?
- If you studied in a different country, what do you think would be your biggest problem?
- If you could change one thing in your life, what would it be?
- If, one day, you became famous, what do you think you'd be famous for?
- How will you celebrate if you pass all your exams this year?

Reading and Use of English | Part 7

1 Work in pairs. You are going to read extracts from four reports written by secondary-school students from different countries. Each student has written about an educational exchange he/she went on to another country. Before you read, discuss these questions.

1 How do you think students benefit from going to school in another country for a term (or even a year)?
2 What problems do each of the pictures show?
3 If you were doing an educational exchange, how would you deal with each problem?

2 Now <u>underline</u> the main idea in each question 1–10.

Which person

was surprised by the different approach to education?	1
enjoyed cooperating with their host family?	2
believes they are more adult as a result of the exchange?	3
feels the exchange has helped to equip them for the future?	4
felt a responsibility to take as much advantage as possible of exchange?	5
had a different attitude to attending school while abroad?	6
wanted a change from their normal school life?	7
had not expected to be able to do an exchange?	8
had mixed feelings about the type of school?	9
changed their opinion of people as a result of the exchange?	10

Exam advice

- Before you read the sections, read the questions carefully, <u>underlining</u> the main ideas.
- Read the first section and find which questions it answers.
- Deal with each section in turn in this way.
- If you have any time left at the end, go back and check what you have written and fill in any questions you missed.

3 For questions 1–10 above, choose the students A–D on page 57 and <u>underline</u> the words which give you the answer. The students may be chosen more than once.

4 Work in groups. Look at this post on an international student forum. Think about the experiences of the students you have just read about and decide what Anna should do.

Anna

I'm 16 years old and I'm interested in coming to your country for a few months to learn the language. I know a little of the language, but I'd like to speak it much better because I might decide to study it at university in future. What do you think I should do? Should I do an educational exchange and find a family with people my own age to stay with, or would it be better to stay at home and do an online course or go to a language school in my town?

At school abroad

Have you ever thought of studying abroad? Four students who studied abroad relate their experiences …

A Divya Singh from Cardiff went to Chile

I went to a talk given by a couple of older students who had been on an exchange programme the previous year, and it occurred to me that if I could persuade my mum, this would be just the sort of break from normal school routine that I needed. I filled in my application while holding out little hope of being selected. However I was, and was soon immersed in a totally different educational culture, which helped me to appreciate many aspects of my school back home. Another great advantage of my year abroad was that I picked up Spanish much more quickly than in classes back home and, because my teachers were pretty demanding, I even feel confident writing it now. As a result, I'm considering doing Spanish and Latin American studies at university and perhaps after that going into the diplomatic service.

B Bruce Brown from Sydney went to England

Although my parents had insisted that I went, I knew what a sacrifice they were making to pay for my year abroad, so I was determined to make the most of the opportunity. My host family was really welcoming, but what I found hard to get used to were the seemingly endless days of grey drizzle and the fact that it got dark so early in winter. Even so, I took every chance to get out and meet people, make friends and get a real, in-depth experience of English life. At the same time, I was keen to make an impact at school and get good grades, although I found the schoolwork quite challenging and not really the highlight of my stay. Even so, I learned far more than I expected, made a lot of friends and came away with the impression that the British are a lot more interesting than I had been given to expect by people back home.

C Nelson Grace from Boston went to New Zealand

I lived on a farm on South Island, where my host family had a vast flock of about 3,000 sheep. Being a city boy, the experience of farming life was totally novel, but I loved it and took every opportunity to go out and help with the work of the farm. I also got involved in lots of sporting activities with my school, including sailing, rugby and skiing – all firsts for me. I found New Zealanders so enthusiastic about everything that I used to get up with a buzz of excitement and, unlike back home, I actually looked forward to going into school every day. I also think I matured a lot during my year abroad. I'm not so dependent now on my family or my teachers to make me study, and I've learned to get on with all sorts of different people, even if they're not my type. I've also learned a bit about the value of money!

D Carmen Echevarria from Bilbao went to Scotland

After four years in a state secondary school in Bilbao, it was a huge shock to find myself in a private all-girls school in the Highlands of Scotland, where everyone wore uniforms. Studying there was a complete revelation to me: gone were the hours spent in the evenings memorising huge numbers of useless facts for tests the next day which I would forget as soon as the test was over. Instead, we spent a lot of time discussing issues, solving problems and writing creatively. I missed my friends back home, but really appreciated learning to think in new ways and seeing that education could be so creative. I missed not sharing my classes with boys, but on the other hand, we probably concentrated harder and may have felt more relaxed about the opinions we expressed.

Reading and Use of English | Part 3

1 **EP** Form nouns from these verbs.

Verb	Noun
qualify	1 qualification
intend	2
respond	3
adjust	4
compare	5
exist	6
demand	7
develop	8
behave	9
advise	10
appear	11
know	12

2 **EP** Each of these nouns has been formed from a verb. Write the verb next to each noun.

Verb	Noun
1 agree	agreement
2	assessment
3	feeling
4	involvement
5	investigation
6	confusion
7	preference
8	approval

➜ page 181 Language reference: Word formation

Exam advice

Read the text quickly to see what it is about.

- Read before and after the gap to decide:
  - what meaning the word has
  - what type of word you need (noun, verb, adjective or adverb).
- Think about how you need to change the word in capitals to form the word you need.
- When you have finished, read the completed text to check it makes sense.

3 **EP** Read the text below.

- Decide what type of word (verb, noun, adjective or adverb) you need for each gap.
- Then, use the word given in capitals at the end of some of the lines to form a word that fits in the gap in the same line.

Culture shock for international students

Students going to study in another country usually have to make a number of cultural **(0)** adjustments. . They may find it difficult to form **ADJUST**
(1) .... with local people and they will **FRIEND**
certainly have to get used to a **(2)** .... **VARY**
of new things including food, the climate and the language. An extra difficulty may be the different **(3)** .... which their teachers **EXPECT**
and tutors have of them in **(4)** .... with **COMPARE**
their home country. They may be **(5)** .... for the amount of work they **PREPARE**
have to do on their own or the fact that their tutors are looking for originality and a capacity for **(6)** .... thought rather than an ability **DEPEND**
to memorise large quantities of information. Equally, they may sometimes be surprised by the **(7)** .... of their fellow students who, **BEHAVE**
although usually friendly and **(8)** .... , **WELCOME**
may sometimes seem a little immature. As time passes, international students will find that things become easier and what was unfamiliar to start with will eventually seem normal.

4 Work in groups. How do schools benefit from having visits from exchange students?

Vocabulary

work or job; possibility, occasion or opportunity; fun or funny

1 👁 Candidates often confuse the following words: *work* or *job*; *possibility, occasion* or *opportunity*; *fun* or *funny*. Read these sentences from Listening Part 3 and circle the correct word in *italics*. Then read the definitions on page 183 to check your answers.

1 This is my first student *job / work*, and I'm a part-time hospital porter.

2 It's hard physical *job / work*, but I think I expected that when I started.

3 They have the *possibility / occasion / opportunity* to talk about things outside the hospital.

4 On some *possibilities / occasions / opportunities*, I've also been left on my own in charge of the whole hotel.

5 It isn't a very well-paid *job / work* and it's not exactly fun, but then first *jobs / works* usually aren't.

6 The people are really *fun / funny*, so there are lots of laughs on set.

7 There's even the *possibility / occasion / opportunity* that I'll be given a small part.

2 Circle the correct word in *italics* in these sentences.

1 I know he was trying to be *fun / funny*, but none of his jokes made us laugh.

2 The trip was *fun / funny* – we should do it again sometime.

3 I don't think there's much *possibility / opportunity* of him being chosen for the job.

4 I only wear these smart clothes on special *occasions / opportunities*.

5 Did you get a(n) *possibility / opportunity* to chat to Matt yesterday?

6 She's just filled out a form applying for a summer *job / work*.

7 I'm hoping to study engineering and to find *job / work* in the construction industry when I finish.

8 One of my *jobs / works* was to count the money at the end of the day.

3 Work in pairs. Complete the diagram below by grouping these words which form adjective collocations with *job* and *work* according to meaning. In some cases, more than one answer may be possible.

> badly paid   challenging   demanding   ~~fascinating~~
> ~~full-time~~   ~~hard~~   holiday   manual   office   ~~outdoor~~
> part-time   permanent   pleasant   responsible
> ~~skilled~~   temporary   tiring   tough   weekend
> ~~well-paid~~   worthwhile

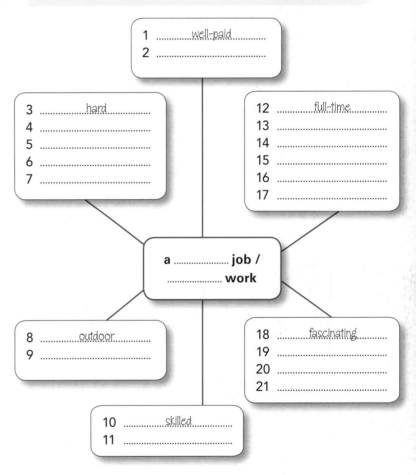

1 ....well-paid.............
2 ....

3 ....hard..............
4 ....
5 ....
6 ....
7 ....

12 ....full-time...........
13 ....
14 ....
15 ....
16 ....
17 ....

a .... job /
.... work

8 ....outdoor...........
9 ....

18 ....fascinating...........
19 ....
20 ....
21 ....

10 ....skilled...........
11 ....

4 Work in pairs. Describe each of these jobs using two or three adjectives from Exercise 3. (Put the adjectives which express your opinion first and the adjectives which express a fact afterwards, e.g. *Being a lifeguard at a swimming pool is a pleasant, outdoor, temporary job.*)

- waiter
- doctor
- social worker
- babysitter
- accountant
- the job you would like to do in the future

Reading and Use of English | Part 5

1 You are going to read an extract from the autobiography of Lucy Irvine, whose first job was in her father's hotel. Before you read, work in groups. What do you think are the advantages and disadvantages of working with your parents?

2 Read the extract quickly to answer these questions.

1 What was Lucy's job?
2 What part of her job involved making things?

Lucy's first job

When I was just 16, my father bought an old guesthouse in the village where we lived and decided to turn it into a luxury hotel. At the early stages of the hotel, he experimented with everything. None
5 of us had ever worked in a hotel before, but my dad had a vision of what guests would like to see. His standards were uncompromisingly high and he believed that in order to achieve those standards the most important thing was work.

10 For a month that summer, my name was down on the duty roster as waitress at breakfast and dinner, which included laying the tables in the dining room beforehand and hoovering and glass polishing afterwards. This gave me the middle of the day free
15 for studying because, predictably, my school report had not lived up to my father's high expectations.

Like all the other waitresses, I was equipped with a neat little uniform and instructions to treat the guests as though they were special visitors in my
20 own home. Although I did not feel comfortable with this, I did not express my feelings. Instead I concentrated all my attention on doing the job as well as, if not better than, the older girls.

I soon learned how to tackle the two most <u>daunting</u>
25 installations in the kitchen: the dishwasher and the chef, Gordon. He had an impressive chef's hat and a terrifying ability to lose his temper and get violent for no clear reason. His breath was strong and fishy, and I avoided close contact with him and always
30 grabbed the dishes he set down with a forbidding expression on my face which was transformed into a charming smile in the brief space between kitchen and dining room.

Breakfast waitressing was, I found, more enjoyable
35 than the dinner shift. The guests came wandering into the dining room from seven thirty onwards, staring with appreciation at the view of sea and islands through the dining-room window. If the day

looked promising, I would note down requests for
40 boats and packed lunches along with their breakfast orders. It was a matter of pride to me that everyone got their order promptly, and I took pleasure in my ability to get on with the people at each table.

It was funny how differently people behaved in the
45 evenings, dressed up and talking with louder, colder voices, not always returning my smile. However, that all changed when Dad, who was keen to make full use of my potential, created a special role for me which made me feel considerably more important.

50 It began with a few modest trays of cakes for the guests' packed lunches and progressed swiftly to fancy cakes for afternoon teas. I found that recipes were easy to follow and it was amusing to improvise. This led to the climax: a nightly extravaganza known
55 as Lucy's Sweet Trolley. Every evening, I made a grand entrance, wheeling before me a trolley carrying the most extraordinary collection of puddings, cakes and other desserts ever to grace a Scottish hotel. Most were things I had invented myself and I had cooked
60 all of them. Some - Jacobite Grenades, Mocha Genghis Khan and Goat's Milk Bavarios to name a few - were undeniably strange. It was Dad's idea that I should dress smartly and stop at each table and recite the name of each dish.

Adapted from *Runaway* by Lucy Irvine

3 Read these questions and copy out (or <u>underline</u>) the parts of the text which provide the answers.

1 In paragraph 1, what does Lucy say the people working at the hotel had in common?
2 What does the writer mean by *daunting* in line 24?
3 What did Lucy do while she carried food to the dining room?
4 Why did Lucy enjoy serving breakfasts more than dinners?
5 What was special about the food on Lucy's Sweet Trolley?

4 For questions 1–6, choose the answer (A, B, C or D) which you think fits best according to the text. Use the words you underlined in Exercise 3 to help you.

1 What did the people working at the hotel have in common?
   A They all understood the guests' expectations.
   B They all shared the same goals.
   C They all lacked experience.
   D They were all hard-working.

2 What does the writer mean by *daunting* in line 24?
   A disgusting
   B frightening
   C interesting
   D strange

3 What did Lucy do while she carried food to the dining room?
   A She smiled at Gordon in a friendly way.
   B She avoided touching Gordon.
   C She checked the food Gordon gave her.
   D She started to look more friendly.

4 Lucy enjoyed serving breakfasts more than dinners because the guests were
   A more demanding.
   B more friendly.
   C more punctual.
   D more relaxed.

5 What was special about the food on Lucy's Sweet Trolley?
   A It was inspired by traditional recipes.
   B It was prepared along with food for picnics.
   C It was made following her father's instructions.
   D It contained a number of new creations.

6 What impression does Lucy give of her job throughout the passage?
   A She found many opportunities to laugh.
   B She looked for ways of doing it better.
   C She found all aspects of it enjoyable.
   D She could do it with little effort.

Exam advice

- First read the text quickly to get a general idea of what it is about.
- Read the first question, find where it is answered in the text and read that section carefully more than once before you read the options A, B, C and D.
- Read each of the options A, B, C and D carefully and choose the one which matches what the text says.

5 Work in pairs.

- Would you enjoy doing a job like Lucy's? Why? / Why not?
- Which parts of her job would you enjoy more and which would you enjoy less?
- Do you think being a waiter is a good holiday job for a teenager? Why? / Why not?

Speaking | Part 2

1 Work in pairs. When you compare photos, you can say what the photos have in common as well as what is different about them. Discuss how you could answer the examiner's instructions below to say:

- which things are similar
- which things are different.

> I'd like you to compare the photographs and say what you think the people are learning from doing these two types of work.

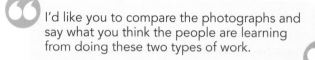

What are the people learning from doing these two types of work?

2 How could you use these words or phrases to talk about the photos?

> a involve   b deal with   c not well-paid   d coaching
> e full-time   f part-time   g keep somebody in order
> h work under pressure   i keep cool

3 ▶21 Listen to Nikolai and Antonia doing this part of the test. Which photo do they use each word or phrase with? Write 1, 2 or B (both) by each word or phrase (a–i).

4 Which of these strategies (a or b) does Nikolai use when doing the task?

a He describes the first photo and answers the question before moving on to the second photo and doing the same.

b He points out similarities as well as differences between the two photos and switches between them as he answers.

5 Listen again. Which of these phrases does Nikolai use? Tick (✓) the ones you hear.

> - Both photos show … ✓
> - Both the jobs in the photos involve … / … neither of them …
> - Anyway, the first photo shows …
> - While the girl in the first photo …
> - … whereas in the second photo … / … whereas the boy's …
> - Another thing in the second photo is …
> - I think both can …
> - On the other hand …
> - not just … but also …

6 **Pronunciation:** sentence stress (2)

We can use stress to contrast ideas or information.

1 Which ideas or information does Nikolai contrast in this sentence?

Anyway, the first photo shows a girl serving young people in a restaurant, whereas in the second photo a boy is working with children.

2 ▶22 Listen to the sentence and <u>underline</u> the stressed words.

3 **23** Decide which words are stressed in these sentences. Then listen to check your answers.

- The girl's job may be full time, // whereas the boy's is probably part time.
- The girl can learn how to keep customers happy, // while the boy has to keep children in order.
- He'll probably learn not just to deal with children, // but also their parents.
- I'd prefer to coach children than work in a restaurant // because really I enjoy being in the fresh air more than being indoors.

4 Work in pairs. Student A: read the first half of each sentence up to each // using the same stress as above. Student B: read the second half of the sentence using the same stress as above.
Student A: The girl's job may be full-time …
Student B: … whereas the boy's is probably part-time.

7 Work alone.

- Write three sentences to compare the photos and say which job you think is more difficult. Use phrases from Exercise 5 in your sentences.
- When you are ready, work in pairs and take turns to read your sentences aloud using stress to contrast your ideas.

8 Work in pairs.

> *Student A:* Do the speaking task in Exercise 1 on page 66.
> *Student B:* Time your partner and make sure they speak for one minute.

9 Work in pairs.

> *Student B:* Follow the examiner's instructions in the next column.
> *Student A:* Time your partner and make sure they speak for one minute.

Then change roles.

Here are your photographs. They show people doing different part-time jobs. I'd like you to compare the photographs and say what you think the people might enjoy about doing these jobs.

What do the people enjoy about doing these jobs?

Exam advice

- Compare the general differences between the two photos and also spend time answering the printed question.
- You can talk about one photo first and then the other (as you saw in Unit 2), or both at the same time (as in this unit).
- Keep speaking till the examiner says 'Thank you'.

Grammar
Countable and uncountable nouns

1 👁 Most of these sentences contain mistakes which are often made by candidates. Two of them are correct. Find and correct the mistakes.

1 Could you please send me some informations about the job?
2 I hope you don't mind if I give you an advice about how to apply for the job.
3 She's just found a work as an ambulance driver.
4 Public transport is still the best way to get around the city.
5 The hotel also provides accommodations for its employees.
6 Congratulations! The news about your job is very good.
7 He works in a shop selling furnitures.
8 Sorry to hear about the accident. Did it do many damages?
9 Unfortunately, when we arrived at the airport terminal, we couldn't find our luggages.
10 Everyone loves the band, because they play such fantastic musics.

➡ page 165 Language reference: Countable and uncountable nouns

2 👁 Candidates often make mistakes with countable and uncountable nouns. Circle all the *uncountable* nouns in each list.

1 (accommodation) hotel (luggage) suitcase (scenery)
2 advice information knowledge news suggestion
3 accident bus damage transport
4 bed furniture
5 dish food meal
6 homework job service task work
7 equipment tool
8 instrument music

3 Complete these sentences by writing a word from the box in the gaps. In some cases, more than one answer may be possible.

piece bit deal number amount

1 Can I give you a .... of advice about shopping in this town?
2 During the storm, quite a large .... of trees were blown down.
3 Have you brought that .... of equipment I asked for? The amplifier, I mean.
4 I've just been given a great .... of news – I've passed my exams!
5 Seb put a great .... of effort into organising the party.
6 There were a large .... of guests at the party, judging by the .... of food that was eaten!

Articles

4 Look at the underlined examples from the reading text in extracts 1–6. Then match them with the rules for articles (*a, an, the*) below (a–f).

1 When I was just 16, my father bought an old guesthouse … (lines 1–2) b
2 … my father bought an old guesthouse in the village where we lived … (line 2)
3 At the early stages of the hotel, he experimented with everything. (line 4)
4 … but my dad had a vision of what guests would like to see … (line 6)
5 … the most important thing was work. (lines 8–9)
6 … the most important thing was work. (lines 8–9)

a No article is used when using uncountable nouns in the singular.
b *a* and *an* are used with singular countable nouns mentioned for the first time.
c *the* is used when it's clear who or what we are referring to from the context.
d No article is used when talking in general and in the plural.
e *the* is used with superlative adjectives and adverbs.
f *the* is used with things mentioned before.

➡ page 163 Language reference: Articles

5 Complete this text by writing *a, an, the* or '–' if no article is needed in the gaps.

I was just 18, and it was **(1)** .... first time I had worked in **(2)** .... office. It was **(3)** .... summer holidays and I had just finished **(4)** .... school. I thought it would be **(5)** .... good way of earning **(6)** .... bit of money before I went to **(7)** .... university in **(8)** .... autumn. I spent most of **(9)** .... day keying **(10)** .... information into the company's database. Although I found **(11)** .... job rather boring, I earned **(12)** .... good salary.

6 ◉ Candidates often make mistakes with articles. Correct the mistakes in these sentences. Some sentences contain more than one mistake.

1 Have you heard a latest news about Bayern Munich in the Champions' League?
2 I bought my first motorcycle at my age of 16.
3 I'm hoping to visit your town the next year.
4 She found a lot of useful information on Internet.
5 My mum had difficulty parking in city centre on Saturday.
6 I think that bicycles are most effective means of transport.
7 The money can cause a lot of problems.
8 I really enjoy listening to the music of all sorts on my iPod.
9 When I visit the foreign cities, I really like the shopping for clothes.
10 I'm having wonderful time with my friends.
11 I've got a plenty of spare time at this moment, so we can have a dinner together if you like.
12 We can provide an accommodation for you in a comfortable hotel.

Reading and Use of English | Part 2

1 Read this article quickly, ignoring the gaps. What activities does the programme include?

A new summer programme

This summer, a group of 16-year-old students are taking **(0)** ...part... in a three-week programme designed to teach them new skills and **(1)** .... them used to working with people they have never met before. **(2)** .... things go according to plan, in two years' time, nearly one in six teenagers will be involved in the programme with **(3)** .... eventual aim of offering it to **(4)** .... young person in the country. **(5)** .... far, our group has spent two weeks living **(6)** .... from home (many for the first time), initially on an outdoor course, with activities **(7)** .... as rock climbing, rafting and trekking, and then spending a week in self-catering accommodation where they are planning and setting up a volunteering project. At the moment, the students are putting their plans into action not **(8)** .... by cooking for themselves, but also by organising a night outside sleeping rough in order to raise money for a local homeless shelter.

Adapted from *The Independent*

2 Read the text again and think of the word which best fits each gap (1–8). Use only one word in each gap. There is an example at the beginning (0).

3 Check or complete your answers using these clues.

  1 a verb
  2 a conditional
  3 an article
  4 a synonym of *all*
  5 a synonym of *up to now*
  6 the opposite of *at home*
  7 a synonym of *for example*
  8 *not* .... *but also*

4 Work in groups.

  1 Do you think all 15–17-year-olds should get experience of:
   • living away from home?
   • doing outdoor activities?
   • cooking for themselves?
   • helping other people?
   Why? / Why not?
  2 Which of the experiences above are the most useful for them to have?

Writing | Part 2 A letter or email

1 Read this writing task and <u>underline</u> the three points you must deal with in your reply.

> You have received an email from an English friend, Rosie. Read this part of the email.
>
> > I'm doing a college project on jobs students do. Can you help me by describing the sort of jobs students do in your country, any problems they have and the best way to find a good student job?
> >
> > Thanks,
> >
> > Rosie
>
> Write your **email**.

2 Work in pairs. Discuss what you can say to answer the three points. Note down your ideas as you speak.

3 Write a brief plan for your reply (in note form).

  • How many paragraphs do you need?
  • What ideas or information will you include in each paragraph?

Listening | Part 2

1 Work in pairs. You are going to hear Gary giving a talk about adventure racing as part of a school project. Read this text and discuss what type of information you need for each gap.

Adventure racing

Gary participated with his (1) .... in his first adventure race last year.

Adventure racing became popular as a sport in the (2) .... , although there were races before that.

In many adventure races, there must be a balance of (3) .... in each team.

Gary thinks teams which contain (4) .... are more successful.

Although some races take place in urban areas, most happen in (5) ....

Teams are really alone on the race because there are almost no (6) .... in the area where they race.

Gary's ambition is to do a race called the (7) .... Race in New Zealand.

Some races may take up to (8) .... to complete.

Gary thinks (9) .... must be the hardest thing in long races.

Adventure racing is considered (10) .... by many athletes from other sports as well.

2 ▶24 Listen and, for questions 1–10, complete the sentences with a word or short phrase.

Exam advice

Before you listen:

- look at the incomplete sentences, including any words which come after the gap.
- think about what type of information you need for each gap (a date, a job, etc.).
- think about what type of word(s) you need for each gap (a noun (phrase), verb (phrase), etc.).

3 Work in groups.

- What do you think are the advantages of racing in teams?
- What are the main difficulties of adventure racing?

Vocabulary
Verb collocations with sporting activities

1 Complete these extracts from Listening Part 2 by writing an appropriate verb in the correct form in the gaps.

1 Adventure racing is a sport you .... in teams.
2 Anyway, it's not like just .... jogging or running or something like that.
3 The races are .... in all sorts of different places.
4 The majority are .... in mountains or deserts.
5 Many people who are at the top of their sport in other fields are now .... because they find that, rather than .... as individuals … they need to work as a team.

2 Use the table of collocations below to complete these sentences. In some cases, more than one answer may be possible.

1 I think local governments should .... competitions for schools in their area where any student over 15 can ....
2 I would encourage people to .... swimming two or three times a week because I think it's an excellent way of .... exercise.
3 People who enjoy team sports often .... basketball or football, whereas people who enjoy individual sports .... golf or .... windsurfing.

verb	sport
hold / organise / compete in / enter / take part in	a race / a competition / a tournament / a championship
do / take	exercise
go*	jogging / cycling / skiing / swimming / windsurfing
play**	football / golf / basketball
do***	sports / athletics / gymnastics / judo / weightlifting

* for sports that end in -ing and are usually or often done outdoors
** for sports which are considered games
*** for other sports which do not use go or play

3 Work in pairs.

- How do you take exercise?
- What sports have you tried, and how much did you enjoy them?

Reading and Use of English | Part 6

1 Work in pairs. You are going to read an article by an adventure racer. Before you read the whole article, read the title and the subheading in *italics*. What do you expect to find out by reading the article?

2 Read the article quite carefully and make a short note in the margin about the subject of each paragraph. An example has been done for you.

Are you ready for an adventure race?

Rebecca Rusch has competed in several Eco-Challenge races, where teams of four men and women race non-stop over a 500 km course which includes trekking, canoeing, horse riding, scuba diving, mountaineering and mountain biking.

need for experience

Obviously, I did not feel so ready for the early races in my career as the races we have done recently. There is a lot to be said for just gaining experience. Just getting out there and getting your feet wet teaches you the right skills and attitude.

It's often not the most physically prepared or the fittest teams that win. The ones who <u>come first</u> are the teams who race intelligently and adapt to unexpected situations. **1** ☐ The only way to develop <u>those qualities</u> is to get out and race or do long training trips with your team-mates and friends.

Adventure races are such a huge challenge that when you enter a race you always think, "Am I ready? Did I train enough? Did I forget something?" I remember one race in particular, <u>my very first Eco-Challenge</u> and only my second race ever. **2** ☐ A 24-hour race seemed like an eternity to me. My background was cross-country running in high school and college where a two- or three-mile race seemed long. Most of <u>my fear</u> was due to lack of experience and knowledge. I really had no idea what I was getting into because I had never done a <u>24-hour race</u> before. **3** ☐

In preparation <u>for Australia</u>, I tried to approach my training in a methodical way. Looking back, I wasn't methodical at all. In fact, what I did involved simply running, biking and paddling a kayak as much and as hard as I could. I was also

working at the same time. In reality, I was training <u>a couple of hours a day</u> during the week to get fit and at weekends training with the team for perhaps <u>four hours</u>. **4** ☐ I spent the rest of the time worrying about how slow I was.

So, we went to Australia and entered the race. We didn't plan a strategy at all, but just ran as fast as possible from the start. I just tried to keep up with <u>my team-mates</u>, who were more experienced than I was. **5** ☐ It was a furious 36 hours. We arrived at a few of the check points in first place and were among the top five. I knew we didn't belong there.

To cut a long story short, two of my team-mates decided not to continue the race after just a day and a half. <u>One</u> was suffering hallucinations and feeling ill. He was just too tired to carry on. **6** ☐ We had been going so fast that he felt uncomfortable asking us to stop so he could take care of his blisters. The other two of us, feeling fresh still, had to drop out with the rest of our team. Four days later, we watched in disappointment as the winners crossed the finishing line. I knew that our team had not been prepared or realistic about the pace we could keep, but not finishing that race was the most valuable lesson I could have learned.

I promised then to come back one day and finish the race. That was seven years (and thousands of race miles) ago.

Adapted from *Adventure Sports Journal*

Grammar

Infinitive and verb + -ing

1 These sentences (some of which are from the article you have just read) are examples of when to use the infinitive and when to use the verb + -ing form. Decide which sentence (a–i) is an example (1–10) for each of the rules on this page. You can use some of the sentences as examples for more than one rule.

 a **Not finishing** that race was the most valuable lesson I could have learned.
 b I promised then **to come back** one day and finish the race.
 c In fact, what I did involved simply **running, biking** and **paddling** a kayak as much and as hard as I could.
 d There is a lot to be said for just **gaining** experience.
 e I was training a couple of hours a day during the week **to get fit**.
 f There are medical teams **to take care of** injured runners.
 g He was just too tired **to carry on**.
 h It's no use **entering** a race if you haven't prepared properly.
 i Two of my team-mates decided **not to continue** the race after just a day and a half.

3 Six sentences have been removed from the article. Read the sentences below one by one. As you read each sentence:

- underline words and phrases which you think refer to something in the article
- decide which gap (1–6) it fits.
  There is one extra sentence which you do not need to use.

 A Another had severe problems with his feet.
 B I kept my mouth shut and followed them.
 C We won it even so, and were invited to compete in the Eco-Challenge in Australia.
 D His encouragement helped me to complete it.
 E That was how much I had prepared.
 F When I did it, I felt totally afraid and unprepared.
 G To achieve this, you have to be flexible and patient.

4 Work in pairs.

- Do you prefer team sports or individual sports? Why?

Exam advice

- Pay attention to pronouns (*we*, *that*, *it*, etc.), adverbs (*however*, *even so*, etc.) and other reference words/ phrases in the sentences which have been removed. Decide what they refer to before you place the sentence in a gap.
- Work methodically through the sentences, reading them and placing them one by one when you're sure they are right.

Using the infinitive and verb + -ing
The **infinitive** is used:

1 to say why you do something (sentence ......*e*......)
2 to say why something exists (sentence ....)
3 after *too* and *enough* (sentence ....)
4 after these verbs (there is a more complete list on page 166): *agree, appear, ask, arrange, decide, expect, fail, help, promise* (sentences .... and ....)
5 The negative is formed by placing *not* before the infinitive (sentence ....)

The **verb + -ing** is used:

6 after prepositions (sentence ....)
7 as subjects or objects of a verb (sentence ....)
8 after these verbs (there is a more complete list on page 166): *admit, enjoy, finish, involve, mind, postpone, risk, suggest* (sentence ....)
9 after these expressions: *it's no good, it's not worth, it's no use, it's a waste of time, spend time, can't help* (sentence ....)
10 The negative is formed by placing *not* before the verb + -ing (sentence ....)

➡ page 166 Language reference: Infinitive and verb + -ing forms

2 Complete these sentences by writing the verb in brackets in the correct form in the gaps.

1 Carlos has suggested .... (*start*) a five-a-side football team. What do you think?
2 I don't think the weather is good enough .... (*go*) sailing this afternoon.
3 We've decided .... (*hold*) the race early in the morning before it gets too hot.
4 .... (*train*) is essential if you want to perform well.
5 I've joined a gym .... (*get*) myself fitter.
6 If you train too hard, you risk .... (*injure*) yourself before the race.
7 It's no good .... (*run*) in a marathon if you're not wearing the right shoes.
8 She was disqualified from the race for .... (*push*) an opponent.

3 Circle the correct form in *italics* in each of these questions.

1 What sport would you advise someone *to do / doing* in order to make friends?
2 What sport would you choose *to learn / learning* if you had plenty of time and money?
3 If someone needed to get fit, what sport would you suggest *to do / doing*?
4 What sports do you avoid *to take part in / taking part in* and why?

4 Work in pairs. Ask and answer the questions in Exercise 3, giving your opinions.

5 ⊙ Candidates often make mistakes with the infinitive and verb + *-ing*. Some of these sentences are correct. Find and correct the mistakes.

1 Students are not allowed running along school corridors.
2 Few people choose spending their time taking exercise.
3 The Internet means that we spend more time sitting at home, but we cannot imagine to live without it.
4 Being fit and healthy does not mean to run 20 km a day.
5 Many students would prefer to cycle to school than go by school bus.
6 Many people only think about take exercise when they are overweight.
7 Unless they try to compete as a team, they will not succeed to win the competition.
8 Doing a sport is a good alternative if you are bored to sit and read a book.
9 It may be good to use a bicycle instead of going by public transport.
10 There are several good reasons for ride a bike.

Reading and Use of English | Part 4

1 Work in pairs. For questions 1 and 2, choose the correct answer A–D. Why are the other answers incorrect?

1 Why don't we start jogging if we want some exercise?
   TAKING
   He suggested .... in order to get some exercise.
   A that they should take up jogging
   B taking up jogging
   C to take up jogging
   D going jogging
2 She won the match without difficulty.
   EASY
   She found .... the match.
   A it easy to win
   B that it was easy to win
   C she could easily win
   D it simple to win

2 Now do these Part 4 questions. Use the clues below each question to help you.

1 Marianne prepared for the race by training every evening.

READY

Marianne trained every evening .... for the race.

• Can you think of an expression with *ready* which means *prepare*?
• Why did Marianne train every evening?
• Do you use the verb + *-ing* or an infinitive to say why she trained every evening?

2 I found it impossible not to laugh at his efforts.

HELP

I .... at his efforts.

• You need an expression with *help* which means 'find it impossible'.
• Your answer needs to be in the same tense.

3 Cycling on the pavement is prohibited.

USE

Cyclists .... the pavement.

• How do you use *allowed* to mean it's prohibited?
• Do you use the verb + *-ing* or an infinitive after *allowed*?

3 Now do these Part 4 questions.

1 We'd like all our students to participate in the sports programme.

PART

We are keen on all our students .... the sports programme.

2 Buying the equipment for this sport is cheaper than hiring it.

MORE

It's .... the equipment for this sport than to buy it.

3 You should have phoned her to tell her the game was cancelled.

GIVE

You were supposed .... to tell her the game was cancelled.

4 Mateo managed to win the race.

SUCCEEDED

Mateo .... the race.

5 'I'll never get angry with the referee again,' said Martin.

TEMPER

Martin promised never .... the referee again.

6 Tanya found windsurfing easy to learn.

DIFFICULTY

Tanya .... to windsurf.

Exam advice

▪ Use the word in **CAPITALS** without changing it.
▪ Count the words. Contractions (*isn't*, *don't*, etc.) count as two words.
▪ Read both sentences again at the end to check that they mean the same and contain all the same information/ideas.

4 Check your answers by looking at these clues for each of the questions in Exercise 3.

1 Did you use a fixed phrase which means *participate*?
2 Have you used an opposite of *cheap*? Did you use an infinitive or a verb + *-ing*?
3 Did you use an expression which means *phone* (*give her a …*)?
4 *Managed* is followed by an infinitive. Is *succeeded* also followed by an infinitive? Do you also need a preposition?
5 Can you remember an expression with *temper* which means *become angry*?
6 You cannot write *did not have any difficulty in learning* because it's seven words.

Listening | Part 4

1 Work in pairs. You will hear an interview with someone who went on a paragliding course. Before you listen, look at the photo.

- Do you think paragliding is a risky sport?
- Would you like to try it? Why? / Why not?

2 Read these questions and <u>underline</u> the main idea in each one.

1 Why did Hannah want to try paragliding?
   A She had seen other people doing it.
   B She wanted to write an article about it.
   C She was bored with the sport she was doing.

2 Why did Hannah choose to do a paragliding course in France?
   A The location was safer.
   B The course was cheaper.
   C The weather was better.

3 Hannah says that the advantage of learning to paraglide from the sand dune is that
   A you are unlikely to fall in the sea.
   B you can land comfortably on the sand.
   C you cannot fall too far.

4 How did Hannah spend the first morning of her course?
   A She learned to lift her paraglider.
   B She flew to the bottom of the dune.
   C She watched other people paragliding.

5 When she started flying, her instructor
   A shouted at her from the ground.
   B talked to her over the radio.
   C flew next to her.

6 When you land after paragliding, it feels like
   A jumping from a seat.
   B falling from a horse.
   C falling from a bicycle.

7 What, for Hannah, is the best reason to go paragliding?
   A It's exciting.
   B It's unusual.
   C It's quiet.

3 ▶ 25 For questions 1–7, listen and choose the best answer (A, B or C).

Exam advice

- When you listen, wait until the speaker has finished talking about an idea before you choose your answer.
- Listen for the same idea to be expressed, not the same words.

Vocabulary

look, see, watch, listen and *hear*

1 ◉ Candidates often confuse the following words: *look, see* and *watch*, and *listen* and *hear*. Complete these sentences from Listening Part 4 by writing *look, see, watch, listen* or *hear* in the correct form in the gaps.

1 I spend my life .... people doing different sports.
2 I was .... down the course, planning my next shot or something, when I .... these paragliders floating down.
3 In fact, I .... to my instructor, Chantalle, through an earphone.
4 It was generally very quiet, calm and civilised, except when she raised her voice to shout at other flyers to keep away from me. And then you really .... her!

2 ◉ Read the definitions on page 184. Then circle the correct word in *italics* in these sentences.

1 I *looked at / watched* my watch and saw that it was time to leave.
2 I really enjoy *looking at / watching* horror films.
3 We live near a motorway and can *listen to / hear* the traffic non-stop.
4 I've been *looking at / watching* our holiday photos.
5 Did you *watch / see* Buckingham Palace when you were in London?
6 She knew the policeman was *looking / watching* what she did.
7 Ivan was in the kitchen, so he didn't *listen to / hear* the telephone when it rang.
8 Marisa looks so relaxed when she's *listening to / hearing* music on her MP3 player.

Speaking | Part 3

1 Before you start this speaking section, look at the work you did on Speaking Part 3 on pages 37–38. Work in pairs. Read the examiner's instructions and the speaking task below. Then take about two minutes to do the task together.

> I'd like you to imagine that your college is interested in getting students to do more sport. Here are some ideas they are thinking about and a question for you to dicuss. First, you have some time to look at the task. Now talk to each other about why these ideas might encourage students to do more sport.

A visit to the [na]tional athletics [c]hampionships

A talk by a professional footballer

How could these activities encourage students to do more sport?

A weekend [do]ing adventure sports

A school sports day

Free membership of a sports club

2 Look at this checklist. Which things did you do?

		yes	no
1	Talk about all of the activities.		
2	Listen to each other and respond to what the other person says.		
3	Ask each other's opinion.		
4	Interrupt each other.		
5	One student tried to speak much more than the other.		

3 ▶26 Now listen to Miguel and Irene doing the speaking task from Exercise 1. Which of the things on the checklist in Exercise 2 did they do?

4 Listen to Miguel and Irene again and write each of these phrases in the correct column in the table below.

> How do you think …?   Well, perhaps …   Yes, and …
> I imagine students would see …   Maybe, but …
> What about …?   I suppose that might be …
> I suppose so, but …   Yes, I see what you mean.
> That's a good point, and …   Do you really think …?
> That's true.   Yes, good idea.   You're right.   Yes, but …

suggesting ideas	asking your partner's opinion	agreeing	disagreeing
	How do you think …?		

5 Pronunciation: intonation (2)

You will make a good impression in the exam if you sound interested and enthusiastic about what you discuss. You can use intonation to show your interest.

1 ▶27 Listen to how the voices rise and fall on the highlighted words.

Miguel: Well, perhaps this could be organised in a more adult way, you know, with some serious sports for people who were interested and less serious activities for other people. That way everyone could get involved.

Irene: Yes, good idea, and people could be organised into teams and it could all be made quite competitive and enjoyable at the same time. When I think about it, it could be really successful.

2 Now work in pairs and read the extract aloud. Take turns as Miguel and Irene.

6 Work in pairs. Follow the examiner's instructions for the second part of Speaking Part 3.

> Now you have about a minute to decide which idea your college should choose.

7 Work in pairs.

1 Take about two minutes to do the first part of this speaking task.

> I'd like you to imagine that a town wants young people to spend their free time in ways which are useful for them. Here are some ideas that they are thinking about and a question for you to discuss. Talk to each other about how these ideas would provide useful ways for young people to spend their free time.

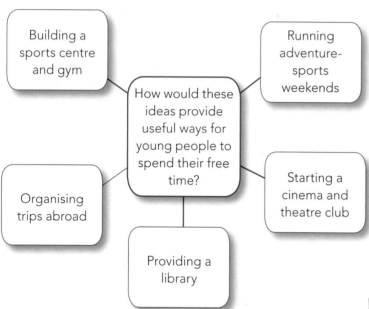

Building a sports centre and gym

Running adventure-sports weekends

How would these ideas provide useful ways for young people to spend their free time?

Organising trips abroad

Starting a cinema and theatre club

Providing a library

2 Now follow the examiner's instructions for the second part of Speaking Part 3.

> Now you have a minute to decide which two facilities the town should build.

Exam advice

When you discuss the first part of the task, you needn't talk about all of the options, but you should make suggestions, ask your partner's opinion and respond to your partner's ideas.

When you discuss the second part of the task, it's not necessary to reach agreement, but you should:

- discuss which option(s) to choose and give reasons for choice(s)
- listen and respond to what your partner says. Don't be afraid to disagree politely – this can lead to a good discussion.

Writing | Part 2 An article

1 Read this writing task and underline the points you must deal with in your answer.

You see this notice on your college noticeboard.

The editors of the college magazine would like contributions to the magazine on the following subject:

A great way to keep fit.

Describe a sporting activity or form of exercise you enjoy, how you started and why you would recommend it to other people.

The writer of the best article will receive ten tickets to the local cinema.

Write your article.

2 Work in pairs.

- Discuss the ideas each of you could express to deal with the points you have underlined in the task.
- Which ideas would you use in your article?

3 Read the article on page 83, which was written by Nacho Pallas.

- What does he enjoy about his way of taking exercise? Why?

Rugby: rough but fun

I love playing rugby. I started playing the game at school when I was just nine years old. It was compulsory to do a sport three afternoons a week, and in winter the boys had to play rugby. I immediately found I enjoyed it, *despite* not being as big as other boys my age. *However*, I was quite athletic, so I could often run past my opponents and score points by being more agile than them.

Although it's quite a rough game with complicated rules, it keeps you fit because you have to run for 80 minutes, so you also have to train several times a week. For people who are competitive and enjoy playing in a team, it's great fun. You can play it at any level, but if you want to win a trophy, you'll need someone to coach you so that you learn the best tactics and learn to work effectively together.

Although you can sometimes get hurt, I would recommend the game to anyone who enjoys ball games, running and keeping fit. *However*, if you decide you don't want to actually play, it's a great sport for spectators as well.

4 Look at the structure of the article. In which paragraph does Nacho deal with these points?

1 He describes a sporting activity.
2 How he started.
3 Why he would recommend it.

5 Study how the words and phrases in *italics* in Nacho's article are used. Then complete these sentences by writing *although, however* or *despite* in the gaps.

1 .... the swimming pool is quite far from where I live, I try to go there three times a week.
2 .... being given tickets to the football match, we decided to watch it on TV.
3 .... I'd love to be a professional footballer, I don't think I'm talented enough.
4 He was very easy to talk to .... being a famous tennis star.
5 Ten per cent of British teenagers dream of becoming sports stars. .... , very few will achieve their ambition.
6 I won the game .... I'd never played badminton before.
7 .... feeling very tired, she managed to finish the race.
8 I didn't enjoy the match. .... , our opponents played very well.

➡ page 168 Language reference: Linking words for contrast

6 (EP) Study how Nacho used the words in the box in his article. Then use them in the correct form to complete the sentences below.

> athletic opponents competitive rough trophy
> coach spectators

1 Although Valery enjoys .... sports, he prefers taking exercise on his own.
2 Ice hockey is a .... game where players often get hurt.
3 If I was more .... , I might be able to win a few more races.
4 Our .... for the next match are last year's champions.
5 We need someone to .... our team so that they learn to play better.
6 Few .... watch adventure sports because they take place in remote areas.
7 We're rated as one of the top teams despite never having won a single ....

7 Now write your own answer to the writing task in Exercise 1.

- Before you start writing, make a brief plan.
- Try to use structures and vocabulary you have studied in this Writing section and this unit.
- Write between 140 and 190 words.
- Read through your article when you have finished to improve it and to check it for mistakes.

Exam advice

- Write a plan before you start writing the article.
- Organise your ideas into paragraphs, and use linking words such as: *however, despite, in addition, for example* and *on the other hand*.

Before you write:

- think about what the people reading the article will find interesting, enjoyable or useful
- write a plan by:
  – <u>underlining</u> all the points you must deal with
  – organising your ideas into paragraphs so that you cover everything you've been asked to do. Often each underlined point will form the topic of a paragraph.

Reading and Use of English | Part 7

1 You will read a newspaper article about five actors at the beginning of their careers. Before you read, discuss this question in pairs.

- What are the advantages and disadvantages of working as an actor?

2 Read questions 1–10 and <u>underline</u> the main idea in each question.

Which actor

believes actors must be ready to accept negative comments?	1
feels that they have learned a lot from people already working in the theatre and TV?	2
says that listening to other people's suggestions improves their acting?	3
has always been excited by having people watching their acting?	4
had planned to enter a different profession before training to become an actor?	5
prefers working in theatre rather than in cinema or television?	6
did not want to work outside the theatre initially?	7
feels worried about performing in front of some important people?	8
originally tried to train as an actor somewhere else?	9
wasn't so interested in acting in the theatre initially?	10

3 Now read the newspaper article. For questions 1–10, choose from the people A–E.

Exam advice

- Many of the sections may say quite similar things. You will have to read carefully to decide which section answers the question exactly.
- Guess difficult words from the context when you think it will help you to answer a question.
- <u>Underline</u> phrases in the texts which give you the answers and check them against the questions.

Starting off

1 Work in groups. Look at the photos and compare these different types of star. Talk about:

- income/money
- preparation and training
- length of career
- the advantages and disadvantages of being famous.

2 If you could be a star, what sort of star would you like to be? Why?

4 Work in groups.

- Have you ever performed in public (e.g. acting, speaking in public, dancing, doing a sport)?
- How did you feel about the experience? What did you enjoy about it? What did you dislike?

Five young actors

The curtains open in the theatre as a group of young actors make their way on to the stage. These are some young Edinburgh-based actors doing the final performance of their drama course.

A Scott Hoatson

22-year-old Scott is already a step ahead of his classmates, as he has been offered a year-long contract with the National Theatre of Scotland's under-26 theatre group. He was discovered by someone from the theatre while performing in plays in Edinburgh and St Andrews, but he admits the students' final performance in front of directors and agents is still nerve-wracking. "It's so important for all of us. The fact that there are artistic directors from the big theatres who come to watch makes it such a big opportunity. There's so much happening in Scotland at the moment. There are a lot of opportunities up here, so it makes sense to stay closer to home. When I started the course, I thought that stage acting was the only thing I wanted to do, but now I want to do everything I can – whether it's on stage, TV, film or radio."

B Kim Gerard

21-year-old Kim got her first taste of performing as a ballet dancer when she was just two and has been hooked on performing ever since. Although her ballet days are now behind her, she admits that it gave her a great introduction to the profession. "It was just so exhilarating to get up on stage and perform in front of an audience. Acting is the only thing that I have ever really wanted to do, and this course has let me do my training close to home. Even though I'd done some theatre before, I always wanted to get into TV. I really liked the idea of being a famous, well-paid TV star in a drama series. But now, I've realised acting on stage is just as good."

C Allan Scott-Douglas

Although 23-year-old Allan has been interested in performing since his early teens, it was only in his second year of a primary teaching degree at Edinburgh University that he decided to pursue a career as an actor. "I kind of got into it by accident," he admits. "I was more of a singer, but I ended up doing musical theatre and absolutely loved it. I'm pretty much open to anything. I suppose my heart will always belong to theatre, as there's a live audience there in front of you, but the film and TV work we've done has been great fun too, so I'd love to do some more. If you want to achieve your ambitions as a young actor, you've got to go where the work is. If I'm offered a job down in London, there's no way I'd ever be able to turn it down."

D Romana Abercromby

26-year-old Romana says she got involved with a lot of drama productions when she was still at school. "When I left school, I realised that it was the only thing I wanted to do. I tried applying to drama schools down in London, but after being rejected by them, I took a year out to go travelling. This course has given us so many useful skills and brought us into contact with so many actors and directors who have told us all about the industry. And we've been able to gain some experience with TV as well as stage acting, which has been great. When it comes down to finding work, if it's in Scotland, that's great, but I'd love to travel around, too."

E Neil Thomas

20-year-old Neil was just seven years old when he joined an after-school youth theatre company, which gave him his first taste of acting on stage. "I went once or twice a week and adored it," he says. "I was always keen to show off at school, so it was the perfect outlet for me to perform properly. I've had the chance to do a lot of different types of acting, and the training has been invaluable. It's intense, but everyone knows that's the nature of the career and you have to be prepared. People will give you all sorts of advice about your acting, which helps you to strip away your bad habits. In our profession, you have to be prepared for brutal criticism, because that's what you'll expect when you start working."

Adapted from *The Scotsman*

Vocabulary

Verb collocations with *ambition, career, experience* and *job*

1 Complete these extracts from Reading and Use of English Part 7 by writing a word or phrase from the box in the correct form in the gaps.

achieve   gain   offer   pursue   turn it down

... it was only in his second year of a primary teaching degree at Edinburgh University that he decided to **(1)** .... a career as an actor.

If you want to **(2)** .... your ambitions as a young actor, you've got to go where the work is. If I'm **(3)** .... a job down in London, there's no way I'd ever be able to **(4)** ....

And we've been able to **(5)** .... some experience with TV as well as stage acting, which has been great.

2 **EP** Complete these groups of collocations by writing *an ambition, a career, experience* or *a job* in the gaps.

1 *gain / get / have / lack* ....
2 *apply for / find / leave / look for / offer / turn down* ....
3 *abandon / build / launch / make / pursue / start out on* ....
4 *abandon / achieve / fulfill / have / realise* ....

3 Complete Dean's story by writing a verb from Exercise 2 in the correct form in the gaps. For some gaps, more than one answer may be possible.

I've always enjoyed performing in front of people and I'd like to **(1)** .... a career as an actor. If I could **(2)** .... my first ambition of going to drama school, I'd **(3)** .... the knowledge and experience which is needed if I'm going to **(4)** .... a job in the theatre. Acting is a very competitive profession, and you have to **(5)** .... your career step by step until, hopefully, a well-known director recognises your talent and **(6)** .... you a job which really **(7)** .... your career on the stage.

4 Work in pairs. Tell each other about your ambitions and the careers each of you would like to follow.

play, performance and *acting; audience, (the) public* and *spectators; scene* and *stage*

5 Candidates often confuse these words: *play, performance* and *acting; audience, public* and *spectators; scene* and *stage*. Circle the correct word in *italics* in each of these sentences. Then check by looking at the text in Reading and Use of English Part 7 again.

He was discovered by someone from the theatre while performing in **(1)** *plays / performances* in Edinburgh and St Andrews, but he admits the students' final **(2)** *acting / performance* in front of directors and agents is still nerve-wracking.

When I started the course, I thought that stage **(3)** *acting / playing* was the only thing I wanted to do.

It was just so exhilarating to get up on **(4)** *stage / scene* and perform in front of **(5)** *a public / an audience*.

Speaking | Part 4

1 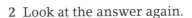 **29** In Speaking Part 4, the examiner will ask you questions which encourage you to give your opinions on topics related to Part 3. Read and listen to Antonia and Peter answering the examiner's question. Underline the words or phrases they use to speak in general.

Examiner: Do you think schools should teach subjects such as dance, drama or music?

Antonia: Well, I think generally speaking schools should teach these subjects to small children so that they can find out if they like them. I think these subjects help children to learn how to express themselves. But I don't think generally it's so important for older children or teenagers to do these subjects because they tend to have lots of other things to study. So, on the whole, I guess these subjects should be voluntary, not compulsory as children get older.

Examiner: Peter, do you agree with Antonia?

Peter: Generally, yes, but I feel it's a pity when students don't have time for the subjects they enjoy.

2 Look at the answer again.

1 How does Antonia give a balanced answer?
2 What reasons does she give?
3 Which of these things does Peter do?
a He just says he agrees.
b He says he agrees, but adds his own opinion.
c He says he agrees and gives a reason.

3 Work alone. Think of general things you can say to give a balanced answer to this question. Then in pairs take turns to ask and answer this question.

- Do you think that schools should teach subjects such as painting and photography? Why? / Why not?

4 Pronunciation: grouping words and pausing (2)

We tend to pause between groups of words which form a meaning together, for example: *The family had a small shop / just round the corner from where we live, / and one day my aunt was working there on her own.*

1 Look back to Exercise 4 in the Speaking section on page 46. Then use a (/) to mark where you think Antonia and Peter pause in their answers in Speaking Exercise 1.

2 ▶ **29** Now listen again and check your answers.

3 Work in pairs. Take the part of Antonia or Peter and read their answers aloud.

4 Note down your own ideas to answer the examiner's question in (Speaking) Exercise 1 and think where you will pause as you speak. Then take turns to answer the question.

5 (EP) Read these questions. Then decide which phrases in the box you could use in your answer to each question. Some phrases can be used for more than one answer.

1 Do you think that all young people should learn to play a musical instrument? Why? / Why not?
2 What things do young people learn from acting in plays?
3 What are the advantages of seeing a film in the cinema instead of on television?
4 Should newspapers and magazines pay so much attention to singers' and actors' lives and relationships? Why? / Why not?
5 Which do you think is the purpose of television: to entertain or to educate people? Why?

a celebrity ....
a compulsory/voluntary activity ....
avoid/cause a scandal ....
develop their acting/musical abilities ....
develop their artistic expression ....
develop their musical knowledge ....
help society develop ....
disturb/protect someone's privacy ....
interrupt a film with advertisements ....
make people aware of problems ....
the media ....
when the film is released ....
a tabloid (newspaper) ....
work in a team ....

6 Work alone and think how you can give balanced, general answers to each question in Exercise 5. Then work in pairs and take turns to ask and answer the questions.

Exam advice

- Many of the questions will be general questions of opinion; give your opinion and support it with reasons and or examples.
- Don't be afraid to give your honest opinion – there are no right or wrong answers.
- Listen carefully to what your partner says: you may be asked if you agree.

Writing | Part 1 An essay

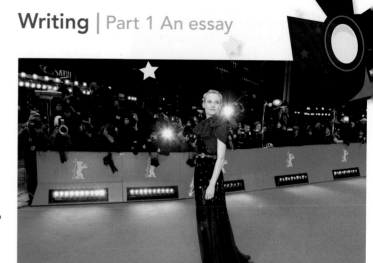

1 Read this writing task and underline the key points you must deal with.

> In your English class, you have been talking about the advantages of being famous as a film star.
>
> Now your English teacher has asked you to write an essay.
>
> Write an essay using **all** the notes and give reasons for your point of view.
>
> **Essay question**
> Being famous as a film star has both advantages and disadvantages. Do you agree?
>
> **Notes**
> Write about:
>
> 1. media attention
> 2. lifestyle
> 3. .... (your own idea)
>
> Write your **essay**.

2 Work in groups. Discuss the advantages and disadvantages of being famous as an actor or film star. While you discuss, you should:

- note down the main points of your discussion
- cover all three notes in the essay task in Exercise 1.

3 Work alone and write a brief plan for your essay. In your plan, you should have:

- the number of paragraphs
- the main idea of each paragraph.

4 Look back to page 60, Exercises 4 and 5. Then write your own opening paragraph. When you have finished, work in pairs and compare your paragraphs.

5 Work in pairs. Read this opening paragraph.

- How does it compare with yours?

> Many young people dream of achieving fame as actors or film stars. However, it is a life which has both advantages and disadvantages.

6 Javier wrote a balanced essay to answer the question in the writing task. Read the essay. Then work in pairs to answer questions 1–6 below.

a Many young people dream of achieving fame as film stars. However, it is a life which has both advantages and disadvantages.

b <u>There are three main advantages</u>. Firstly, if actors are well-known, people will want to watch their films and if their films are popular, they will be offered more jobs in the future. Also, they live exciting and glamorous lives with plenty of foreign travel and luxury. There is no doubt that most actors find this very enjoyable. Finally, fame and success go together.

c <u>On the other hand, fame brings disadvantages for actors too.</u> First, many film stars have little privacy or time to themselves because they are always being followed by reporters and photographers. Next, people with glamorous lifestyles meet other glamorous people and this can sometimes cause problems with, for example, their family relationships. Finally, they have to work very hard to be successful and this may lead to considerable stress.

d <u>To conclude,</u> I think for film stars the advantages of being famous outweigh the disadvantages because being well-known is a result of their professional success. However, they need common sense to deal with the disadvantages.

1 Are Javier's ideas about being famous similar to yours?
2 How does he balance his arguments in the essay?
3 What is the purpose of the <u>underlined</u> phrases in the essay?
4 Highlight words and phrases he uses to link ideas together throughout the essay.
5 In which paragraph (a–d) does Javier give his own opinion?
6 Why is it important to make your opinion clear?

7 Work alone.

1 Write a second paragraph where you outline the advantages you discussed in Exercise 2. Start it using an introductory sentence.
2 Write a third paragraph where you balance the advantages of the second paragraph with the disadvantages. Start it with an introductory sentence as well.

8 Write your answer to the writing task below.

- Follow the stages of <u>underlining</u>, thinking of ideas and planning that you have practised.
- Use Javier's answer in Exercise 6 as a model.
- You should write between 140 and 190 words.

> In your English class, you have been talking about the advantages and disadvantages of a career in music or acting.
>
> Now your English teacher has asked you to write an essay.
>
> Write an essay using **all** the notes and give reasons for your point of view.
>
> **Essay question**
> There are both advantages and disadvantages to a career as a musician or an actor. Do you agree?
>
> **Notes**
> Write about:
>
> 1. *doing something you enjoy*
> 2. *becoming well known*
> 3. *.........* *(your own idea)*
>
> Write your **essay**.

Exam advice

- To make your argument easy to follow, you can start paragraphs with a short sentence which says what the paragraph is about.
- If you decide to write a 'balanced essay', try to have the same number of points in favour as against, or advantages as disadvantages.
- The writing task will not be complete unless you express your personal opinion clearly.

Vocabulary and grammar review Unit 7

Word formation

1 **EP** Read this text. Use the word given in capitals at the end of each line to form a word that fits in the gap in the same line.

Adventure racing

The teams that come first are the ones who
race **(0)** ...intelligently... and adapt to the sort of   **INTELLIGENT**
(1) .... situations which arise in these   **PREDICT**
races. The teams who do well show both flexibility
and **(2)** .... Unfortunately, our   **PATIENT**
(3) .... for the race in Australia weren't   **PREPARE**
methodical in any way. In fact, as a beginner, I
was so **(4)** .... that the training I actually   **EXPERIENCE**
did was **(5)** .... to run and cycle as much   **SIMPLE**
and as hard as I could. When we actually did the
race, one of my team-mates became just too tired
to continue. We had been going really fast without
taking any rests, and he had been **(6)** ....   **WILL**
to ask us to take a break. I knew that our team
had not been prepared or **(7)** .... about   **REAL**
the pace we could keep. Not finishing that race
was the most **(8)** .... lesson I could have   **VALUE**
learned.

Grammar

2 Complete the sentences by writing the verb in brackets in the infinitive or verb + -ing form in the gaps.

1 Can I suggest .... (take) a break in about ten minutes?
2 Did you manage .... (get) in touch with her?
3 Do you want me .... (invite) her?
4 He's considering .... (change) his course of studies.
5 He absolutely refuses .... (have) anything to do with them.
6 He admitted .... (steal) the money.

7 He persuaded them .... (finish) the job.
8 I expect .... (become) very rich one day.
9 I really don't mind .... (work) at weekends.
10 It's no good .... (ask) him anything. He's really unhelpful.
11 Toya enjoys .... (work) in an internet café.
12 You know it's not worth .... (spend) so much money on a meal like that.

3 Complete the second sentence in each question so that it has a similar meaning to the first sentence, using the word given in capitals. Do not change the word given. You must use between two and five words, including the word given.

1 You can't go skydiving until you're 18 years old.
   ALLOWED
   People under 18 .... skydiving.
2 He didn't want to get sunburnt, so he stayed in the shade.
   AVOID
   He stayed in the shade .... sunburnt.
3 Paola hates windsurfing when the weather is cold.
   BEAR
   Paola .... when the weather is cold.
4 Could you please turn your mobile phone off?
   MIND
   Would .... your mobile phone off?
5 You might have an accident if you don't take all the safety precautions.
   RISK
   If you don't take all the safety precautions, ... an accident.
6 The weather is so wet that it's not worth going for a walk today.
   POINT
   The weather is so wet that there's .... for a walk today.

Vocabulary and grammar review Unit 8

Vocabulary

1 Choose the best word, A, B, C or D, for each gap.

1 The flying display attracted about 50,000 ..... despite the rain.
   A public B assistants C spectators D audience

2 As a police officer, I get a lot of questions from members of the ..... asking how to get to one place or another.
   A people B public C audience D spectators

3 During the musical, the ..... clapped at the end of every single song.
   A audience B spectators C public D attendants

4 British actress Amanda Haslett gave a superb ..... as Lady Macbeth at the Globe Theatre last night.
   A play B act C performance D acting

5 If you're interested in a career in ..... , you must be prepared to work hard for little money.
   A acting B playing C performance D stage

6 That play is much better on the ..... than in the film version.
   A theatre B play C scene D stage

7 Vera is thinking of pursuing a ..... in the music industry.
   A work B job C career D position

8 It's more important to do a job you enjoy than one where you ..... a lot of money.
   A win B earn C gain D pay

Grammar

2 Complete each of the sentences below by writing a word or phrase from the box. In some cases, more than one answer may be possible. You can use the words and phrases more than once.

> although despite even though however
> in spite of whereas while

1 .... Eva wanted to pursue a career in acting, she couldn't find a job.

2 Max gave a wonderful performance in the school concert .... his headache.

3 .... Jason dreams of being a footballer, Eva wants to work in the theatre.

4 .... not being very talented, she became a highly successful Hollywood star.

5 They spent millions on the film. .... , not many people were interested in going to see it.

6 I enjoy watching documentaries .... my brother prefers soap operas.

7 He insisted on playing loud music .... it was nearly two o'clock in the morning.

8 People of all ages go to rock concerts, ... classical music concerts are mainly attended by people over 50.

3 For questions 1–6, complete the second sentence so that it has a similar meaning to the first sentence, using the word given. Do not change the word given. You must use between two and five words, including the word given.

1 Although it was dangerous, she went swimming.
   THE
   In spite .... she went swimming.

2 The theatre was full, despite the high price of the tickets.
   EXPENSIVE
   Although .... , the theatre was full.

3 Although he felt ill, he went to work.
   DESPITE
   He went to work .... well.

4 She enjoys her job in spite of her low salary.
   EVEN
   She finds her job enjoyable .... low.

5 'I've been asleep all afternoon.'
   HAD
   Helen admitted that .... whole afternoon.

6 'I'll phone when the concert finishes.'
   CALL
   Martin said he .... end of the concert.

Starting off

1 Work in pairs. Find nine things which might make people happy by matching these words and phrases.

1	being admired	a	a loving family
2	being part of	b	in your studies or work
3	doing really well	c	by the people around you
4	falling	d	live well
5	having enough money to	e	friends
6	having lots of	f	in a nice neighbourhood
7	having lots of time to spend	g	in love
8	living	h	on the things you enjoy doing
9	not having to	i	work too hard

2 Which of the things in Exercise 1 do you think are essential for happiness? Which do you think are not so important?
Are there any other important things which make people happy?

3 Work in pairs. Take turns to do the task below.

- Student A should look at photos 1 and 2.
- Student B should look at photos 3 and 4.

The photos show people who are happy. Compare the photos and say why you think the people might be happy.

Why might the people be happy?

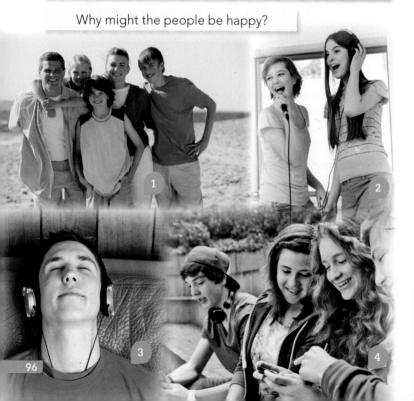

Reading and Use of English | Part 5

1 You are going to read an article by a psychologist about happiness. Read the article quickly to find out what he thinks makes people happy.

Article	Video	Picture gallery

The secrets of happiness

Mihaly Csikszentmihalyi has devoted his life to studying happiness. He believes he has found the key.

I've been fascinated by happiness most of my life. When I was a small boy, I noticed that though many of the adults around me were wealthy and educated, they were not always happy and this
5 sometimes led them to behave in ways which I, as a child, thought strange. As a result of this, I decided to understand what happiness was and how best to achieve it. It was not surprising, then, that I decided to study psychology.

10 On arrival at the University of Chicago 50 years ago, I was disappointed to find that academic psychologists were trying to understand human behaviour by studying rats in a laboratory. I felt that there must be other more useful ways of
15 learning how we think and feel. Although my original aim had been to achieve happiness for myself, I became more ambitious. I decided to build my career on trying to discover what made others happy also. I started out by studying
20 creative people such as musicians, artists and athletes because they were people who devoted their lives to doing what they wanted to do, rather than things that just brought them financial rewards.

25 Later, I expanded the study by inventing a system called 'the experience sampling method'. Ordinary people were asked to keep an electronic pager for a week which gave out a beeping sound eight times a day. Every time it did so, they
30 wrote down where they were, what they were doing, how they felt and how much they were concentrating. This system has now been used on more than 10,000 people, and the answers are consistent: as with creative people, ordinary
35 people are happiest when concentrating hard.

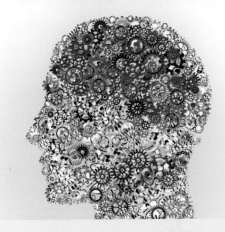

After carrying out 30 years of research and
writing 18 books, I believe I have proved that
happiness is quite different from what most
people imagine. It is not something that can
40 be bought or collected. People need more than
just wealth and comfort in order to lead happy
lives. I discovered that people who earn less
than £10,000 are not generally as happy as
people whose incomes are above that level. This
45 suggests that there is a minimum amount of
money we need to earn to make us happy, but
above that dividing line, people's happiness has
very little to do with how much poorer or richer
they are. Multi-millionaires turn out to be only
50 slightly happier than other people who are not
so rich. What is more, people living below the
dividing line and in poverty are often quite happy
too.

I found that the most obvious cause of happiness
55 is intense concentration. This must be the
main reason why activities such as music, art,
literature, sports and other forms of leisure have
survived. In order to concentrate, whether you're
reading a poem or building a sandcastle, what
60 you need is a challenge that matches your ability.
The way to remain continually happy, therefore,
is to keep finding new opportunities to improve
your skills. This may mean learning to do your
job better or faster, or doing other more difficult
65 jobs. As you grow older, you have to find new
challenges which are more appropriate to your
age. I have spent my life studying happiness and
now, as I look back, I wonder if I have achieved it.
Overall, I think I have, and my belief that I have
70 found the keys to its secret has increased my
happiness immeasurably.

Adapted from *The Times*

Exam advice

When a question asks what a word or phrase refers to:
- read carefully what is said in the preceding sentence
- make sure you understand the reference before you read the options.

2 For questions 1 and 2, the sentences in the article which give you the answers have been <u>underlined</u>. Read the questions and the underlined sentences. Then choose the answer (A, B, C or D) which you think fits best according to the underlined sentences.

1 What does *this* in line 6 refer to?
   A the writer's decision to study psychology
   B the writer's interest in happiness
   C the writer's observations of adults
   D the writer's unhappy childhood
2 What sort of people did the writer choose to concentrate on at the start of his career?
   A People who were clearly happier
   B People with more freedom
   C People whose main aim in life was not making money
   D People whose objective was to become richer

3 Now, for questions 3–6, choose the answer (A, B, C or D) which you think fits best according to the text.

3 The 'experience sampling method' showed in general that
   A creative people are happier than other people.
   B uncreative people are just as happy as creative people.
   C people's happiness depends on who they are with.
   D people are happier when they are very focused on an activity.
4 *that dividing line* in line 47 refers to a division between
   A living more comfortably and less comfortably.
   B poor countries and rich countries.
   C happy people and unhappy people.
   D millionaires and poor people.
5 According to the writer, people concentrate more when they are doing
   A something which they find enjoyable.
   B something which they find difficult but possible.
   C something which they find quite easy.
   D many things at the same time.
6 What impression do you have of the writer of the text?
   A He has become happier by studying happiness.
   B He has been unhappy most of his life.
   C He has always been a happy person.
   D He has only been happy for short times.

4 Work in groups.
   - Did anything surprise you about what the writer says makes people happy? If so, what? If not, why not?

Vocabulary

achieve, carry out and devote

1 Complete these sentences from Reading and Use of English Part 5 by writing the correct form of *achieve*, *carry out* or *devote* in each gap.

1 Although my original aim had been to .... happiness for myself, I became more ambitious.
2 They were people who .... their lives to doing what they wanted to do, …
3 After .... 30 years of research and writing 18 books, I believe I have proved that happiness is quite different from what most people imagine.

2 ◉ Write the nouns in the box by each verb they can form collocations with.

> ~~an aim~~   an ambition   energy   an improvement
> an instruction   an objective   an order   one's life
> research   success   a test   a threat   time

1 achieve   an aim, …
2 carry out
3 devote … (to)

3 Complete these sentences by writing collocations from Exercise 2 in the correct form in each gap. In some cases, more than one answer may be possible.

1 Last year, my uncle .... a lifelong .... to visit New York.
2 Scientists have been .... to discover the cause of the disease.
3 The exercise is quite easy, so you won't need to .... very much .... to doing it.
4 Igor felt very tired because he had .... a lot of time and .... to the project.
5 My mum said she'd stop my pocket money if I was home late, but I don't think she'll .... her ....
6 In the army, you have to be obedient and .... immediately.

stay, spend and pass; make, cause and have

4 ◉ Candidates often confuse the following words: *stay*, *spend* and *pass*; *make*, *cause* and *have*. Read these sentences and circle the correct word in *italics*. Then check your answers by reading the definitions on page 184.

1 Remember, your behaviour will *have / cause* an effect on other people.
2 I'm very sorry if I've *made / caused* you any problems.
3 I have *passed / spent* my life studying happiness.
4 Yesterday, I *spent / stayed* two hours listening to the radio.
5 I really enjoy late-night films on TV when I can *stay / be* awake.
6 The news that her sister had had a baby *made / had* her very happy.

5 Now complete each of these sentences using *stay*, *spend*, *pass*, *make*, *cause* or *have* in the correct form.

1 I decided to .... the afternoon in the park.
2 Colin played a game on his phone to .... the time while he was waiting for the train.
3 We should be able to go camping because they say the weather is going to .... like this for the rest of the week.
4 Your talk was excellent and .... a powerful impact on the other students.
5 How did you .... the weekend? Did you enjoy yourself?
6 I .... two hours today trying to finish my homework.
7 The bus strike has been .... problems for students trying to get to school.
8 The bad sound quality .... the film very difficult to understand.
9 Using up-to-date materials can .... a dramatic effect on the amount students learn.
10 Our maths teacher .... the whole lesson explaining algebra to us.

6 Which verb – *make*, *cause* or *have* – forms a collocation with each of these nouns? In some cases, more than one verb–noun collocation is possible.

> an accident   a change   an effect   an impact
> an impression   a problem   trouble

7 Complete these sentences by writing a collocation from Exercise 6 in each of the gaps. In some cases, more than one answer may be possible.

1 A dog ran onto the road and would have .... if I hadn't reacted quickly.
2 Amalia obviously .... a good .... on the examiners because they gave her a Grade A.
3 I hope I haven't .... you .... by coming to stay unexpectedly.
4 I .... that she's not very organised. Otherwise, she'd hand her work in on time.
5 Living in the country .... a nice .... after spending the last three years living in a city.
6 Your choice of subjects at university will .... a big .... on your future career.

Listening | Part 1

1 You are going to hear people talking in eight different situations. Before you listen, work in groups. Discuss whether you agree with these statements or not.

- Your first impression of a person is usually formed by what they say, not how they look.
- In general, people marry someone quite similar to them rather than someone very different.
- Young people nowadays are generally more intelligent than their grandparents were.
- Few people are afraid of flying in planes and getting in lifts. More people are afraid of heights.
- Everyone sometimes has a dream where they're flying, falling or running.

2 Now work in pairs. Read questions 1 and 2 and match the words and phrases in the box with each of the options A, B and C in the two questions. (For some options there may be more than one word or phrase.)

> actual words   body language   character
> things in common   gestures   hobbies   intonation
> people we like   appearance   mirror

1 You hear an expert giving advice about meeting people for the first time. What has the most impact?
  A how you sound
  B how you look
  C what you say

2 You hear a man and a woman talking about successful relationships. The man thinks the most important factor in successful relationships is
  A similar personalities.
  B the same friends.
  C similar interests.

3 ▶02 Now listen and for questions 1 and 2, choose the best answer (A, B or C). Then say which words and phrases you heard from the box in Exercise 1.

4 ▶03 Listen and, for questions 3–8, choose the best answer (A, B or C).

3 You hear a psychologist in the UK talking about intelligence. What does she say?
  A The human brain is changing.
  B Scores in intelligence tests are rising.
  C Exams are getting harder.

4 You overhear a boy calling a friend on his mobile phone. Why is he calling his friend?
  A to complain about her behaviour
  B to explain a problem
  C to change an arrangement

5 You overhear a man talking about things which frighten people. What frightens him?
  A using an escalator
  B taking a flight
  C using a lift

6 You hear a girl talking to a boy about a dream. She has read that the dream means
  A she's worried about lack of success.
  B her life is in danger.
  C she has to escape from something.

7 You overhear two students talking about a classmate. Why are they discussing her?
  A To organise something for her.
  B To see if they can help her.
  C To point out her faults.

8 You hear a boy and a girl talking about the boy's free-time activities. What do they agree about his personality?
  A He's friendly and sociable.
  B He prefers his own company.
  C He's creative and adventurous.

Exam advice

- Listen to the whole piece before you choose: the answer may depend on the general idea rather than a few words.
- If you are not sure about the answer after listening the first time, try to decide which answers you think are wrong before you listen the second time.

5 Work in pairs.

- When you feel stressed, what do you do to relax?
- Talk about someone in your family. What do you think their free-time activities might show about their personality?

Grammar
Modal verbs to express certainty and possibility

1 Read these extracts from Listening Part 1 and look at the underlined modal verbs. Then answer the questions below.

- That's right! I think I <u>must have</u> got the problem when I was trapped in one as a kid. I <u>can't have</u> been there for more than ten minutes, but I was trembling when I came out.
- Well, the interpretation I've heard is that you <u>may</u> be afraid of failing in some way. You know, there are all sorts of interpretations for other dreams, for example that you <u>could</u> find something subconsciously threatening and your dream <u>might</u> be sort of pointing that out to you.

1 Which of the underlined verbs do we use when we:
- are certain something is true? (1) ....
- are certain something is not true? (2) ....
- think something is possibly true? (3) .... , (4) .... and (5) ....
2 Which of the underlined verbs refer to
a the present?
b the past?

➡ page 170 Language reference: Modal verbs – expressing certainty and possibility

2 👁 Candidates often make mistakes with modal verbs. Four of these sentences contain mistakes with modal verbs. However, one is correct. Find and correct the mistakes.

1 I think the school play was lovely. You may have really enjoyed acting in it!
2 He's had a really good sleep, so he mustn't be tired any more.
3 The road is very busy, so cross it carefully or you can have an accident.
4 I have a lot of homework to do, so I may go to bed late.
5 She lives in a really nice house, so her mum and dad can be earning a lot of money.

3 Complete these sentences by writing a suitable modal verb and the verb in brackets in the correct form (present or past) in the gaps. In some cases, more than one answer may be possible.

1 Everyone in the class .... (work) incredibly hard because you have all passed the exam!
2 I think she .... (be) a really happy person because she's always smiling and laughing.
3 Jamie woke up in the night screaming. He .... (have) a nightmare.
4 I don't know why Irina hasn't arrived yet. She .... (have to) stay on late at school, or she .... (stop) on the way home to see some friends.
5 I don't know how old the teacher is, but he looks quite young, so he .... (be) more than 25.
6 They say it .... (rain) at the weekend, so we won't be able to play football on Saturday.

4 Work in pairs. Look at these two pictures and, using *may, might, must, could* and *can't*, say what you think

- has happened or is happening in each picture
- the people are feeling and why.

Reading and Use of English | Part 4

1 Work in pairs. In Reading and Use of English Part 4, you have to complete a sentence so that it has a similar meaning to the first sentence, using the word given. You must write between two and five words. Look at questions 1–5 and the different answers students wrote (a–c).

- Decide which is the correct answer.
- Say why the other answers are wrong.

1 'I spoke to Maria yesterday,' Paola said.
   HAD
   Paola said she .... day before.
   a had had a conversation with Maria the
   b had spoken to Maria the
   c spoke to Maria the

2 Although the music outside was loud, we managed to sleep.
   DESPITE
   We managed to sleep .... outside.
   a despite of the loud music
   b despite the loud music
   c despite they played loud music

3 I'll forget the number if I don't write it down.
   NOT
   I will .... I write it down.
   a remember the number if
   b not remind the number unless
   c not remember the number unless

4 You needn't give me your homework tomorrow.
   HAND
   It is .... your homework to me tomorrow.
   a not necessary for you to hand
   b not needed handing in
   c not necessary to hand in

5 It is possible that Eva collected the parcel from the post office.
   MAY
   Eva .... up the parcel from the post office.
   a may have collected
   b could have taken
   c may have picked

6 'You should try harder at maths,' my teacher said.
   MORE
   My teacher advised .... an effort at maths.
   a that I do more
   b me to make more of
   c making more of

Exam advice

Think about:

- whether you need an expression, e.g. *he changed his mind*
- whether you need a phrasal verb, e.g. *give up*
- what grammar you will need, e.g. do you need to change from active to passive or put something into reported speech?

You should try to spell your answers correctly.

2 For questions 1–6, complete the second sentence so that it has a similar meaning to the first sentence, using the word given. Do not change the word given. You must use between two and five words, including the word given.

1 My grandma hates it when people make a noise in her house.
   STAND
   My grandma can't .... in her house.

2 'Don't forget to lock the front door, Karl,' said his wife.
   REMINDED
   Karl's wife .... the front door.

3 Sven enjoyed the film despite missing the beginning.
   MANAGE
   Although Sven .... the beginning of the film, he enjoyed it.

4 I'm sure Annabel wasn't in London all weekend.
   HAVE
   Annabel .... in London the whole weekend.

5 How long did it take you to write the essay?
   SPEND
   How long .... the essay?

6 It's possible that my brother has discovered that I have borrowed his bike.
   MAY
   My brother .... out that I have borrowed his bike.

Speaking | Part 2

1 Look at this speaking task. Then complete Peter's answer below with words or phrases from the box which he uses to compare or speculate about what he can see.

> Why have the people decided to do these activities?

could be   exactly what   looks as if   may have decided
must   perhaps   ~~seem~~   unlike   different   who appears

Examiner: Here are your photographs. They show young people doing difficult activities. I'd like you to compare the photographs and say why you think the people have decided to do these activities. All right?

Peter: The first photo shows young people walking up a mountain. They **(1)** .... to be tied together with ropes and they **(2)** .... be resting, or **(3)** .... they've been waiting for one of the group to catch them up. They may be part of an adventure activity which they're doing from their school or college and they may have been climbing for quite a long time. The second photo shows a

(4) .... situation. The girl seems to be working with equipment in a factory. I'm not sure **(5)** .... she's doing, but she **(6)** .... building a machine or something. There's a man **(7)** .... to be supervising her. The girl in the first photo **(8)** .... to climb the mountain because she wants a new experience, or she just enjoys being in the mountains even though she looks a bit tired. The girl in the second photo **(9)** .... she's starting a new job and learning to do something. She looks as if she's quite warm from her work, **(10)** .... the girl in the first photo.

2 ▶04 Now listen to check your answers.

➡ page 168 Language reference: *look, seem* and *appear*

3 Work in pairs. Look at the examiner's instructions and the photos. Then complete the sentences on page 103 with your own ideas.

Here are your photographs. They show people celebrating at different events. I'd like you to compare the photos and say what you think the people are enjoying about the different situations.

> What are the people enjoying about the different situations?

Speculating about photos

1 In the first photo, the people look as if …
2 The old man seems to be …
3 They are probably going to …
4 In the second photo, the people appear to be …
5 They could be …
6 Unlike the first photo, …
7 In both photos, the people seem …

4 Pronunciation: sentence stress (3)

We can use sentence stress to emphasise certain words in a sentence.

1 ▶05 Look at this sentence from Peter's answer in Exercise 1 and listen to it.

- Underline the words emphasised in **a** and the words emphasised in **b**.
- How does the different emphasis change the meaning of what he says?

a The girl seems to be working with equipment in a factory. I'm not sure exactly what she's doing, but she could be building a machine or something.

b The girl seems to be working with equipment in a factory. I'm not sure exactly what she's doing, but she could be building a machine or something.

2 Work in pairs. Take turns to read either sentence a or sentence b aloud to your partner. Your partner should listen and say which sentence you are reading.

3 ▶06 Listen to the extract from Peter's answer again and underline the words each speaker emphasises. Then discuss how the different emphasis changes the meaning.

A: The girl in the first photo may have decided to climb the mountain because she wants a new experience, or perhaps she just enjoys being in the mountains even though she looks a bit tired. The girl in the second photo looks as if she's starting a new job and learning to do something. She looks as if she's quite warm from her work, unlike the girl in the first photo.

B: The girl in the first photo may have decided to climb the mountain because she wants a new experience, or perhaps she just enjoys being in the mountains even though she looks a bit tired. The girl in the second photo looks as if she's starting a new job and learning to do something. She looks as if she's quite warm from her work, unlike the girl in the first photo.

4 Work in pairs. Decide which words you would like to emphasise in the extract. Take turns to read the extract aloud. While you listen to your partner, underline the words he/she emphasises.

The girl in the first photo may have decided to climb the mountain because she wants a new experience, or perhaps she just enjoys being in the mountains even though she looks a bit tired. The girl in the second photo looks as if she's starting a new job and learning to do something. She looks as if she's quite warm from her work, unlike the girl in the first photo.

5 Look at the sentences you completed for Speaking Part 2 Exercise 3 and decide which words you would like to emphasise when you speak. Then work in pairs and take turns to read your sentences aloud.

5 Look again at the answer in Pronunciation Exercise 3. How many words or phrases can you find which mean *a little*?

6 Now take turns to do the task in Speaking Part 2 Exercise 3. When talking about people's feelings, use words or phrases which mean *a little* where appropriate.

7 Work in pairs. Take turns to do the speaking tasks on page 104.

- While you listen to your partner doing the speaking task, think about the things he/she is doing well and the things he/she could do better.
- When he/she has finished, give feedback and suggestions. If necessary, look at the checklist in Exercise 2 on page 24 to give you ideas.

Exam advice

- When you're not sure how to answer the question in the task, use phrases which allow you to speculate. Practise these before you go to the exam.
- Spend about half the time comparing the photos and half the time answering the question..

Task 1

Here are your photographs. They show people who have just done something special. I'd like you to compare the two photographs and say how you think the people feel about what they have just done.

Task 2

Here are your photographs. They show people in frightening situations. I'd like you to compare the two photographs and say why you think the people are frightened in these situations.

How are the people feeling about what they have just done?

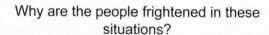

Why are the people frightened in these situations?

Writing | Part 2 A report

1 Work in pairs. Read this writing task, <u>underlining</u> the things you must deal with in your answer. Which do you think the money should be spent on?

The college where you study has been given a large amount of money to spend either on improving the classrooms or on students' social activities. The director of your college has asked you to write a report describing the benefits of both ideas and saying which one you think should be chosen and why.

Write your **report**.

2 Answer these questions.

1 Who will read your report?
2 Should you write in an informal or a formal style?
3 What things must you include in your report?

3 Read the report below. Write one verb from the box in the correct form in the gaps.

> benefit   contain   ~~discuss~~   find   improve   make
> participate   recommend   reduce   spend

Our college money

Introduction

The purpose of this report is to **(1)** .... whether the money which has been given to the college should be **(2)** .... on improving the classrooms or on students' social activities and to **(3)** .... a recommendation.

The classrooms

The college classrooms are well equipped with the latest technologies. Each classroom already **(4)** .... computers with internet connection and an interactive whiteboard. However, the furniture needs replacing because students who attend class all day **(5)** .... it uncomfortable, and this affects their concentration. Furthermore, the classrooms would **(6)** .... from an air-conditioning system, and this would also **(7)** .... the quality of students' work.

Social activities

The college already has a social programme with a wide range of activities for students to **(8)** .... in. If money was spent on this, it would **(9)** .... the cost of the activities for the students and they would be able to take part in more of them.

Recommendation

I **(10)** .... spending the money on new furniture and an air-conditioning system as this would have a beneficial effect on students' work in class.

4 Work in pairs.

1 What recommendation does the writer make to the college director?
2 How can the college director find things quickly in the report if he/she doesn't have much time?
3 Has the report dealt with everything in the writing task?
4 What is the purpose of each section?
5 Which tenses are used? Why?
6 Does the report use contractions (*it's, we'll*)? Why? / Why not?

5 Complete these ways of making recommendations and suggestions by putting the verb in brackets into the correct form.

1 I recommend .... (*install*) a new air-conditioning system.
2 I suggest .... (*spend*) money on improving the social programme.
3 I suggest that the college should .... (*buy*) new furniture for the classrooms.
4 It would be a good idea .... (*equip*) all the classrooms with computers.

6 Work in pairs. Write four more sentences making recommendations or suggestions for your own college or language school.

7 Work in pairs. Read this writing task. How do you think the money should be spent?

> Your town has a large amount of money available to spend on improving the area around your school. Your English teacher has asked you to write a report suggesting how it can be improved.
>
> Write your **report**.

8 Do the writing task. Write between 140 and 190 words. Follow these steps:

- <u>Underline</u> the points you must deal with in your report.
- Think and write a plan for your report. This should include sections and section headings.
- Write your report following your plan and using the report in Exercise 3 as a model.
- When you have finished, check it for mistakes.

Exam advice

- Think about who will read the report and if you need a formal or an informal style.
- If you decide to divide the report into sections, decide what sections you need and what the section headings should be.

10 Spend, spend, spend?

Starting off

Work in groups.

1 Look at the pictures. Which of these things would you enjoy buying? Where would you buy each of them? Would you buy any of them online?

2 How should teenagers pay for each of these things? Choose from options a–c.

a from money given to them by their parents when it is asked for

b from a weekly allowance given by their parents

c from money they have worked for and earned themselves

Reading and Use of English | Part 2

1 Work in groups. You are going to read an article about shopping in the UK. Before you read, discuss these questions.

• What are the advantages and disadvantages of shopping online?

• Why is it a problem for a town when local shops have to close?

2 Read this article in one minute ignoring the gaps. What does the writer say are the advantages of using local shops and shopping online?

Shopping online versus shopping locally

Most people want a busy shopping street (0) ....in.......... their town with butchers, bookshops, boutiques, cafés and restaurants, (1) .... makes it depressing to see so many shops becoming vacant. Experts predict that (2) .... to 40% of shops will be forced to close in the next five years.

No one wants to see their high-street shops disappear, (3) .... why would people want to shop locally? Internet shopping sites offer discount prices along with 24/7 shopping and deliveries. (4) .... to a recent report, some products, such as toys, are as (5) .... as 60% cheaper online.

Local shops should be more (6) .... clubs which provide personal service and social relationships, and each shop should be seen (7) .... something unique. To meet this need, in some parts of the world shops shut for hours during the day, then do excellent business in the evening, when they aim to give customers (8) .... more satisfying experience than they would ever have from shopping online.

3 Work alone. Decide which word best fits each gap. Where you are not sure, think of the type of word (preposition, article, etc.) you need. When you have finished, compare your ideas with the rest of the group.

4 Work in pairs.

- Do you or members of your family ever buy things online? If so, what are your favourite websites for online shopping?

Exam advice

- Answer the questions you find easy first. Go back to the more difficult questions later.
- Pay careful attention to the meaning of the text to help you think of the right word.
- Read to the end of each sentence before deciding what the missing word might be.
- Answer all the questions. If you can't decide what word to write, think what type of word you need (preposition, pronoun, etc.) and guess.
- When you have finished, check your answers by reading the completed text again.

Grammar
as and *like*

1 Look at these sentences (a–c) and answer the question below.

- **a** Tom has two jobs: he's a teacher and a football referee. As a teacher he's very easy-going, but as a referee he's really strict.
- **b** Mark is a social worker, but he spends so much time with young people that sometimes he feels like a teacher.
- **c** Shops should be more like clubs which provide personal service and social interaction, and each should be seen as something unique.

Which, *as* or *like*, means …
1 he is / they are (a teacher / something unique, etc.)?
2 he is similar to / they are similar to (a teacher / club, etc.)?

➡ page 163 Language reference: *as* and *like*

2 Complete these sentences by writing *as* or *like* in the gaps.

1 He has a weekend job .... a shop assistant.
2 He was regarded by his teachers .... one of the most brilliant students they had ever taught.
3 Tanya's father gave her a car for her 18th birthday .... she'd done so well in her exams.
4 I find subjects .... physics and chemistry very difficult.
5 I shall be on holiday next week, ... you know.
6 I'm afraid I don't study .... much .... I should.
7 I'm speaking to you .... a friend.
8 My English teacher is lovely. She's .... a mother to me!
9 Several cities in Switzerland, such .... Zurich and Berne, have reputations .... excellent places to live.
10 How embarrassing! Donna came to the party wearing exactly the same clothes .... me!

Reading and Use of English | Part 5

1 Work in groups. You will read a story called 'My greatest influence' written by a teenager from Texas. Before you read, discuss these questions.

- Who or what has had the greatest influence on you?
- How have they / has it influenced you?

2 Read the story quite quickly to find out what happens.

My greatest influence
By Rachel S., Colleyville, Texas

Sundays, I walk to the supermarket. Mother hands me the grocery list and puts money in my pocket, hoping it will be enough. She's had a hard day, and I've had a hard week. Nothing out of the ordinary happens when I get to the
5 store. I grab the bread, some milk, and other things on the list. As I turn to head out, I see it, all pinks and yellows. It looks gorgeous in the window, and I'm sure if I were to try it on, it would be a perfect fit. I smile for a moment and turn away, bitter that I could never own such a dress as
10 that. Instead, I grab the last item and check out.

Outside, traffic zooms by, an artificial breeze across my face. The sun beats down, making me sweat. These paper sacks in my arms are not the easiest things to carry. Yet, even with all these distractions, I cannot stop thinking
15 about that pretty sundress in the window of the market. It is not fair that I can never have what I want. I work so hard to help my family and yet I get nothing in return, just another grocery list or errand to do.

In my anger, I fail to realize the tear that had been growing
20 along the bottom of one of the sacks. Its contents spill out everywhere so that I must drop everything else just to chase after the soup cans and apples rolling across the sidewalk. Suddenly, I see a pair of hands that do not belong to me. They hold out to me a can of green
25 beans. I follow them up the forearms, from the shoulders, and to the face of this stranger. His skin is tanned and wrinkled from so many years in the sun. His clothes are mismatched, borrowed or stolen. But his eyes are soft and kind.

30 I pause in silence, only able to stare at him. "Huh … thanks," I say, coming to my senses, and I take the can from him. No other words are spoken as he continues to help me recover my purchases and get back on my feet. There is an awkward silence between us. Not knowing what
35 else to say in this sort of situation, I tell him "thank you" one more time and am on my way because I have many

other chores to finish. Suddenly, he speaks for the first time, and all he says is "Have a good day, ma'am." And then he gives me the biggest, most gap-toothed smile I
40 have ever seen. Right then, he looks years younger—and feel a fool.

Look at me, feeling sorry for myself because I do not get what I want! Do I not think others are in the same boat, worse? I am but one person out of the billions that exist
45 this earth, so who am I to think that I deserve more than already have?

To say that I try to follow the example of just one person would be to oversimplify things. The human character is much more complex than that. Just as our world is shap
50 by many different outside sources, so, too, have I been influenced by many familiar and unfamiliar faces.

It is not a matter of who, but what, has been the greates influence in my life. I do not wish to be that homeless ma on the street, for he has taught me with one genuine sm
55 that my life is enough, and that there are worse things or there than not having a pink and yellow sundress. But it his selfless character that continues to mold me.

My mother will hand me the grocery list today. I will make the same journey to the supermarket, and most likely, I w
60 get the same items as last time. And I will probably see something I want but cannot have. But before I start to fe sorry for myself, I will remember the kind stranger with th gap-toothed grin, I'll grab the last item, and check out.

Source: www.teenink.com 'My Greatest Influen

3 For questions 1–6, choose the answer (A, B, C or D) which you think fits best according to the text.

1 What impression do we have of Rachel in the first paragraph?
   A She enjoys doing the family shopping.
   B She comes from a family with not much money.
   C She never buys herself new clothes.
   D She is in a hurry to get home.

2 She feels angry as she walks home because
   A she is expected to do too much.
   B she dislikes the area where she lives.
   C her family pay little attention to her.
   D she is not rewarded for her effort.

3 Rachel only speaks briefly to the man who helps her because
   A she thinks he has a criminal past.
   B she has never met him before.
   C she doesn't like the way he's dressed.
   D she's in a hurry to do other work.

4 What does Rachel mean by 'others are in the same boat' in line 43?
   A She has similar ambitions to other people.
   B She deserves to be treated the same as other people.
   C She lives in similar circumstances to other people.
   D She can share her problems with other people.

5 Who, according to Rachel, has had the greatest influence on her?
   A the homeless man
   B her mother
   C many different people
   D her family as a whole

6 Which of these phrases best summarises the lesson Rachel has learned?
   A She shouldn't complain about her situation.
   B She shouldn't envy other people.
   C She can be poor but happy.
   D She should value her family more.

4 To understand a text, you often need to understand exactly what the writer is referring to at different points in the text. Which noun phrase (a or b) does each of these words/phrases refer to?

1 it (line 2)
   a the grocery list
   b the money

2 it (line 6)
   a the list   **b** the dress

3 these distractions (line 14)
   a the traffic, the sun, the sacks
   b the dress, the window, the supermarket

4 everything else (line 21)
   a the other sacks   **b** the spilled contents

5 them (line 25)
   a the soup cans and apples   **b** the hands

6 him (line 30)
   a the stranger   **b** a friend

7 others (line 43)
   a other people   **b** other strangers

8 that (line 49)
   a following the example of just one person
   b oversimplifying things

9 what (line 52)
   a a familiar face   **b** one genuine smile

Exam advice

- The answers to the questions come in the same order in the text, so, for example, you will locate the answer to question 2 after question 1.
- The final question may refer to the whole passage: in this case, consider the general message, but also skim the text for words which support your choice.

5 Work in groups.

- Do you think Rachel was right to feel angry that she couldn't have the dress? Why? / Why not?
- If they can afford it, how much pocket money should parents give their children at these ages: 13, 15 and 18? Why?
- What is the best age for young people to have their own bank account? When should they have their own credit card?
- Should young people be encouraged to save? Why? What for?
- Do you think teenagers should earn some of the money they need by doing housework or taking a part-time job? Why? / Why not?

Vocabulary
arrive, get and *reach*

1 ⊙ Candidates often confuse *arrive, get* and *reach*. Circle the correct word in *italics* in each of these sentences. Then check your answers by reading the definitions on page 185.

1 Nothing out of the ordinary happens when I *arrive / get / reach* to the store. I grab the bread, some milk, and other things on the list.
2 The plane was late taking off and has only just *arrived / got / reached*.
3 When they *arrived / got / reached* the top of the mountain, they were unable to see anything due to the thick cloud.

2 Complete these sentences with *arrive, get* or *reach* in the correct form. In some cases, more than one answer may be possible.

1 Stop writing when you have .... 190 words.
2 The traffic was so bad that they didn't .... to the concert till after it had started.
3 She's driving home and she'll phone me when she .... there.
4 What time do you normally .... to school in the morning?
5 When they .... at the hotel, they went straight to their rooms.
6 When you .... the end of the road, turn left.

3 Complete the sentences below with an adverb / adverbial phrase from the box to form collocations with *arrive*.

finally   in time   on time   safe and sound   shortly
unannounced

1 Mum was worried that we might have an accident because of the snow, but we arrived home .... , much to her relief.
2 Sandy was late for the refreshments, but he arrived .... to hear the speeches.
3 The airline has a great reputation for punctuality, with 90% of flights arriving ....
4 The train that will be arriving .... at Platform 13, just two minutes after its scheduled time, is the Orient Express from Paris.
5 Uncle Kamal arrived .... in the middle of lunch, so we had to set an extra place for him at the table.
6 We were very late because of the traffic and when we .... arrived, the shop was closed.

Listening | Part 4

1 Work in pairs. You are going to hear a student interviewing two teenagers about a new shopping centre they've been researching for a school project. Before you listen, why do many people prefer shopping centres? Make a list of your ideas.

2 ▶07 Listen to the interview once. How many of your ideas from Exercise 1 do they mention?

3 Read questions 1–7. How many can you answer already?

1 Where is the shopping centre situated?
  A in the city centre
  B on the edge of the city
  C in the countryside

2 The location was chosen because
  A it would not harm the environment.
  B it was easy to get permission to build there.
  C it was easy for people to reach.

3 What is the main attraction of the shopping centre?
  A It's a convenient place to do the shopping.
  B It's attractive to the whole family.
  C It offers high-quality goods at low prices.

4 Kerry particularly enjoys the shopping centre's
  A feeling of luxury.
  B good security.
  C friendly atmosphere.

5 Salim says families argue when they go shopping because
  A they don't enjoy the same things.
  B they can't agree on what to buy.
  C they find each other's company stressful.

6 How are the shops organised?
  A Each shop in the centre chooses its own location.
  B Each section of the centre has a variety of shops.
  C Similar shops in the centre are located near each other.

7 What innovation does Salim describe for making shopping easier?
  A electric vehicles
  B moving walkways
  C automatic delivery systems

4 Listen again. For questions 1–7, choose the best answer (A, B or C).

4 Pronunciation: intonation (3)

We tend to use more intonation on stressed words than on unstressed words.

1 ▶ **17** Work in pairs. Look at this extract from Antonia's answer. <u>Underline</u> the words you think she stresses. Then listen to check your answers.

OK, so both photographs show people doing things which might be good for their sanity, sorry, I mean their health. In the first photo I can see someone who looks as if he's, um, what's the word, he's commuting by bicycle in busy traffic.

2 ▶ **18** Listen to the extract with two different intonations.

- In which version, a or b, does the speaker sound more certain and confident?
- Does the voice rise or fall on the final stressed word in each sentence? What does this show?

3 Take turns to read the extract in Exercise 1 aloud. Your partner should say whether your intonation is more like version a or b.

4 ▶ **19** Decide which words will be stressed in these two extracts. Then listen to check your answers.

a I'd say there are some problems with the idea of health in the first photo because of the danger from the traffic, especially because he's cycling in the night, I mean the dark, and the, um, I can't think of the word, but it's a type of smoke which comes from the cars.

b On the other hand, if you live in the city, it's a good way of getting exercise. In the second photo, the kids should remember that they need to eat a mixed, sorry, a balanced diet, not just salad and fruit.

5 Does the speaker sound more certain and more confident in extract a or b? Why? Take turns to read these extracts aloud.

5 ▶ **20** Work in pairs.

- Student A: Listen to the examiner's instructions and do the Speaking Part 2 task in Exercise 2.
- Student B: Listen and complete the checklist in Exercise 2 for your partner. When your partner has finished, give feedback.

6 ▶ **21** Now, Student B should listen to the examiner's follow-up question and answer it.

7 ▶ **22** Work in pairs. Student B should listen to the examiner's instructions and do this task. Student A should complete the checklist in (Speaking) Exercise 2 and give feedback at the end.

Why is it important for these people to deal with their problems?

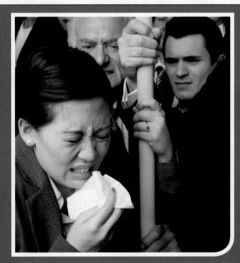

8 ▶ **23** Now Student A should listen to the examiner's follow-up question and answer it.

Writing | Part 1 An essay

1 Work in groups. Look at this discussion question. Discuss and note down at least three healthy or unhealthy aspects for each discussion point (a–e). When you have finished, change groups and report what your group decided.

> Do you think modern lifestyles are healthy or not?
> Talk about:
> a   the environment and health
> b   diet
> c   work activities
> d   information, e.g. about exercise, diet
> e   free-time activities.

2 Work in pairs. Read the writing task in the next column.

- <u>Underline</u> the main ideas in the task.
- Decide which points from your discussion you would include in your answer and write a plan.

> In your English class, you have been talking about whether modern lifestyles are healthy or not.
>
> Now your English teacher has asked you to write an essay.
>
> Write an essay using **all** the notes and give reasons for your point of view.
>
> **Essay question**
> Modern lifestyles can seriously endanger our health. Do you agree?
>
> **Notes**
> Write about:
>
> 1. *food*
> 2. *physical activity*
> 3. .... *(your own idea)*
>
> Write your **essay**.

3 Work in pairs. Discuss what the strong points and weak points of this essay are. Then say what comments you would write at the end if you were this student's teacher.

> It seems strange that although we know a lot about how to live healthily, many people continue to do things which may be harmful to their health.
>
> There are many parts of our lifestyles which enable us to live healthily. For instance, we all know about the importance of eating a balanced diet and taking regular exercise. Moreover, in rich countries we have easy access to good-quality fresh food and suitable sports facilities, so it should be easy to adopt healthy living habits.
>
> However, there are things which prevent people from having a healthy lifestyle. For example, industry and traffic have led to serious environmental pollution. What is more, we spend a lot of time sitting down, and this often means we have less time for activities which keep us fit. For example, there are many people who spend many hours sitting in front of computers working, studying, or playing computer games. In addition, many people do not eat the right sort of food.

4 Work in pairs. Read these concluding paragraphs and decide which one is most suitable for the essay in Exercise 3. Why?

1 All in all, I believe that we have to find ways of living which are as healthy as possible. Also, I think people should try to drive more carefully.

2 In conclusion, I would agree with the statement because although we have plenty of opportunities to follow a healthy lifestyle, in practice we often choose a less healthy alternative.

3 To summarise, modern lifestyles have good and bad aspects, but the lifestyle we choose depends on us. However, often our health depends on factors which we cannot control.

5 Match each of these teacher's comments (a–c) to one of the concluding paragraphs in Exercise 4.

a A good brief final paragraph where your opinion is clearly stated and you summarise the main arguments of your essay.

b This concluding paragraph doesn't seem to sum up the arguments you expressed in the main part of the essay, but it sums up other arguments. What a pity, because it's well written!

c You're giving an opinion which is not exactly connected with the essay question. Also, your final sentence introduces a new argument which hasn't been dealt with in the main part of the essay, so it's not really a conclusion.

6 If you're not sure how to begin a paragraph, you can begin with a sentence which:

- says what the paragraph will contain
- relates the paragraph to the previous paragraph.

Look at the opening sentences (a and b) from the sample answer in Exercise 3.

1 What will each paragraph contain?
2 Which word relates one of the paragraphs to the previous paragraph?

a There are many parts of our lifestyles which enable us to live healthily.

b However, there are things which prevent people from having a healthy lifestyle.

7 Write opening sentences for paragraphs which will contain:

1 three advantages of living in the country
2 some disadvantages of living in the country
3 reasons exercise is important
4 dangers of taking too much exercise.

8 Work in groups. Discuss whether you agree or disagree with the essay question in Exercise 9. You can talk about:

- diet
- sport and exercise
- free-time activities.

9 Do this writing task. Write between 140 and 190 words. Before you write, make a plan.
When you write, you can use the essay in Exercise 3 as a model.

In your English class, you have been talking about how interested young people are in health and fitness.

Now your English teacher has asked you to write an essay.

Write an essay using **all** the notes and give reasons for your point of view.

Essay question
Young people generally don't pay enough attention to their health and fitness. Do you agree?

Notes
Write about:

1. physical exercise
2. other habits which affect health
3. .... (your own idea)

Write your **essay**.

Exam advice

- Your concluding paragraph should summarise your opinion and the reasons for it.
- Don't include new arguments or ideas in your final sentence because you won't be able to support them with reasons or examples.
- Be careful not to spend too long on Part 1, or you won't have time to do Part 2 well.

12 Animal kingdom

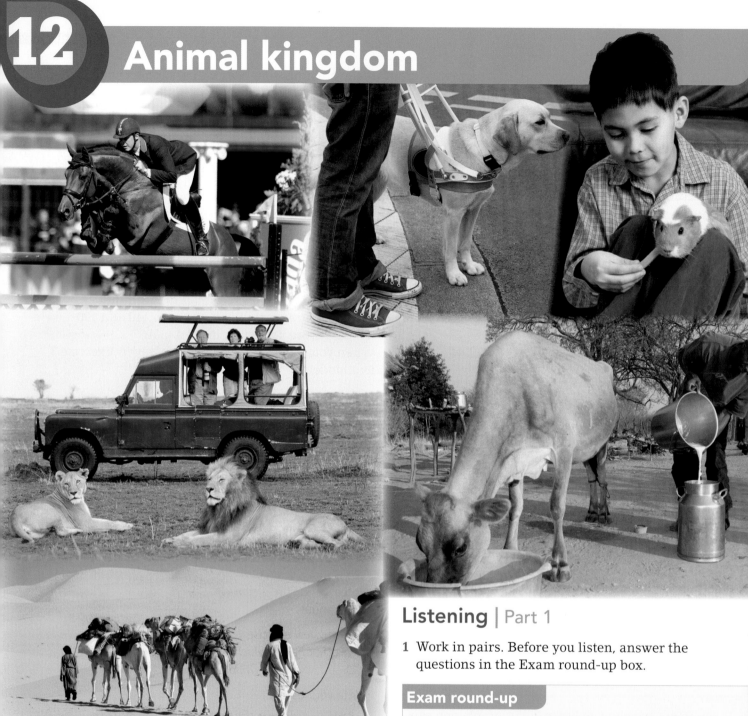

Starting off

Work in pairs.

Imagine you are planning an article for your college magazine on the importance of animals in our lives. First, discuss what role each animal in the photos plays in our lives and how these roles benefit people.

Then decide which two photos would be best for the magazine article.

Listening | Part 1

1 Work in pairs. Before you listen, answer the questions in the Exam round-up box.

2 ▶24 You are going to hear people talking in eight different situations. For questions 1–8, choose the best answer (A, B or C). As you hear the question, <u>underline</u> the main idea.

1 You overhear a conversation between two women about animals. Which animal does she think her family will choose?
  A a cat
  B a dog
  C a horse

2 You hear part of a television programme about zebras. What does the presenter say about their appearance?
  A All members of a family of zebras have the same stripes.
  B Zebras can recognise each other by their stripes.
  C Male and female zebras have similar stripes.

3 You overhear a conversation between a boy and a girl about birds in the girl's garden. How does the girl's mother feel about birds?
  A She enjoys watching them.
  B She likes feeding them.
  C She worries about them.

4 You overhear part of a conversation in which a girl and a boy are talking about dogs. What is the boy doing?
  A recommending having a dog
  B complaining about his dog
  C suggesting where to keep a dog

5 You hear a woman giving part of a lecture about animal rights. She says zoos
  A are no longer necessary in modern times.
  B should only be for endangered species.
  C should be closely supervised.

6 You hear a girl talking about some animals she worked with. When she was with them, she felt
  A frightened.
  B relaxed.
  C strange.

7 You hear a boy talking about hippos. What does he say about them?
  A They are more dangerous than he previously thought.
  B They often attack people for no reason.
  C They are easily frightened.

8 You hear a woman talking to her husband about a circus. She is talking to him in order to
  A make a suggestion.
  B make a complaint.
  C remind him of something.

Vocabulary

avoid, prevent and *protect; check, control, keep an eye on* and *supervise*

1 👁 Candidates often confuse the following words: *avoid, prevent* and *protect; check, control, keep an eye on* and *supervise.* Circle the correct word in *italics* in these extracts from Listening Part 1.

  1 I mean, we'd have to *check / control / supervise* her quite closely to start with to make sure she was safe. At least until we know she can *check / control / keep an eye on / supervise* it.
  2 … we really got him to *avoid / prevent / protect* us from burglars.
  3 Well, all that barking might *avoid / prevent / protect* a burglary.
  4 … the more modern zoos need to be strictly inspected to make sure that the animals are kept in the best conditions possible. That way diseases and other problems can be *avoided / prevented / protected.*
  5 I had to *check / control / keep an eye on* them as well, because they could be quite rough when playing with each other …

2 Read the definitions on page 185. Then complete these sentences (1–10) by writing one of the words in the correct form in the gaps. In some cases, more than one answer may be possible.

  1 This cream is perfect for .... you from insect bites.
  2 Can you .... the children while they're in the swimming pool, please, to make sure they're safe?
  3 You need to .... your dog, especially when you're walking with it in busy streets.
  4 The new law .... people from building houses near the National Park.
  5 There was a man who was .... the tickets as people walked into the stadium.
  6 I think we should set out early to .... the worst of the traffic.
  7 You ought to be wearing a hat to .... your head from the sun.
  8 It's the chemistry teacher's responsibility to .... students when they're doing experiments to make sure nothing explodes!
  9 Make sure you .... your answer for mistakes before you hand it in.
  10 We should always respect the forces of nature because we will never be able to .... them.

3 Complete each of the sentences below with an adverb/verb collocation from the box in the correct form.

> avoid … at all costs   check … carefully
> closely supervise   heavily protect
> narrowly avoid   properly protect   strictly control
> successfully prevent

1 Ben .... the bear from attacking them by making a lot of noise.
2 Juan .... an accident when a dog ran in front of the car.
3 Rhinos are an endangered species and need to be .... by game wardens.

4 The number of visitors to the game reserve is .... to avoid upsetting the animals.
5 Tourists visiting the park need to be .... to make sure they don't go near the wild animals.
6 When it rains heavily, you should .... crossing the river .... , as the current can be very strong.
7 You need to .... your route .... on the map before you start, as you could easily get lost.
8 The camp is .... with a high fence and an alarm to prevent dangerous animals from getting in.

Grammar
Third conditional and mixed conditionals

1 Look at this sentence from Listening Part 1 (extract 7) and then decide whether the statements (1–3) are true (T) or false (F).

If he hadn't reacted quickly, the hippo would have killed him.

1 The man reacted quickly.
2 The hippo killed him.
3 The speaker is talking about the past.

2 Now look at these sentences and answer the questions below.

a *I think if they'd had more acrobats, we'd have enjoyed the circus more.*
b *I think if they had more acrobats, we'd enjoy the circus more.*

Which sentence (a or b) … ?
1 means: *They don't have enough acrobats, so we don't enjoy the circus very much.* ....
2 means: *They didn't have enough acrobats, so we didn't enjoy the circus very much.* ....
3 has this form: *if* + past simple, *would* + infinitive ....
4 has this form: *if* + past perfect, *would have* (*been/done/ enjoyed*, etc.) ....
5 is second conditional (see pages 54–55) ....
6 is third conditional ....
7 has the same form as *If he hadn't reacted quickly, the hippo would have killed him* in Exercise 1 ....

➡ **page 165 Language reference:** Conditionals – third conditional

3 ☉ Candidates often make mistakes with tenses in third conditional sentences. Complete each of these sentences by writing the verb in brackets in the correct form.

1 If Martin had concentrated on his work, he .... (*finish*) it earlier.

2 If I .... (*know*) that the train was going to be so late, I .... (*catch*) an earlier one.

3 If there had been a swimming pool in the garden I .... (*go*) swimming in it.

4 John could have spoken to Emma if the phone .... (*not be*) broken.

5 We wouldn't have become friends unless you .... (*sit*) next to me on the school bus.

6 If you had been there, you .... (*enjoy*) yourself, too!

7 Sorry! I .... (*not make*) so much noise if I'd known you were asleep.

8 We .... (*not hear*) the burglar downstairs unless the dog had barked.

4 Work in pairs. Answer these questions in any way you like.

- What would have happened if you'd got up an hour later this morning?
- Where was the last place you went on holiday? What would you have done if you hadn't gone on holiday there?
- What was the last exam you passed? What would have happened if you'd failed the exam?

5 If you want to talk about past and present time in the same conditional sentence, you can combine second conditional with third conditional. Look at these two extracts from Listening Part 1. Which part of each sentence (a or b):

- is second conditional, and which part is third conditional?
- refers to present time and which part refers to past time?

1 Probably, if we lived in a safer area, (a) they wouldn't have bought a dog. (b)

2 I'd be happier, (a) if my parents had bought a house in the country. (b)

➡ **page 165 Language reference:** Conditionals – mixed conditionals

6 Complete these sentences by writing the verb in brackets in the correct form (second or third conditional) in the gaps.

1 My dad doesn't have a car, so he didn't drive me to my dancing lesson yesterday. If my dad .... (*have*) a car, he .... (*drive*) me to my dancing lesson yesterday.

2 Katie feels nervous about the test because she didn't study last weekend. If she .... (*study*), she .... (*not feel*) nervous about the test.

3 Our dog barks too much, so we didn't take him on holiday with us. If our dog .... (*not bark*) so much, we .... (*take*) him on holiday with us.

4 Karl was very rude to me, so we are no longer friends. If Karl .... (*not be*) so rude to me, we .... (*still be*) friends.

7 For questions 1–4, complete the second sentence so that it has a similar meaning to the first sentence, using the word given. Do not change the word given. You must use between two and five words, including the word given.

1 Marcelo often misses school, so his teacher did not let him go on the school trip.
ALLOWED
If Marcelo went to school more often, his teacher .... to go on the school trip.

2 We were late leaving home, so we missed the concert.
EARLIER
If we .... , we would not have missed the concert.

3 I did not ask my geography teacher any questions in class because she is quite frightening.
LESS
If my geography teacher was .... asked her some questions.

4 Franz did not understand because the guide spoke too quickly.
MORE
If the guide .... , Franz would have understood.

Reading and Use of English | Part 1

1 Work in pairs. You will read a short article by someone who worked in a circus. Before you read, discuss these questions.

- Are circuses popular in your country? Why? / Why not?
- What other traditional forms of entertainment are popular in your country? Why?

2 Before doing Reading and Use of English Part 1, answer the questions in the Exam round-up box.

3 Read the article quickly without paying attention to the gaps. What animals do Nell and Toti have in their circus?

My sister's circus

My sister and brother-in-law, Nell and Toti, (0) ...own... a circus. It is (1) .... Giffords Circus, and it tours some of the loveliest parts of south-west England. Circuses have always been a part of Nell's life, even when we were children. When she (2) .... Toti, she had already worked in (3) .... circuses in Britain and Europe. She had ridden elephants, but what she really (4) .... for was a circus of her own. If the word 'circus' (5) .... you of clowns and lions, think again. The show is (6) .... on traditional travelling circuses and aimed at a rural (7) ....
There are no wild animals, but horses play a leading role in performances, which are a mixture of theatre, dance, traditional circus acts and clowns. I had visited Nell at the circus a lot, but this time I was going to (8) .... the summer there.

Adapted from the *Daily Telegraph*

Exam round-up

How much do you remember about Reading and Use of English Part 1? Complete the information below with these words and phrases.

*eight   after   all the questions   the text quickly
you have finished   the options*

1 There are .... questions in this part. You must choose A, B, C or D.
2 Read .... before attempting the questions.
3 Read the words before and .... the gaps carefully.
4 Try all .... in the gaps before deciding.
5 Read the text again carefully when ....
6 Answer ....

4 For questions 1–8, read the text again and decide which answer (A, B, C or D) best fits each gap. There is an example at the beginning (0).

0	A belong	B keep	C (own)	D possess
1	A called	B known	C named	D titled
2	A encountered	B knew	C met	D saw
3	A few	B number	C plenty	D several
4	A desired	B longed	C wanted	D needed
5	A recalls	B recollects	C remembers	D reminds
6	A based	B built	C put	D set
7	A spectator	B public	C viewer	D audience
8	A be	B pass	C spend	D stay

5 Work in pairs.

- Many people think it's cruel to use animals in circuses. Do you agree?
- Do you think it's cruel to keep animals in zoos? Why? / Why not?

Writing | Part 2 A letter or email

1 Work in pairs. Read this exam task and discuss the questions below.

> You have received a letter from your British friend, Les. Read this part of the letter.
>
> > I'm thinking of visiting your country this summer. I'd be interested in seeing some beautiful scenery. Also, we'd like to see some wildlife. Can you advise me on where to go, what to see and the best way of getting around?
> >
> > Best wishes,
> >
> > Les
>
> Write your **letter**.

1 What three things must you deal with in your letter?
2 What advice would you give Les about your country?
3 What style would you use: formal or informal? Why?

2 Work in pairs. Write a plan for your letter.

3 Read Manolo's reply to Les's letter and answer these questions.

1 How does Manolo show that he has read Les's letter?
2 Has he answered all three things from the question? What advice did he give about each?
3 Does he give reasons for his advice?
4 What style does he use: formal or informal?

4 Find and <u>underline</u> these ways of giving advice in Manolo's letter.

1 *I'd advise you* + infinitive
2 *You should* + infinitive (without *to*)
3 *If I were you, I'd / I would ...*
4 *The best idea would be* + infinitive
5 *Make sure that ...*

5 Write five similar sentences using each of the five phrases in Exercise 4 once to give advice to Les for visiting your country.

6 Write your own answer to the question.

- Use Manolo's letter as a model.
- Write between 140 and 190 words.

Exam advice

- If you're writing a letter/email to a friend, use an informal style with contractions.
- Start in a friendly way with a phrase like *It's good to hear from you* or *I'm glad you're thinking of coming*, etc.
- Finish with something friendly like *I hope you enjoy yourself* or *Looking forward to seeing you.*

Dear Les,

I'm very glad to hear that you're thinking of visiting my country this summer. You can see beautiful countryside and scenery all over the country, although it varies a lot, depending on the region.

If you want somewhere that's not usually too hot in summer, I'd advise you to go to Asturias, in the north of Spain. It's a region which has some fantastic mountains as well as green countryside and beautiful rivers. You should visit the 'Picos de Europa', which are really spectacular mountains and canyons. All the paths are clearly marked, which makes walking quite safe, and you're sure to see a lot of wildlife while you're there. You may even see bears and wolves if you're lucky!

If I were you, I'd hire a car to get around. The best idea would be to hire it online before you leave home. Make sure that you take warm clothes and a raincoat as we can have heavy rain, even in summer.

I hope you enjoy your holiday and have good weather!

Best wishes,

Manolo

Vocabulary

1 Complete sentences 1–10 below with a word from the box in the correct form in the gaps.

> check-up   cure   diagnose   fit   get over   heal
> infection   prescription   put on   treatment

1 After a brief examination, my doctor .... that I was suffering from a slight infection.
2 As long as you keep the cut clean, it should .... on its own quite soon.
3 Farouk has been having .... in hospital following an accident he had last month.
4 She's spent the last two or three days in bed because of a minor .... she picked up at school.
5 I have to be quite careful what I eat so that I don't .... too much weight.
6 It's a good idea to keep .... by doing regular exercise – at least 40 minutes a day.
7 Rana's doctor has given her a .... for antibiotics to treat her illness.
8 Take this medicine. It should .... you in a couple of days.
9 You may not be very ill, but it's still worth going to the doctor for a .... to make sure it's nothing serious.
10 It took her several weeks to .... her illness, and she missed a lot of classes in that time.

Word formation

2 🄴🄿 Complete each of these sentences by using the word given in capitals at the end of the sentences to form a word that fits in the gap.

1 I'm sorry about the mistake. The trouble is I .... the instructions. **UNDERSTAND**
2 My mum and dad .... of my friends because they make a lot of noise and don't study much. **APPROVE**
3 I felt very .... with the quality of the food at that restaurant and I'm thinking of complaining. **SATISFY**
4 Although she's a little .... , she's very keen and she tries hard. **EXPERIENCE**
5 Luis goes to school even when he's feeling ill because he .... missing lessons. **LIKE**

6 Even though Sandra offered to invite Toni to lunch, he was .... to help her with her essay. **WILL**
7 It feels strange and .... to be chatting with my teachers on Facebook. **NATURE**
8 We got the answers wrong because we were given .... information by the teacher. **LEAD**
9 I don't like to wear .... clothes even when I'm at school. **FASHION**
10 My aunt sent me home because she said my behaviour was .... in her home. **ACCEPT**
11 Teresa is quite .... , so I'm not sure if she'll turn up. **RELY**
12 I want to know the truth, so don't be .... with me. **HONEST**

Grammar

3 Complete the second sentence in each question so that it has a similar meaning to the first sentence, using the word given in capitals. Do not change the word given. You must use between two and five words, including the word given.

1 The boy with the broken arm is still in hospital.
  IS
  The boy .... not left hospital yet.
2 Did the doctor treat this injury?
  ONE
  Is this .... doctor treated?
3 Everyone who lives in the town Paola comes from is very friendly.
  INHABITANTS
  Paola comes from a town .... very friendly.
4 The teacher liked how Jan had answered the questions.
  WAY
  Jan answered the questions .... the teacher liked.
5 His email left us in no doubt about his opinion.
  WHAT
  It was clear to us .... his opinion was.
6 No one finds Chiaro's jokes amusing.
  TELLS
  The jokes .... amuse anyone.

Vocabulary and grammar review Unit 12

Vocabulary

1 For questions 1–6, read this text and decide which answer (A, B, C, or D) best fits each gap.

Due to the destruction of their natural habitats, more and more animals need to be **(1)** .... by creating nature reserves and passing laws. The laws are often designed to **(2)** .... farmers from using land where rare species live. The idea is that humans and animals **(3)** .... coming into conflict by not competing for the same land. Sometimes local people complain about losing farm land to nature reserves. However, jobs are often created for game wardens, whose job is to **(4)** .... the nature reserves to make sure everything functions correctly. Other people get jobs selling tickets to visitors, and there are also jobs for people to **(5)** .... the tickets as the visitors pass the entrance. In nature reserves containing dangerous animals, it may only be possible to visit them by car, and wardens need to **(6)** .... the number of cars entering the reserve to make sure they keep within reasonable limits.

1 A prevented	B protected	C avoided	D defended
2 A avoid	B cease	C prevent	D disallow
3 A avoid	B prevent	C miss	D fail
4 A check	B control	C prevent	D supervise
5 A check	B control	C look	D supervise
6 A check	B control	C prevent	D supervise

Grammar

2 Complete these sentences with the correct form of the verb in brackets. In some sentences more than one answer is possible.

1 The lions wouldn't have attacked us if they .... (not be) so hungry.
2 I wish it .... (be) summer – then we could go to the beach!
3 If my maths teacher .... (be) ill at the moment, we .... (have) a maths test yesterday.
4 If only you .... (not make) so much noise! I can't concentrate on my studies, and it's really annoying me!
5 I wish I .... (live) near the city centre. It's such a long bus ride from here.
6 Where's Candice? I hope she .... (not miss) the train.

7 I wish you .... (speak) more clearly so I could understand you better.
8 I think this soup .... (be) nicer if I'd used a bit less salt, don't you?
9 I hope you .... (change) your shirt before we go out to the restaurant.
10 I know my mother wishes she .... (study) harder when she was my age.
11 We .... (get) to the cinema in time if there hadn't been so much traffic.
12 If you .... (eat) more breakfast this morning, you wouldn't be feeling hungry now.

3 Complete the second sentence in each question so that it has a similar meaning to the first sentence, using the word given in capitals. Do not change the word given. You must use between two and five words, including the word given.

1 We are lost because we did not bring the map with us.
LEFT
If we .... the map behind, we would not be lost now.
2 Magda only did the work because we gave her the money beforehand.
PAID
Magda would not have done the work unless we .... advance.
3 Even if he had worked harder, the result would have been the same.
DIFFERENCE
It would not .... if he had worked harder.
4 It is a pity I do not get on better with my brother.
RELATIONSHIP
I wish I .... my brother.
5 Sasha would like Irina to help him from time to time.
ONCE
Sasha wishes Irina .... a while.
6 Sergei is disappointed because the university rejected him.
TURNED
If the university .... , Sergei would not be disappointed.

Starting off

1 Work in pairs. Match each of these types of place to live with the photos.

   a a villa
   b a chalet in the mountains
   c a block of flats with several storeys
   d a house in a village
   e a housing estate
   f a mobile home

2 Which of these things do you think are important when choosing somewhere to live? Why? / Why not?

> a quiet neighbourhood   a good view
> shops within walking distance   a garden
> parking space   public parks or gardens
> good public transport   a good local school

3 Work in groups. Imagine you are going to live together for a year. Decide which type of place shown in the photos would be best for all of you.

Reading and Use of English | Part 5

1 Work in pairs. You are going to read an extract from a historical novel about a house in Venice. Before you read, look at the painting. Do you think you would have enjoyed life in 18th-century Venice? Why? / Why not?

2 Before doing Reading and Use of English Part 5, answer the questions in the Exam round-up box.

Exam round-up

How much do you remember about Reading and Use of English Part 5? Circle the correct option in *italics* in each of these sentences.

In Reading and Use of English Part 5:

1 there are *six / eight* questions; you must choose the best option: A, B, C or D.
2 you should read *the text quickly before reading the questions / the questions quickly before reading the text.*
3 you should read the options *before / after* reading the section of text where a question is answered.

3 Read the extract quite quickly to find out why the writer thinks the house is in a good location.

My new home in Venice, 1733

Uncle Leo gives me a suspicious look when I call this place the 'Scacchi Palace'. It is really a house, called Ca'Scacchi in Venetian. Anywhere else in the world, this would surely be regarded as a palace, although it is one in need of a little care and attention.

Our house is by the side of the little San Cassian canal and a small square of the same name. We have a door which leads onto the street and two entrances from the water. One runs under a grand, rounded arch into the ground floor of the house, which, as is customary in the city, is used instead of a cellar for storing things. The second is used for our commercial activities and it is situated in another building, which is three storeys high, attached to the north side, towards the Grand Canal.

Finally, there is yet another exit: a wooden bridge, with handrails, runs from the first floor of the house between the two river entrances straight over the canal and into the square itself. Consequently I can wander over it in the morning and find fresh water from the well in the centre of the square while still rubbing the sleep from my eyes. Or I may call a gondola from my bedroom window, find it waiting for me by the time I get downstairs and, just one minute later, be in the middle of the greatest waterway on Earth: the Grand Canal of Venice.

The house is almost 200 years old, I am told, and built of bricks of a rich dark brown colour. It has elegant arched windows and green-painted shutters to keep out the cruel summer heat. I live on the third floor in the third room on the right with a view over the canal and the square. When I lie in bed at night, I can hear the chatter and songs of the passing gondoliers and the conversations in the square nearby. I understand why Uncle runs his business here. The prices are not too steep. The location of the house is near the city centre and easy for our clients to find. Furthermore, the printing trade has many roots in this area of Venice, even if some of the old publishers from the area no longer exist.

Oh sister! I long for the day when I can show you these things instead of struggling to describe them in a letter which may take a long time to reach you in Spain! Venice is like a vast imitation of our old library at home, full of dark corners and unexpected surprises, some very close to me. Last night, while searching in the jumbled corners of the warehouse cellar, I found a single copy of *Aristotle's Poetics*, published in the city in 1502. I raced to Uncle Leo with my discovery and – now here's a victory – a smile almost appeared on his face. 'A find, boy! This'll fetch good money when I sell it down in the market.'

'May I read a little first, sir?' I asked, and felt some anxiety when I made the request. Leo has a frightening manner at times.

'Books are for selling, not reading,' he replied immediately. But at least I had it for the night, since the dealers were by that time closed.

Adapted from *The Cemetery of Secrets* by David Hewson

4 For questions 1–8, choose the answer (A, B, C or D) which you think fits best according to the text.

1 In what way is the house typical of Venice, according to the writer?
A There are several ways of entering it.
B People live and work in the same building.
C The storage area is not below ground.
D It consists of two separate buildings.

2 What does *it* refer to in line 10?
A the family business
B an entrance
C a floor
D a building

3 What does the writer say about his uncle's printing business in the fourth paragraph?
A His printing business is less expensive than others.
B The business has plenty of customers.
C There are other similar businesses in the district.
D It's the only printing business left in the district.

4 What do we understand about the writer and his sister in the fifth paragraph?
A They both enjoy reading.
B They both used to live in Venice.
C They write to each other often.
D They don't expect to see each other soon.

5 What does the incident with the book show about Uncle Leo?
A He dislikes having the writer in his house.
B He has a good sense of humour.
C He has problems with money.
D His main interest is making money.

6 In the text as a whole, the writer regards Venice as
A a strange and special place to live in.
B somewhere that could never be home.
C a city it's easy to get lost in.
D a place dominated by money.

5 Work in pairs. Take turns to describe a house which you have really enjoyed living in or visiting. You should each speak for about one minute.

- Before you speak, spend a few minutes planning what you are going to say.
- When your partner speaks, listen and think of one or two questions to ask at the end.

Vocabulary

space, place, room, area, location and *square*

1  Candidates often confuse the following words: *space, place, room, area, location* and *square*. Circle the correct word in *italics* in these sentences from Reading and Use of English Part 5.

1 Uncle Leo gives me a suspicious look when I call this *place / area* the 'Scacchi Palace'.
2 When I lie in bed at night, I can hear the chatter and songs of the passing gondoliers and the conversations in the *square / place* nearby.
3 The *place / location* of the house is near the city centre and easy for our clients to find.
4 Furthermore, the printing trade has many roots in this *area / place* of Venice.

2 Look at the definitions on page 185. Then circle the correct word in *italics* in these sentences.

1 We don't have enough *area / space* in our garden to hold the party.
2 I hope I will have enough *place / room* for all the things I am bringing.
3 Sorry I'm late. I just couldn't find a parking *place / space* anywhere.
4 I'm enclosing a map which shows the *location / place* of my school.
5 It's dangerous to go walking in a mountainous *area / place* without the correct equipment.
6 The animals in this zoo have a lot of *area / space* to move around.
7 The concert will take place in the main *square / place* in front of the cathedral.
8 The *area / space* of forest where they're going to build a new shopping centre is over 500 years old.
9 There isn't enough *place / space* to build more houses in this neighbourhood.
10 It's fine for you to stay at our place, as we've got loads of *room / place*.

3 Work in pairs. Write *area, place, room* or *space* in the gaps to form collocations, e.g. *hiding place*. Then discuss what each of them means, e.g. *A hiding place is a place to hide or to hide something.*

1 *hiding / market / meeting* ....
2 *floor / green / office / parking / personal / public* ....
3 *head / leg / standing* ....
4 *dining / penalty / picnic / play / reception* ....

4 Complete these sentences by writing one of the collocations from Exercise 3 in the gaps.

1 Teachers get angry when students leave their cars in their personal ....
2 If someone makes you feel uncomfortable by standing too close to you, we say that they have entered your ....
3 I love my school. It's surrounded by .... with lots of trees and lawns.
4 I'm tall, and the seats on the plane didn't have enough ....
5 There are lots of stalls in the .... selling fresh fruit and vegetables.
6 When you go to the country, it's good to find a .... where you can sit and eat a sandwich.

Listening | Part 2

1 Work in pairs. You are going to hear a student giving a talk to his classmates about his house, which he claims is haunted. Before you listen, do you think it's possible for houses to be haunted? Why? / Why not?

2 Answer the questions in the Exam round-up box.

Exam round-up

How much do you remember about Listening Part 2? Say whether these statements are true (T) or false (F). If a statement is false, correct it.

1 In Listening Part 2, you hear a conversation.
2 There are eight questions.
3 You will need just one or two words for each gap.
4 You hear the actual words you need to write.
5 You must spell your answers correctly.
6 Before you listen, read the questions as quickly as possible.
7 When you finish, make sure your answers form grammatical sentences.

3 Now read these sentences and predict what type of information or what type of words you need for each gap, e.g. question 1 is probably *a length of time*.

Jeff has lived in the house for **(1)** ....
He thinks his house is haunted because of the **(2)** .... which people have had there.
His **(3)** .... saw medieval soldiers.
Another guest saw furniture moving in the **(4)** ....
When doing homework, Jeff has felt a person **(5)** .... him .
His mother decided to convert the **(6)** .... into a study.
An expert told them the house was built on the site of a **(7)** ....
His father recently had a **(8)** .... installed.
One of the workers saw a man with **(9)** .... on his clothes.
His father is normally at home **(10)** ....

4 ▶31 For questions 1–10, listen and complete the sentences with a word or short phrase.

5 Work in groups. Would you be happy to live in a house with a reputation for being haunted? Do you know of any haunted houses?

Grammar
Causative *have* and *get*

1 In Listening Part 2, Jeff describes two changes to the house. What were they? Listen again if necessary.

2 Look at these sentences and answer the questions in the next column.

  1 a She turned the old garage at the back of the house into a study.
    b She had the old garage at the back of the house turned into a study.

  2 a Then my dad checked the whole house.
    b Then my dad got the whole house checked by a specialist.

1 Which sentences (a or b) did you hear in Listening Part 2?
2 Which sentences (a or b) mean ...?
  • he/she did it himself/herself?
  • he/she asked someone else to do it for them?
3 In the b sentences, who do you think did these things?

➡ page 164 Language reference: *Causative have and get*

3 Complete the sentences below by writing the correct form of *have* or *get* and the correct form of one of the verbs in the box in the gaps.

> cut down   deliver   pull out   extend   paint   renew

  1 You'll need .... your passport .... before you go to America next autumn.
  2 She went to the dentist yesterday and .... a tooth .... , so she's not feeling too well today.
  3 We're thinking of .... the house .... blue. What do you think?
  4 There's a tree hanging dangerously over the house, and I think we ought to .... it ....
  5 Our house is too small. If we could afford it, we'd .... it ....
  6 He hates cooking and .... all his meals .... from the restaurant opposite.

4 For questions 1–4, complete the second sentence so that it has a similar meaning to the first sentence, using the word given. Do not change the word given. You must use between two and five words, including the word given.

  1 Someone stole my bag during the bus journey.
    HAD
    I .... I was on the bus.
  2 A professional photographer is taking a photo of Stephan.
    PICTURE
    Stephan .... by a professional photographer.
  3 Marianne wants the hairdresser to change the colour of her hair.
    DYED
    Marianne wants to .... at the hairdresser's.
  4 The college rejected Pascual's application.
    TURNED
    Pascual had .... by the college.

Reading and Use of English | Part 2

1 Work in pairs. Look at the photo. Would you like to live here? Why? / Why not?

2 Before doing Reading and Use of English Part 2, answer the questions in the Exam round-up box.

Exam round-up

How much do you remember about Reading and Use of English Part 2? Complete the following sentences with the words and phrases in *italics*.

eight   before and after   one word ONLY   general idea grammar   the completed text

1 There are .... questions in this part.
2 The words you need are .... words: articles, pronouns, auxiliary verbs, etc. and parts of fixed phrases (e.g. *take part in*) or phrasal verbs (e.g. *make up*).
3 First, read the text quickly to get a .... of what it's about.
4 Read .... the gaps to decide what type of word you need.
5 Answer every question with .... , and check your spelling.
6 When you have finished, quickly read .... to check.

3 Read this article quickly, ignoring the gaps. Do you think you'd enjoy living on a houseboat?

Living on a houseboat

When we first moved onto our houseboat on the River Crouch, there (0) ...was... a big storm. The lights swung backwards and forwards (1) .... though we were at sea, but in (2) .... of the bad weather, not a single cup fell off the shelves. In fact, in the four years (3) .... we moved from our small house in the town nearby, (4) .... anything has been broken.

The boat is huge: 20 metres long and 4 metres wide. (5) .... to my dad, it is about four times the size of the house we had before. The kitchen (6) .... up about half of the main living space and it is not separated from the rest of it, so that whoever is cooking doesn't feel left (7) .... Our friends often (8) .... round to see us after we have been to school. In the living area, there is even room for a ping-pong table.

Adapted from *The Observer*

4 Now think of the word which best fits each gap. Use only one word in each gap.

5 Work in pairs.
- Do you think it's important for a house to have plenty of space? Why? / Why not?
- What things would you like to have room for in your house? Why?
- Would you like to live in a different place? If so, where? If not, why not?

Speaking | Part 2

1 Work in pairs. Before doing Speaking Part 2, answer the questions in the Exam round-up box.

Exam round-up

How much do you remember about Speaking Part 2? Say whether the following statements are true (T) or false (F). If a statement is false, correct it.

1 Each candidate must speak alone for about one minute.
2 You have to compare four photos and answer a more general question about them.
3 You should compare the photos in detail.
4 You should spend about half the time on the photos and half the time on the printed question.
5 After your partner has spoken, you will be asked a question about the same photos.

2 Work in pairs. Look at the speaking task on the right and the examiner's instructions. Then brainstorm words and phrases you could use to talk about each photo.

Here are your photographs. They show two different places to live. I'd like you to compare the photographs and say what you think it is like for the people to live in each of these places.

3 Look at these words and phrases. Which could you use with the first photo (1), which with the second photo (2) and which with both (B)?

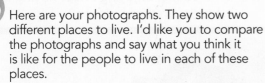

close to nature .... environment .... fresh air ....
hi-tech .... maintain a lifestyle .... occupants ....
organic food .... a rural setting ....
spend quality time .... social life ....
sophisticated entertainment .... pollution ....

4 Work in pairs. Take turns to speak for a minute about the photographs following the examiner's instructions.

What is it like for the people to live in each of these places?

5 ▶ 32 Work in pairs. Listen to Peter and Martyna doing the task, then say whether the statements on this checklist are true (T) or false (F).

	Checklist	T	F
1	Peter spends a lot of time describing what he sees in each photo.		
2	He outlines the main idea of each photo.		
3	He concentrates on answering the question more than comparing the details of the photos.		
4	He compares what it would be like to live in each place.		
5	He mentions things which he thinks are similar about the people in both photos.		
6	He uses language which shows he is imagining the lifestyle in each photo.		
7	He uses a good range of vocabulary to express his ideas.		
8	He uses short, simple sentences.		
9	Martyna gives a long, detailed answer to her question.		

6 Pronunciation: linking (2)

In order to speak more fluently, you sometimes put a consonant between the first and the second word when the second word begins with a vowel.

1 33 Listen to these extracts from Peter's answer. In the highlighted phrases, what consonant is used in the extracts to link:

a the yellow highlighted words?
- with the occupants, a family standing in the garden
- On the other hand, living in the city flat might be quite exciting

b the green highlighted words?
- where they grow their own vegetables
- Money and success in your career are not so important as being close to nature and the countryside
- which is probably busier and more stressful

c the blue highlighted words?
- Money and success in your career are not so important
- The family in the second photo must need to earn quite a lot of money

2 Work in pairs. Take turns to read Peter's phrases in Exercise 1 aloud.

3 34 In the gaps in these sentences, write the consonant which you think can link the two words. Then listen to check your answers.

1 We live further........away from the........old town.
2 Does he........ever........answer your questions?
3 Our........aunt comes to stay........at our house just now........and then.
4 Fewer........and fewer shops in our........area are........open at weekends.
5 Many........of you are busy........and in a hurry.
6 The........end of the story is more........exciting than the beginning.

4 Work in pairs. Take turns to read sentences 1–6 in Exercise 3 aloud.

5 Write three or four sentences as part of your answer to the task in (Speaking) Exercise 2.
- Think about how you can link words in the sentences using consonants.
- Then work with a partner and take turns to read your sentences aloud.

7 Work in pairs. Choose either Task A or Task B. Then discuss what you can say to do the task in a similar way to Peter (see questions 2–7 from the checklist in (Speaking) Exercise 5).

8 Change partners and work with someone who chose the other task.
- Take turns to do your tasks.
- While you are listening to your partner, use questions 2–7 from the checklist in (Speaking) Exercise 5 as a checklist.
- When your partner has finished, use all the questions from the checklist in Exercise 5 to give him/her feedback.

Task A

Here are your photographs. They show people on holiday in different places. I'd like you to compare the photographs and say what you think the people are enjoying about having a holiday in these places.

What are the people enjoying about having a holiday in these places?

Task B

Here are your photographs. They show old people living in two different types of place. I'd like you to compare the photographs and say which place you think is better for old people to live.

| Which place is better for old people to live? |

Grammar
Expressing obligation and permission

1 Work in pairs. You will hear five students who are staying with host families while studying in Britain. Before you listen, make a list of things students who stay with a host family in your country should and shouldn't do, e.g. *You should keep your room tidy. You shouldn't come home too late.*

2 Look at these sentences and then answer the questions below.

A *I can* invite my friends to dinner sometimes.
B *I have to* help with the housework.
C *I can't* take food from the fridge.
D *I'm supposed to* be back home early.
E *They let me* borrow their car.
F *They won't let me* do any cooking.

1 Which phrases in *italics* have a similar meaning to:
  a I must? ....
  b I'm not allowed to? ....
  c I'm allowed to? ....
2 Which phrase (a or b) has a similar meaning to *I'm supposed to* in D?
  a I must be
  b I should be, but sometimes I'm not

3 35 Listen and, for questions 1–5, choose which sentence in Exercise 2 (A–F) best summarises what each student says. There is one extra letter which you do not need to use.

1 Miguel	☐	4 Nikolai	☐
2 Irene	☐	5 Antonia	☐
3 Martyna	☐		

4 Which speaker said each of these sentences? If necessary, listen again to check.

1 *I don't have to* do anything around the house.
2 *I had to* buy the food and cook it.
3 *They don't allow me to* have big parties.
4 Apparently, *I was supposed to* phone to say I wasn't coming.
5 *They didn't let me* invite a couple of friends to dinner the other day.
6 *I needn't* clean the bathroom or do any shopping.

5 Work in pairs. Copy this table into your notebook. Complete it using the phrases from Exercises 2 and 4.

	obligation	prohibition	permission	no obligation
present				
past				

➡ **page 171 Language reference:** Modal verbs – expressing obligation, prohibition and permission

6 Complete the second sentence so that it has a similar meaning to the first sentence, using the word given. Do not change the word given. You must use between two and five words.

1 'You can't go to the club,' Steve's father told him.
   ALLOW
   Steve's father did .... to go to the club.
2 When you do the exam, it's not necessary to copy out the question.
   HAVE
   You .... copy out the question when you do the exam.
3 I shouldn't wear shoes inside the house.
   SUPPOSED
   I .... off my shoes before I enter the house.
4 You can't enter the room marked 'Private'.
   ALLOWED
   You .... into the room marked 'Private'.
5 Diane wouldn't lend Celia her car.
   LET
   Diane refused .... her car.
6 We were not allowed to use dictionaries during the exam.
   LET
   They did .... dictionaries during the exam.

Writing | Part 2 An article

1 Work in pairs. Before working on Writing Part 2, answer the questions in the Exam round-up box.

Exam round-up

How much do you remember about how to do Writing Part 2? Put these tasks in the correct order by writing a number 1–6 by each.

a Check what you have written, looking for specific mistakes you know you make. ☐

b Organise your notes into a plan. ☐

c Read all the questions and quickly choose the one you think you will find easiest. ☐

d Think and make notes. ☐

e Underline the things you must deal with in your answer. ☐

f Write your answer (140–190 words) following your plan. ☐

2 Work in groups of three. Read this writing task and discuss the questions below.

You see this announcement in your college magazine.

My ideal home

If you could choose the type of house you would like to live in and its location, where would you live, what sort of house would it be and what features would it have?

The best articles will be published in the next issue of our magazine.

Write your **article**.

1 What would be the ideal location for your house?
2 What sort of house would you choose?
3 What features would your ideal house have?

3 Work in pairs with someone from another group.

- Take turns to give a short talk describing your ideal house.
- When your partner finishes speaking, ask a few questions to find out more details.

4 Look at the writing task again and discuss these questions.

1 Who will read your article?
2 What style would be suitable for this article?
3 Which of these should your article particularly use: present simple, *going to/will*, conditional? Why?
4 What information must it contain?
5 How can you make the article interesting for your readers?

5 Read the sample answer below to the writing task, ignoring the gaps.

1 How does this ideal home compare with your own?
2 Has the writer answered the question completely?

My space, my place

I dream of living in a small, stylish modern flat in a historic old building near the centre of a large city **(0)** ..such.. as Barcelona or Bologna. What a change that would be **(1)** .... the ordinary suburban house **(2)** .... I'm living now! I could live like a sophisticated girl-about-town, dropping into art galleries, smart boutiques and street cafés with all my glamorous friends who live nearby popping in from time to time.

What would the flat be like? Well, for a start, I'd live on my **(3)** .... , so I'd be able to do **(4)** .... I wanted whenever I wanted. The flat would be hi-tech, with the heating and lighting controlled automatically, a cosy bedroom, a light, airy sitting room, and a handy little kitchen. Ideally, it would **(5)** .... a small balcony with a **(6)** .... plants where I could sit out in the sun.

I wouldn't need much space, as **(7)** .... as I had room to keep my books and clothes. **(8)** .... I had all these things, I'd be happy for years.

6 Complete this plan for the sample answer in Exercise 5 by writing the notes in *italics* below beside the correct paragraphs.

Para. 1: ....
Para. 2: ....
Para. 3: ....

Advantages of ideal flat
Characteristics of flat
Conclusion: room for my things
My present accommodation
Type of flat and location

7 Complete the sample answer by writing one word in each of the gaps.

8 Work in pairs. Discuss whether these statements are true (T) or false (F).

		T	F
1	The article uses plenty of adjectives.		
2	It uses conditional tenses.		
3	The writer mentions the furniture she would need.		
4	You can tell something about the writer's personality and tastes from the article.		
5	There are plenty of relative clauses.		
6	The writer doesn't say where she lives now.		

9 Write your own article.

- Before you write, decide what features of the sample answer on the left you could also use. Then think and write a plan.
- When you write, follow your plan.
- Write 140–190 words.

Starting off

1 Work in pairs. Write one of the verbs from the box in the correct form in each of the gaps below to complete the descriptions of festivals and celebrations. Use each verb once only.

> celebrate commemorate dress up gather round
> hold let off march perform play wearing

1 We hold a festival every March to .... the arrival of spring.
2 People in our region .... in **traditional costumes** and then they .... one of our **traditional dances**.
3 People .... through the town in a spectacular **parade** to .... a famous battle.
4 In many parts of the town, residents .... **street parties**.
5 **Bands** .... dance music all night long.
6 Crowds .... **street performers**.
7 During the festival, we .... **fireworks**.
8 People from the town go out in the streets .... **disguises**.

2 Find the words and phrases in bold in Exercise 1 illustrated in the photos on this page and the next.

3 Look at the photos again. They show different events which take place during festivals.

1 Why do people do these different things at festivals?
2 Which type of activity is most enjoyable for people to watch?
3 Which country do you think each of the photos was taken in?

4 Take turns to talk about a festival in your town or country.

- What does the festival celebrate?
- What happens during the festival?
- Do you participate? Why? / Why not?

Listening | Part 4

1 Work in pairs. You are going to hear an interview with a street performer at festivals, including one called the Hat Fair. Before you listen discuss these questions.

- What sort of things do street performers do?
- Do you enjoy watching street theatre? Why? / Why not?

2 Answer the questions in the Exam round-up box.

Exam round-up

How much do you remember about Listening Part 4? Complete the following sentences with the words and phrases in *italics*.

seven   general ideas   an interview   underline
different words

1 Listening Part 4 is .... or a conversation between two or more speakers.
2 There are .... questions; you must choose A, B or C.
3 Read the questions carefully and .... the main ideas. These will be expressed using .... from the question.
4 Listen for .... as well as specific information.

3 ▶ 36 Now listen, and for questions 1–7, choose the best answer (A, B or C).

1 Why is the festival called the Hat Fair?
  A It was started by local hat-makers.
  B Many participants wear hats.
  C Street performers collect money in hats.

2 What does Max most enjoy about the Hat Fair?
  A the type of audiences he gets
  B the other street performers he meets
  C the shows he can do

3 How did Max start in street theatre?
  A He lost his job in a circus.
  B He did it while he was at university.
  C He learned it from his father.

4 What do audiences enjoy most about Max's act?
  A the jokes
  B the acrobatics
  C the danger

5 According to Max, what makes street performers perform well?
  A They earn a lot of money.
  B They are paid by results.
  C They enjoy their work.

6 What does he say is usually the main problem with street theatre?
  A the weather
  B the location
  C the police

7 According to Max, how does the Hat Fair help the city?
  A It attracts visitors to the town.
  B It encourages people to work together.
  C It helps people to relax together.

4 Work in pairs. Sometimes towns and cities discourage street theatre. Why do you think this is?

Grammar
The passive

1 The passive is formed by the verbs *be* or *get* + a past participle (*eaten, done, played,* etc.). Read the following extracts from the recording script and <u>underline</u> the verbs in the passive.

  a I've been told the fair was only started in 1974, as a way of encouraging street performers like myself.

  b A hat's passed around so that the performers can earn a living.

  c They really seem to love it when they're being made a fool of by other people in the crowd.

  d I actually went to quite a famous circus school in Canada as a teenager where I was taught juggling and acrobatics.

  e Here we're given the main shopping street, which is fine. In other places, if you haven't got permission, you'll get moved on by the police.

2 Work in pairs. In which extracts (a–e) does the speaker do the following? (You can use the extracts for more than one answer.)

  1 He tells us who or what does/did the action.
    In extract c and part of extract e (the police)

  2 He uses the passive because he doesn't know who or what does/did something.

  3 He uses the passive because he doesn't need to say who or what does/did something because it's obvious from the situation or context.

  4 He uses the passive because what happens is more important than who does it.

➡ page 177 Language reference: The passive

3 Rewrite these sentences in the passive, starting with the words given.

  1 They founded our school in 1904.
    Our school ....

  2 Someone has stolen my wallet!
    My wallet .... !

  3 You won't be able to email me while they are repairing my laptop.
    You won't be able to email me while my laptop
    ....

  4 Have you heard? They've given me a place on the course!
    Have you heard? I ....

  5 If you hadn't done the work, your teacher would have told you off.
    If you hadn't done the work, you ....

4 👁 Candidates often make mistakes when they use the passive. Correct one mistake in each of these sentences.

  1 First of all, I'd like to show you a castle, which ~~might be built~~ in the 16th century. *might have been built*

  2 I was expecting the performer to be Danny Brook, but you didn't even mention that he was going to replace by someone else.

  3 I'm writing to you now because I've been told that is going to be read on the radio a short story by Agatha Christie.

  4 Moreover, how could we acquire a knowledge of the universe if the computer weren't invented?

  5 Ekaterina's story, which has already published in the school magazine, is really fun to read.

  6 Also, museums display many old things which have been using in the past.

  7 To sum up, nobody wants to be revealed their private life in public.

5 Read this text quickly to find out what happens at the Egyptian festival of Sham el Nessim.

Sham el Nessím

A large number of contemporary Egyptian traditions **(1)** .... said to have their origins in very ancient times. These include the holiday which is known **(2)** .... Sham el Nessim. This holiday may have **(3)** .... celebrated as early as 4,500 years ago. It is thought **(4)** .... have been the first festival to celebrate the beginning of the spring.

Nowadays, in the early morning of Sham el Nessim millions of Egyptians come out to crowded public parks and other open areas. Young men swim in the Nile and families generally enjoy the cool breeze of spring.

Sham el Nessim **(5)** .... also celebrated by eating traditional foods and these include salted fish, coloured eggs, sunflower seeds and raw onions. The reason for each of these foods **(6)** .... eaten is supported **(7)** .... a different myth. For example, offerings of fish are believed to **(8)** .... been made to the ancient gods and by **(9)** .... this a good harvest was ensured. Salted fish symbolised welfare to the ancient Egyptians and in ancient times fish **(10)** .... easily caught by being trapped in natural pools created by the movement of the Nile.

6 For questions 1–10, read the text again and think of the word which best fits each gap. Use only one word in each gap.

7 Look at this sentence from the text about Sham el Nessim and answer the questions below.

It is thought to have been the first festival to celebrate the beginning of spring.

1 What does the sentence mean?
  a People think that this was the first festival that celebrated the beginning of spring.
  b It used to be the first festival to celebrate spring.
2 It follows the pattern 'subject + passive verb + infinitive'. Other verbs which can be used in this way include: believe, report, say, consider, expect. Which other two sentences in the text follow the same pattern?
3 The sentence could also be expressed as follows: It is thought that this was the first festival to celebrate the beginning of spring. How would the other two sentences be expressed using this pattern instead?

➡ page 177 Language reference: The passive – the passive with reporting verbs

8 Rewrite the following sentences beginning with the words given.

1 Sham el Nessím is thought to have marked the start of the spring festival in ancient Egypt.
  It is thought …
2 Eating salted fish is known to have been a custom of the ancient Egyptians.
  It is known …
3 It is reported that five thousand people joined in the festivities.
  Five thousand people are reported …
4 It is said that our festival has the best fireworks in the world.
  Our festival is said …

9 For questions 1–6, complete the second sentence so that it has a similar meaning to the first sentence, using the word given. Do not change the word given. You must use between two and five words, including the word given.

1 People believe that the festival originated in the 18th century.
  HAVE
  The festival .... in the 18th century.
2 People expect that she will be chosen as carnival queen.
  BE
  She is .... as carnival queen.
3 The festival is said to be more popular than ever.
  THAT
  It is .... more popular than ever.
4 They think Channel 4 is the only channel which will broadcast the opening ceremony.
  THOUGHT
  Channel 4 .... the only channel which will broadcast the opening ceremony.
5 People think that Carnival is the best festival of the year.
  CONSIDERED
  Carnival .... the best festival of the year.
6 We know the festival started more than three thousand years ago.
  BACK
  The festival is known .... three thousand years.

Reading and Use of English | Part 6

1 Answer the questions in the Exam round-up box.

2 Work in groups. You will read an article about a Peruvian festival. Before you read, look at the festival in the photos.

- What do you think is happening?
- Would you enjoy a festival like this? Why? / Why not?

3 Six sentences have been removed from the article. Read the article (but not the missing sentences) quite carefully. As you read:

- think about and perhaps quickly note down the subject of each paragraph.
- underline any words and phrases before and after the gaps which may refer to the missing sentences (one has been done for you as an example).

The world's highest festival?

Where the writer was going

It felt as if we had been climbing for hours. I stopped to catch my breath as a wave of dizziness swept over me in the thin mountain air. I stood to one side of the path to let the mass of travellers with us pass. I was trekking with Marco, my guide to experience the festival of Qoyllur Rit'i which takes place at 4,300 metres in the southern Andes of Peru, a festival which few foreign tourists see.

As I looked back down the trail we had climbed and up towards where we had to go, I marvelled at the colourful sight. Entire families wearing local costumes were travelling to this unique festival from all over Peru. Among them there were old men, mothers with small babies and children all following the same route. Many of them had horses and donkeys to carry their food, blankets, cooking pots and tents. **1** ☐ Others had made their way on foot through the mountains for days to attend this remarkable event.

We continued our upward ascent for another hour and a half before reaching the Sinakara valley. There we looked down on a flat plain of open grassland crossed with streams from the glaciers and overlooked by snow-topped mountain peaks. Right across this flat piece of ground people were putting up shelters and tents of blue plastic to protect themselves from the freezing mist and rain. **2** ☐ The air of excitement, even from our vantage point more than a mile away, was palpable.

We chose a spot between two icy streams to put up our tent. While thus occupied, one of the many women dressed in the traditional costume of a wide-brimmed hat, woolly jacket, skirt and stockings came to sell us some very welcome hot soup and fish. **3** ☐

Not far away in another open market, people were buying tiny houses, cars or small pictures showing a baby or a wedding. Marco explained that these represented something the pilgrims desired. **4** ☐ This, they believed, would ensure that what they wished for would come true in the year ahead.

After dining in a makeshift restaurant and sampling the dancing and partying, we went to bed fully clothed inside our sleeping bags. **5** ☐ The ukukus, men wearing black masks and costumes, had left the encampment in the early hours to climb the nearest mountain by the light of the full moon. **6** ☐ In the dawn light, we watched them winding their way back down like a great black serpent. As they descended, they were joined by groups of dancers in bright traditional costumes. They performed wherever there was a space. Although there did not seem to be anyone organising them or any timetable, the whole festival had become a huge harmonious celebration.

5 👁 Candidates often make mistakes with punctuation. Ulli's answer in Exercise 4 is missing ten commas. Punctuate it correctly by placing the ten commas.

➡ page 177 Language reference: Using commas

6 Work in pairs. Ulli connects her ideas by using words which refer to other parts of her essay. What does each of the <u>underlined</u> words in her essay refer to?
1 'they' refers to people.

➡ page 178 Language reference: Using *it, this, that* or *they*

7 👁 Candidates often make mistakes with *it, this, that* and *they* when referring to other parts of their writing. Complete these sentences by writing *it, this, that* or *they* in the gaps. In some cases, more than one answer may be possible.

1 In my opinion, going to live concerts is better. .... gives you the chance to really connect with the band.
2 Listening to live music is better, but on the other hand .... is more expensive.
3 A further disadvantage is that when young people want to go to a concert, ... cannot always afford the ticket price.
4 During the tour, the band performed in Paris and Berlin, but .... had played in Amsterdam before ....
5 The band's tour had various problems: the bus broke down and some of their equipment was stolen. On top of all .... , there was a storm on the night of the concert.
6 Many live concerts are held late at night. .... leads to complaints from people living nearby who cannot sleep.
7 The sound quality of the recording is not very good, and in addition to .... , it is quite expensive.
8 I am not very keen on being in large crowds. In spite of .... , I would never miss a concert by my favourite band.

8 Work alone. Do this writing task.

In your English class, you have been talking about the advantages and disadvantages of going to the cinema rather than watching films on DVD or television.

Now your English teacher has asked you to write an essay.

Write an essay using **all** your notes and give reasons for your point of view.

Essay question
Is it better to watch films at the cinema or at home?

Notes
Write about:

1. quality
2. cost
3. .... *(your own idea)*

Write your **essay**.

Vocabulary

1 Circle the correct word in *italics* in these sentences.

1 You can leave your car in the parking *space / place* just outside my house.

2 Bring your family to stay with us! We've got plenty of *room / place* for all of you.

3 He loves travelling and the first thing he does when he arrives in a new *location / place* is take a photo.

4 The university campus is in an excellent *location / space* surrounded by countryside, but within easy reach of the city centre.

5 The schools are excellent in this *area / location*, so it might be a good place to buy a house.

6 There's an empty *place / room* at that table if you want to sit there.

7 We may have to take two taxis because I don't think there's *space / place* in one for all of us.

8 You can buy international newspapers at the newsagent's in the main *square / place*, just behind the station.

9 I found the flight uncomfortable because there wasn't enough leg *place / room*.

10 She's got a good hiding *place / room* for the money she keeps in her bedroom.

Grammar

2 For questions 1–8, read this text and think of the word which best fits each gap. Use only one word in each gap.

3 For questions 1–6, complete the second sentence so that it has a similar meaning to the first sentence, using the word given. Do not change the word given. You must use between two and five words.

1 We're hoping to employ someone to build a tennis court for us in the garden.
HAVE
We're hoping to .... for us in the garden.

2 Make sure that someone checks the car before you buy it.
HAVE
Make sure that .... before you buy it.

3 Magda must tidy her room each morning.
CLEAR
Magda has .... her room each morning

4 They make us do three hours of homework a day in this school.
HAVE
We .... three hours of homework a day in this school.

5 In this restaurant, you should pay for your food when you order it.
SUPPOSED
In this restaurant, you .... for your food when you order it.

6 Speaking is forbidden during the exam.
ALLOWED
You .... during the exam.

---

home | news | search | living green | stories | advice | contact

LIVING IN CAVES

Wherever people live, they need to protect themselves (0) ......*from*...... the weather, and ever (1) .... humans started to walk the Earth, they have lived in caves. To start with, they (2) .... use of natural caves, but they soon ran (3) .... of these. It then became simpler for them to create their own caves (4) .... to build shelters using other materials or techniques. On volcanic islands, for example, people found the rock was soft (5) .... to dig into, and (6) .... are places in the world where these

artificial caves are still inhabited.
Modern-day caves have some unexpected advantages. For anyone who has ever visited (7) .... , the benefits are immediately apparent: they will have found that the cave is isolated from noise and has a generally pleasant temperature. It is not too hot in the summer, while it stays warm in the winter. (8) .... is more, a modern cave is likely to contain all the modern household gadgets that make life comfortable.

Vocabulary and grammar review Unit 14

Word formation

1 **EP** Read this text. Use the word given in capitals at the end of the lines to form a word that fits in the gap in the same line.

Getting work experience is a good
way for young people who are still at
school to see whether they will enjoy a
particular career. Future (0) ...employers...   **EMPLOY**
like to see work experience on CVs and
it can be a good way to see whether,
for example, someone will enjoy being a
(1) .... before they start on a law   **LAW**
degree. They get the chance to consider
various (2) .... for a future career   **POSSIBLE**
with working professionals whose advice
they will find (3) .... helpful when   **SPECIAL**
thinking about the different choices they
will have to make. Work experience often
involves uncomfortable situations but
people who do it learn how to behave
(4) .... in front of clients and   **SUIT**
how to take (5) .... for things in   **RESPOND**
the workplace. Appearance is important
and they need to dress (6) ....   **APPROPRIATE**
whether they are going for a job as an
air-traffic controller or an IT specialist
or a job which is perhaps less technical
but equally (7) .... such as a sales   **DEMAND**
(8) .... or teacher.   **REPRESENT**

2 Complete each of the following sentences by
using the word given in capitals at the end of each
question to form a word that fits in the gap.

1 Tanya has a .... as a very hard-working student.
   REPUTE
2 In this airline, we make sure that we follow all the
   .... procedures in order to avoid accidents.
   SAFE
3 My teacher just looked at me in .... when I
   answered all the questions perfectly. **AMAZE**
4 We have expressed our .... with the work,
   which was very badly done. **SATISFY**

5 Visitors are often confused to find the .... of
   two streets with similar names in the town. **EXIST**
6 If only Maria would tell us the .... instead of
   trying to deceive us with obvious lies! **TRUE**
7 Pierre swam the .... of the river in five minutes.
   WIDE
8 The .... of a swimming pool has made the hotel
   much more popular. **ADD**
9 Can you tell the .... between this fake
   Rolex and the original one made in Switzerland?
   DIFFER
10 I have several other .... in July, so I won't be
    able to go on holiday then. **OBLIGE**

Grammar

3 For questions 1–6, complete the second sentence so
   that it has a similar meaning to the first sentence,
   using the word given. Do not change the word given.
   You must use between two and five words, including
   the word given.

1 It is almost certain that the flight will arrive on time.
   EXPECTED
   The flight .... on time.
2 Thieves entered my house last night.
   BROKEN
   My house .... thieves last
   night.
3 According to reports, seven firefighters were injured in
   the fire.
   REPORTED
   Seven firefighters .... been
   injured in the fire.
4 It's five months since my car was serviced.
   BEEN
   My car .... five months.
5 According to many people, she's living in Mexico.
   SAID
   She .... in Mexico.
6 There were very few cakes left by the end of
   yesterday's party.
   EATEN
   Almost every .... by the end of
   yesterday's party.

Language reference

Contents

Adjectives with -ed and -ing

There are many adjectives which are formed with -ed or -ing. Some adjectives do not have both forms, e.g. *living* but not ~~lived~~.

- Adjectives with -ed express how the person feels about something:
  *I was **fascinated** by the photos of her trip to Australia on her Facebook page.*
- Adjectives with -ing are used to describe the person or thing which produces the feeling:
  *Have you seen that **amazing** video on YouTube? (I felt amazed when I saw it.)*

➡ See also page 176: Spelling

Articles

The indefinite article

We use *a* or *an*:

- with singular, countable nouns mentioned for the first time:
  ***A blue car** came round the corner.*
  *We have **a new chemistry teacher**.*
- to talk about jobs:
  *His mother's **a doctor**.*

We do not use *a* or *an* with uncountable nouns or plural countable nouns:
Knowledge makes people powerful.
More women go to university in this country than men.

- Use *an* before words which begin with a vowel sound: ***an** app*, ***an e**mail* (but not when the letters 'u' or 'e' produce a 'y' sound: ***a u**seful tool*, ***a Eu**ropean student*, ***a u**niversity*).
- When 'h' is silent, use *an*: ***an h**our*, ***an h**onest man*

The definite article

The is used:

- with things we have mentioned before or when it's clear who or what we are referring to from the context:
  *I've got two new teachers. **The maths teacher** is from California and **the English teacher** is from Ireland.*
  *Could you go to **the** bank for me, please? (i.e. the bank we always use)*
- when referring to particular things:
  *I love music, but I don't like **the music my sister listens to**.*
- with things which are unique: ***the Internet**, **the moon***
- with adjectives to express groups:
  *In this country, **the rich** are growing richer and **the poor** are growing poorer.*
- with nationalities:
  the French, the Spanish, the Italians

- with superlative adjectives:
  the best**, **the longest
- with ordinal numbers (e.g. ***the** first, **the** second, **the** third*) used as adjectives:
  *Manolo won **the first prize** and Igor won **the second**.*
- with names of countries which include these words *Republic, Kingdom, States* or *Emirates*:
  The** Czech **Republic**, **The** United **Kingdom**, **The** United **States**, **The** United Arab **Emirates
- with names of rivers, mountain ranges, seas and oceans:
  the Nile, the Alps, the Mediterranean, the Pacific
- with many common expressions:
  *at **the** moment, at **the** age of 15, in **the** end, on **the** one hand … on **the** other hand*

Do not use *the*, *a* or *an*:

- when talking in general and in the plural:
  Teachers are not paid enough.
  I can't imagine offices without computers.
- with many common expressions:
  in bed/hospital/prison/school: He's in bed.
  at home/university/work: I'm at university.
  (go) to bed/hospital/university/work: What time do you go to work?

as and like

as

We use *as*:

- to say someone or something is that thing, or has that function:
  *He works **as a nurse**.*
  *She uses email **as a way of** keeping in touch with friends.*
  *Can I give you some advice **as a friend**?*
- to mean *the same as* before a subject + verb or a past participle:
  *Things happened exactly **as I had predicted**.*
  *The exam was **as expected** – very difficult!*
- to mean 'because':
  ***As** tomorrow is a public holiday, I will not be giving you any homework to do.*
- after certain verbs including *describe* and *regard*:
  *The teachers **regard** you **as the best group of students in the school**.*
  *The police **are describing** him **as extremely dangerous**.*
- with adjectives and adverbs to make comparisons:
  *Mike is **not as clever as** his sister.*
- to mean 'for example' in the phrase *such as*:
  *I spent the summer travelling round Europe and visiting lots of places **such as Venice, Florence and Barcelona**.*
- with *the same … as*:
  *You're wearing **the same colour shirt as me**!*

- in the phrases *as far as I know* (I think it's true but I don't know all the facts), *as far as I'm concerned* (this is my personal opinion), *as far as I can see/tell* (this is what I've noticed or understood):
  As far as I know, my grandparents have always lived in the same house.
  *I don't mind how much money you spend on clothes – you can spend all your money on clothes **as far as I'm concerned**.*
  *Arsenal aren't going to win the cup this year **as far as I can see**.*

like

We use *like*:
- to mean 'similar to' (especially after the verbs *be, seem, feel, look, sound, smell* and *taste*):
  *He's eating what **looks like a hamburger**.*
  *This swimming pool is fantastic – the artificial waves mean it's **like swimming in the sea**.*
- to mean 'for example':
  *He enjoys all sorts of adventure sports **like paragliding, windsurfing and canoeing**.*

Causative *have* and *get*

We use *have/get* + something + *done* (*cleaned / fixed / made*, etc.) when we ask someone else to do something for us:
*I've just **had my bike mended**.* (i.e. Someone has mended my bike for me.)
- *get* is less formal than *have*:
  *My dad **has just got some new furniture delivered**.*
- It's not usually necessary to say who did it for us, but it is possible:
  *I'm going to **have my hair dyed blonde** this afternoon **by my sister**.* (i.e. My sister is going to dye my hair for me.)
- *have/get* + something + *done* can be used in any tense or form:
  *I'm going to **get** my suit dry-cleaned for the wedding.*
- We can also use this structure to say we have been the victim of something:
  *Tim **had his wallet stolen** while he was waiting for the bus.*

➡ See also page 177: The passive

Conditionals

Conditional sentences express a condition (*If ...*) and the consequence of the condition. The consequence can be expressed before or after the condition:
If you come to Canada, we can visit Vancouver.
We can visit Vancouver if you come to Canada.

Note: If the condition comes first, a comma is used. If the consequence comes first, no comma is used.

Zero conditional

We use a zero conditional to express:
- things which are always or generally true:
  *If the teacher **is** late, it **sets** a bad example to the class.*
  *People **tend to get** annoyed if/when you **shout** at them.*
- scientific facts:
  *When/If water **boils**, it **evaporates**.*

Note: In zero conditionals, *when* and *if* often mean the same.

First conditional

We use a first conditional to express a future condition we think is possible or likely:
*If I **get** the job, **I'll buy** myself a new car.*
*If you **wash** the car, it **will** look much smarter.*
*I **won't phone** you **unless** it's urgent.*
*You **can have** an ice cream if you **behave** well.*
*You **shouldn't go** swimming **unless** you **think** it's safe.*
*If he **phones, tell** him I'm busy.*

Note: *unless* means 'except if'. We can often use *unless* instead of *if not*:
*I can't watch the football with you **unless I finish my school work** beforehand.* (I can't watch the football with you if I don't finish my school work before the game begins.)

Second conditional

We use a second conditional to express a present or future condition which is imaginary, contrary to the facts, impossible or improbable:
*I **would go** for a walk **if** it **wasn't** so cold.*
*If I **was** as rich as Bill Gates, I **wouldn't work**.* (Being as rich as Bill Gates is imaginary.)
*I **wouldn't fly** in a helicopter **unless** I **was** sure it **was** completely safe.* (This is how I would feel in this situation.)
*We**'d win** more matches **if** we **trained** harder.* (This is contrary to the facts – we don't train hard enough.)

Third conditional

We use a third conditional to talk about:
• something which did not happen in the past and
• its results, which are imaginary.

*If you **had gone** to the concert, you **would have enjoyed** it.*
*If you **had phoned** me this morning, I **would not have been** late for school.*
*If I **had lived** in the 19th century, I **would have gone** to school by horse.* (If I had lived in the 19th century (something which did not happen – I am alive now), I would have gone to school by horse (an imaginary consequence because I didn't live in the 19th century).)

*If he **hadn't reacted** quickly, the hippo **would have killed** him.* (He reacted quickly, so the hippo didn't kill him.)

Note: We can contract the third conditional as follows:
*If **I'd lived** in the 19th century, **I'd have gone** to school by horse.*
*If he **hadn't been** in such a hurry, he **wouldn't** have had an accident.*

We can use *could* and *might* instead of *would*:

*If our team had played harder, they **could have won** the match.* (They had the ability to win the match, but they didn't, because they didn't play hard enough.)
*If our team had played harder, they **would have won** the match.* (They were sure to win, but they didn't because they didn't play hard enough.)
*If the weather had been better, we **might have gone** swimming.* (Swimming was a possibility.)
*If the weather had been better, **we would have gone** swimming.* (Swimming was a certainty.)

Mixed conditionals

When we want to use a conditional sentence to talk about both the past and the present, we can use second conditional in one part of the sentence and third conditional in the other:

If tickets weren't so expensive, | *I'd have gone to the cinema last night.*
2nd conditional (present time) | 3rd conditional (past time)

• The tickets are expensive and that is why the speaker didn't go to the cinema.

If Mar hadn't fallen off her bike, | *she'd be champion now.*
3rd conditional (past time) | 2nd conditional (present time)

• Mar fell off her bike and that is why she isn't champion.

Note: You cannot use zero or first conditionals in mixed conditionals.

Countable and uncountable nouns

Nouns can be either countable [C] or uncountable [U]. However, some nouns can be both countable [C] and uncountable [U], but with a difference in meaning:
*They say it's healthy to drink **tea**.* (tea in general, uncountable)
*Would you like **a tea**?* (a cup of tea, countable)
*Living in a large house **is a lot of work**.* (work in general, uncountable)
*That picture is **a work of art**.* (a particular work, countable)

The grammar for countable nouns is different from the grammar for uncountable nouns.

countable nouns	uncountable nouns
• use *a* or *an* in the singular: *a job, an animal* • can be made plural: *cars, books* • use *some* and *any* in the plural: **some** friends, **any** answers • use *few* and *many* in the plural: **few** students, **many** years	• do not use *a* or *an* • cannot be made plural: *work, music* • use verbs in the singular: *The news **is** good, Music **helps** me relax.* • use *some* and *any* in the singular: **some** food, **any** advice • use *little* and *much* in the singular: **little** information, **much** homework • use other words to refer to a quantity: **a piece of** advice, **a small amount of** money

> 👁 Some common uncountable nouns in English
> accommodation advice behaviour countryside damage equipment experience food furniture homework housework information knowledge luggage media music news paper pollution research scenery smoke software stuff transport work

Infinitive and verb + -*ing* forms
Infinitive

We use the infinitive:
- to say why we do something:
  *I've just gone running **to get some exercise**.*
  *He's taken up tennis **to make friends**.*
- to say why something exists:
  *There's an example **to help you**.*
- after *too* and *enough*:
  *It's **too** cold **to go** swimming today.*
  *He isn't good **enough to make** the national team.*
- We use the infinitive in the following verb patterns:

verb + *to* infinitive	agree appear bother decide demand fail hope learn manage offer plan refuse seem be supposed threaten	She **agreed to meet** him after work.
verb + (somebody/ something) + *to* infinitive	ask choose expect help intend promise want	She **expected to win** the race. I **expect you to play** in the match.
verb + somebody/ something + *to* infinitive	advise allow enable encourage forbid force invite order permit persuade recommend remind teach tell warn	The money **enabled him to go** to university.

- We use these verbs from the lists above to report speech:

advise agree allow ask decide encourage forbid invite offer order permit persuade promise recommend refuse remind tell threaten warn

 See also page 173: Reported speech

Verb + -*ing*

We use a verb + -*ing*:
- after prepositions:
  *He's made a lot of friends **by joining** the tennis club.*
  *We watched a film **about climbing** in the mountains.*

Note: We also use a verb + -*ing* after *to* when *to* is a preposition:
*I'm **looking forward to going** on holiday.*
*She's **used to studying** everything in English.*

- as subjects or objects of a sentence:
  ***Climbing** is safer than it looks.*
  *He decided to take up **running**.*

We use a verb + -*ing* after these verbs:

admit appreciate avoid celebrate consider delay deny dislike enjoy finish imagine involve keep mind miss postpone practise regret risk stop suggest

*I really **enjoyed winning** that match.*
*She **suggested playing** a game of squash after school.*

We can use these verbs from the list above in reported speech:

admit deny regret suggest

 See page 174: Reported speech – reporting verbs

We use a verb + -*ing* after these expressions:

it's no good   it's not worth   it's no use it's a waste of time   can't stand   can't bear   can't help

*It's **not worth joining** that sports club.*
*It's a **waste of time entering** the competition unless you're really fit.*
*I **can't bear watching** my team when they play badly.*

Verbs followed by either an infinitive or a verb + -*ing* with almost the same meaning:

love   begin   continue   hate   prefer   like   start

*I **love playing** tennis. I **love to play** tennis.*
*It **continued raining** all day. It **continued to rain** all day.*

Note: When *love, hate, prefer* and *like* are used with *would*, they are always followed by the infinitive:
*I **wouldn't like to do** an adventure race.*
*I'd **prefer to watch** it on television.*

- *may not* and *might not* (or *mightn't*) in negative sentences (not *can't* or *couldn't* which express certainty):
Frankie is looking very pale. He **may not be** *very well.*
Don't cook any dinner for me because I **might not be** *back in time.*

To express possibility about the past, we use:
- *may have, might have, could have, may not have, might not have* + past participle:
It's unlike Sally to be late. She **may have overslept**, *or she* **might not have remembered** *the appointment.*

Expressing obligation, prohibition and permission

Obligation – *must* and *have to*

We can often use *must* and *have to* without any difference in meaning:
Teachers **must / have to** *try to make their lessons as interesting as possible.*

However, we use:
- *must* + infinitive without *to* in the present tense. For other tenses, we use *have to* + infinitive:
I'd like to go camping, but I **'ll have to** *ask my parents.*
In order to get the holiday job I **had to fill in** *an application form and do an interview.*
- *have to* more often in questions:
Do *we* **have to answer** *all the questions?*
- *must* for a goal (or an obligation) that we give ourselves:
I **must go** *to the supermarket later.*
- *have to* when the obligation comes from someone else:
My teacher has given me a lot of homework which I **have to do** *for Monday.*
- *must* for strong advice:
You **must be** *careful if you stay out late at night.*

Other ways of expressing obligation:
- We use *be supposed to* + infinitive to talk about an obligation which is different from what really happens:
We're **supposed to do** *five writing tasks each term. (But most people only do two or three.)*
Aren't *you* **supposed to be** *in class right now? (i.e. not out here playing football)*
- We use *should* + infinitive without *to* to talk about the right thing to do, but which is different from what really happens:
You **should answer** *using your own ideas, not things you have memorised beforehand.*
- The past of *should* is *should have* + past participle:
You **shouldn't have tried** *to answer all three questions in Writing Part 2!*
- We can use *ought to* to mean 'should':
You **ought to be** *more polite to the people you deal with.*

Prohibition

We use these modal verbs and phrases to express prohibition: *can't, mustn't, not let, (be) not allowed to, don't allow (somebody) to.*
You **can't go** *in there – it says 'No entry!'*
You **mustn't speak** *during the exam – it's forbidden.*
My sister **won't let** *me* **listen** *to her CDs.*
I'm **not allowed to use** *the kitchen in my host family's house.*
My parents **didn't allow** *me* **to play** *computer games when I was small.*

We do not use *don't have to* to express prohibition:
You **mustn't use** *your mobile phone in class. (It's not allowed.)*
Compare this with:
You **don't have to use** *your mobile phone to speak to Fayed. Look! He's over there. (i.e. It's not necessary.)*

In the past, we use: *couldn't, didn't let, wasn't allowed to, didn't allow (somebody) to:*
I **couldn't leave** *the room until the end of the meeting.*
She **wasn't allowed to invite** *her boyfriend to the party.*

We don't use *mustn't* to talk about the past:
I ~~mustn't~~ **couldn't ride** *my bike to school because my mum thought it was dangerous.*
We ~~mustn't~~ **weren't allowed to** *use our dictionary in the exam last week.*

Permission

To express permission, we use: *can (past could), let, am allowed to* and *may (past was/were allowed to).*
You **can** *only* **use** *your phone during the break, not in class.*
Are *we* **allowed to use** *calculators in the maths exam?*
She **let** *him* **borrow** *her bicycle to get to the station.*

We only use *may* in formal situations:
It's not necessary to stay until the end of the examination. When you have answered all the questions, you **may** *leave the room.*

To say that there is no obligation, or it's not necessary, we use: *don't have to, don't need to* and *needn't:*
This is a really good exercise on phrasal verbs for anyone who's interested, but it's not for homework, so you **don't have to do** *it if you don't want to. You* **needn't learn** *all the vocabulary on this page – only the words you think are useful.*

I didn't need to means 'It wasn't necessary and I didn't do it'; *I needn't have* means 'It wasn't necessary but I did it':
I **didn't need to buy** *a newspaper to find out the story because I'd already heard it on the radio.*
What lovely roses! You **needn't have bought** *me so many, but it was very generous of you.*

Prepositions

at, in and on in time expressions

We use *at* with:
- points of time:
  at three o'clock, **at the end of the lesson**, **at midnight**
- mealtimes:
  *We can meet **at breakfast**.*
- *the weekend, Christmas* and *Easter*:
  *Why don't we go to the cinema **at the weekend**?*
- *night* when talking about nights in general:
  *I prefer to study **at night** because it's quieter.*

Note: *on the weekend* is common in American English.

We use *in*:
- for periods of time:
  in 2014, in April, in the summer, in the 19th century
- for parts of the day:
  *Paola often has a short sleep **in the afternoon**. (But Paola slept for two hours **on Sunday afternoon**. See below.)*
- to say the period of time before something happens or how long something takes:
  *I'll be going to university **in six weeks' time**.*
  *He did the writing task **in just 13 minutes**.*

We use *on*:
- for particular dates, days, parts of days or types of days:
  *He was born **on July 13th**.*
  *What are you doing **on Sunday night**?*
  *I got married **on a sunny day** in August.*

at, in and on to express location

We use *at*:
- when we think of a place as a point, not an area (including *at home, at school, at work, at university*):
  *The postman is **at the front door**.*
- to talk about an event with a number of people:
  *I'll see you **at the party** tonight!*
- for addresses:
  *The party is **at 367 Wood Avenue**.*

We use *in*:
- when we think of a place as an area or space:
  *Olga lives **in St Petersburg**.*
  *Sonia lives **in a large house in the country**.*
- for cars and taxis:
  *I love listening to music when I'm **in the car**.*
- normally with *in class, in hospital, in prison, in court*:
  *Patrick is **in hospital** with a broken leg.*
- with people or things which form lines:
  *We stood **in the ticket queue** for four hours.*
- for *the world*:
  *He's reputed to be one of the richest men **in the world**.*

We use *on*:
- to talk about a position in contact with a surface:
  *There's an insect **on your forehead**.*
  *She lay **on the beach** all day.*
- with *coast, road to, the outskirts of, the edge of, border, the way to/from*, etc:
  *We can stop at my village, which is **on the way** to Madrid.*
- with means of transport apart from cars and taxis (see above):
  *I always get frightened **on planes**.*
- for technology:
  *He's been **on the phone** for hours.*
  *I found out about it **on Facebook**.*
- with *left* and *right*:
  *Talk to the student **on your right**.*
- with *premises, farm, floor, island* and *list*:
  *It's **on the fifth floor**.*
  *You're not **on my list** of students for this class.*

at	in	on
at your/my house	in the world	on the beach
at the festival	in the city	on the/a train
at the party	in the mountains	on the island
at the theatre	in the country	on the/a farm
at the/your hotel	in the town	on the outskirts
at the concert	in the sky	on the floor
at my school	in the hotel	on the stage
at the camp	in a car	on the bus
at the university	in this area	on the road(s)
at the beach	in the countryside	on the plane
at the airport	in the street	
at the seaside	in the sea	
	in traffic jams	

Relative pronouns and relative clauses

A clause is a group of words containing a subject and a verb in a tense which form a sentence or part of a sentence. Relative clauses start with these relative pronouns: *who, which, that, whose, where, when* and *why*.

relative clause ↓
The man who phoned you is my doctor.

Defining relative clauses

Relative clauses which tell us which particular person or thing the speaker is talking about are called defining relative clauses. They give essential information:
*The doctor **who treated me** is my cousin.*

The relative clause tells us which doctor we are talking about.

Non-defining relative clauses

Relative clauses which give us extra information are called non-defining relative clauses:

My doctor, **who belongs to the same tennis club as you,** *vaccinated me yesterday.*

We already know which doctor (it's my doctor); *who belongs to the same tennis club as you* does not tell us which doctor we are talking about; it just adds extra information.

There are differences in grammar:

defining relative clauses	non-defining relative clauses
• Don't have commas. • Use the following relative pronouns: *who, which, whose, where, when* and *why.* • Can use *that* instead of *who* or *which.* • *who, which* or *that* can be omitted when they are the object of the clause: *The medicine (– / **which** / **that**) the doctor gave me should be taken twice a day* (the doctor is the subject and – / *which* / *that* the object of the clause).	• Use commas (or pauses in spoken English). • Use the following relative pronouns: *who, which, whose, where* and *when.* • Don't use *that.* • The relative pronoun cannot be omitted.

Reported speech
Tense changes in reported speech

If the reporting verb (*said, told, admitted, warned,* etc.) is in the past, we tend to change the original verb to a past form as well. Here are some changes we make:

present simple → past simple	*'I **live** in Berlin.'*	*She said she **lived** in Berlin.*
present continuous → past continuous	*'I'm **watching** TV.'*	*He said he **was watching** TV.*
present perfect → past perfect	*'I've **seen** the film already.'*	*She said she **had seen** the film already.*
past simple → past perfect	*'I **missed** the concert.'*	*He told me he **had missed** the concert.*
will → would	*'I'll **phone** you soon.'*	*She promised she **would phone** me soon.*

We also change these modal verbs:

can → could	*'I **can understand** German, but I **can't speak** it.'*	*She said she **could understand** German but she **couldn't speak** it.*
may → might	*'I **may give** the book to John.'*	*Sam suggested he **might give** the book to John.*
must → had to	*'I **must cook** dinner.'*	*Tanya said she **had to cook** dinner.*

We do not change these modal verbs in reported speech: *could, would, should, might, ought to* and *used to:*
*'I **would prefer to study** in London.'* → *She said that she **would prefer to study** in London.*

must can change to *had to:*
*'You **must read** this text for the next lesson.'* → *My teacher told me I **had to read** the text for the following lesson.*

But we don't change *must* when:
• it's negative:
*'You **mustn't tell** Katya our secret.'*
→ *Ana told Stefan he **mustn't tell** Katya their secret.*
• it expresses a deduction:
*'Arturo **must** still **be** asleep.'*
→ *She said that Arturo **must** still **be** asleep.*

Note: If the reporting verb is in a present tense, no tense changes are necessary: *'I'll **help** you with your homework.'*
→ *She **says** she**'ll help** me with my homework.*

Questions in reported speech

To report a question, we make the following changes.
• We change the word order in the question to the same as a normal sentence.
• We make the same tense changes as in reported speech (see above).
• We use the same question words (*when, how,* etc.).
• We use a full stop (.), not a question mark (?):
'How long have you been living in London?' → *She asked me how long I had been living in London.*
'When can I phone you?' → *Abdullah asked Magdi when he could phone him.*
• We do not use the auxiliary verbs *do, does* and *did*; the question has the same form as a normal sentence:
'What time does the lesson start?' → *Ludmila asked what time the lesson started.*
• We use *if* or *whether* with Yes/No questions:
'Can I come to your party?' → *Aniela wanted to know **whether** she could come to our party.*

We often use these verbs and phrases to introduce reported questions: *ask, wonder, want to know, enquire.*

Pronoun, adjective and adverb changes in reported speech

We usually make the following changes:

you → he/she/they	'I spoke to **you** earlier.'	He said he had spoken to **her** earlier.
• your → his/her/their • our → their	'I saw **your** brother earlier.'	He mentioned that he had seen **her** brother earlier.
this/that (as pronouns) → it	'You should give **this** to Joan.'	She told him he should give **it** to Joan.
this/that/these/those + noun → the + noun	'**This work** is very good.'	She told him **the work was** very good.

Remember that references to times also need to change in reported speech:
'I saw Adam **this morning.**' → She said she had seen Adam **that morning**.

Other changes include:

present reference	• **today** • **this** week / **this** month / **this** year	• **that** day • **that** week / **that** month / **that** year
future reference	• **tomorrow** • **next** month/ **next** year	• **the next** / **the following** day • **the next** / **the following** month/year
past reference	• **yesterday** • **last** week/ month/year	• **the day before** OR **the previous day** • **the previous** week/month/year OR the week/month/year **before**

Descriptions of place also frequently change: 'Did I leave my book **here**?' He asked if he'd left his book **there**.

Imperatives in reported speech

We use verb + infinitive to report orders and commands:
'**Fetch** that book!' → She asked him **to fetch** the book.
'**Don't look** out of the window!' → She told him **not to look** out of the window.

Reporting verbs

There are many verbs which we can use to introduce reported speech, each followed by different grammatical patterns. You will see that most verbs can be followed by more than one grammatical pattern.

verb + infinitive
- agree: Magda **agreed to look after** the children.
- offer: She **offered to take** the children to the zoo.
- promise: She's **promised to phone** me later.

verb + object + infinitive
- advise: The doctor **advised Mrs Carter to take** a long holiday.
- ask: The neighbours **asked us to turn** our music down.
- invite: Patsy **has invited me to go** to the party with her.
- order: The police **ordered everyone to leave** the building.
- persuade: I **persuaded my mother to take** a holiday.
- remind: Can you **remind me to phone** Stephen?
- tell: Carl **told Jane to close** all the windows.
- warn: They **warned us not to walk** on the ice.

verb + preposition + noun or verb + -ing
- accuse of: Sophie **accused Marcel of stealing** her books.
- admit to: Bill **admitted to the mistake.**
  Sally **admitted to taking** the money.
- apologise for: Tommy **apologised for the accident.**
  Mandy **apologised for being** late.
- complain about: The neighbours **have been complaining about the noise.**
  We **complained about being** given too much homework to do.

verb + noun or verb + -ing
- admit: Danny **admitted the theft.**
  Sue **admitted stealing** the money.
- deny: Silvia **denied the crime.**
  Sean **denied causing** the accident.
- recommend: I can really **recommend this book.**
  I **recommend cycling** as a way of getting fit.
- suggest*: Jasmine **suggested the solution** to the problem.
  Mike **suggested going** climbing at the weekend.

verb + (that) + sentence
- admit: Sally **admitted (that)** she had taken the money.
- agree: The headteacher **agreed (that)** the exam had been too difficult.
- complain: We **complained that** we had been given too much homework to do.
- deny: Pablo **denied that** he had caused the accident.
- explain: She **explained that** she wasn't feeling very well.
- promise: Mandy **promised (that)** she would phone later.
- recommend: The doctor **recommended (that)** I take more exercise.
- say: Robin **said (that)** he was going swimming later.
- suggest*: Liz **suggested (that)** I should try the shopping centre on the edge of town.

verb + object + (that) + sentence

- persuade: *I **persuaded my mother that** she should take a holiday.*
- promise: *Lynn **promised Charlie (that)** she would phone him later.*
- remind: ***Can I remind you (that)** you've got to phone Stephen?*
- tell: *The school **told the students (that)** they had the rest of the day free.*
- warn: *Nobody **warned me (that)** my grandmother was visiting us today.*

Note: *suggest* is never followed by the infinitive. The following patterns are possible:

- *suggest + verb + -ing*:
  *Maria **suggested buying** a new computer.*
- *suggest + noun*:
  *Phil **suggested the idea**.*
- *suggest + (that) + sentence*:
  *Tony **suggested that** they played football that afternoon.*
- *suggest + (that) + should*:
  *Chantal **suggested (that) I should** write a letter.*

Other common patterns are:

- *ask + if/what, etc. + sentence*:
  *She **asked** me **what** I was doing.*
  *He **asked** me **if** I was free.*
- *invite + object + to + noun*:
  *Patsy **has invited me to the party**.*

➡ See also page 166: Infinitive and verb + -*ing* forms

➡ See also page 177: The passive – the passive with reporting verbs

so and such, too and enough

so and such

so and *such* (*a/an*) mean 'very', 'extremely':
*That was **so** kind of you!*
*I've had **such a** nice time.*
We use *so* and *such* (*a/an*) to talk about cause and effect:
*He was **so** late that he missed the beginning of the exam.*
*She gave **such a** good performance that she won an Oscar.*

so + adjective or adverb (+ *that*):	such + adjective + uncountable noun / plural noun (+ *that*)
• He was **so nervous** before the exam **that** he couldn't sleep at all. • That remark was just **so silly**! • He cooks **so well that** I think he'll win the competition.	• She tells **such good jokes**. • Switzerland has **such spectacular scenery that** we always choose it for our holidays.

so + much/many/few/little + noun (+ *that*)	such a/an + adjective + singular countable noun (+ *that*); *such a lot of ...*
• We had **so little money** left at the end of our holiday that we had to sleep on a bench in the station. • Marta makes **so many mistakes** when she's speaking!	• Why did you come in **such an old pair of jeans**? • It was **such a beautiful day** that we decided to go for a picnic. • Elena's got **such a lot of friends** that the telephone never stops ringing.

We also use *such* (+ noun) to mean 'of a similar type':
*When children commit crimes, adults are often shocked. Fortunately **such behaviour** is not as common as newspapers make us believe.*

too and enough

- *too* means 'more than is needed or wanted':
  *She's **too old** to join the police.*
- *enough* means 'as much as is necessary or needed':
  *Have we got **enough eggs** to make a cake?*

too + adjective (+ noun) + (for somebody) (+ infinitive)	adjective/adverb + enough + (for somebody) (+ infinitive)
He's **too young to drive.** That suitcase is **too heavy for me to lift.**	This coffee is **not warm enough!** Please heat it up again. Franz didn't answer the questions **convincingly enough to get** the job. That hotel is **not smart enough for her.**
too + adverb + (for somebody) (+ infinitive); too much / too many + noun + (for somebody) (+ infinitive)	enough + noun + (for somebody) (+ infinitive)
You're driving **too dangerously.** Please slow down. They brought **too much food for us to eat.** I've received **too many emails to answer.**	Have you got **enough money to get** to London? There isn't **enough cake** in the cupboard **for me to give** some to everyone.

Spelling

Spelling changes when adding -ed, -ing, -er and -est to words

We double the final consonant when we add *-ed, -ing, -er* or *-est* to words:

- which are one syllable and end in a consonant-vowel-consonant: *stop – sto**pp**ed, hit – hi**tt**ing, flat – fla**tt**er*
- which have two or more syllables which end in consonant-vowel-consonant and the final syllable is stressed: *admit – admi**tt**ed, occur – occu**rr**ing*

Note: In British English, we always double a final 'l' after a single vowel: *trave**l** – trave**ll**ing, cance**l** – cance**ll**ed*

We don't double the final consonant when:

- there are two final consonants: *send – sending, hard – hardest*
- there are two vowels before the final consonant: *appeal – appealed, mean – meanest*
- the word ends in a vowel: *strike – striking, safe – safest*

- for a verb, the stress is not on the final syllable: *open – opening*
- the word ends in *-w, -x* or *-y*: *slow – slower, relax – relaxing, display – displayed*

When adding *-ed*, a final 'y' after a consonant becomes 'i': *study – studied, lovely – loveliest*
When adding *-ing*, a final 'y' after a consonant does not change: *study – studying*

Note: Notice how the spelling of these words changes: *lie – lying – lied; die – dying – died; lay – laying – laid; try – trying – tried*

Spelling changes when adding prefixes and other suffixes

We normally do not change the spelling of the base word when we add a prefix or a suffix:
*need – un**need**ed, arrange – **arrange**ment*

However:

- we drop the final 'e' when there is a consonant before it and the suffix begins with a vowel (*-er, -ed, -ing, -ance, -ation,* etc.): *irritate – irritating, fame – famous*
- we do not drop the final 'e' when the suffix begins with a consonant: *safe – safety, manage – management*
- a final 'y' becomes 'i': *industry – industrial*

Adding prefixes

When we add a syllable like *un-, dis-,* or *in-* before the word to make it negative, we do not change the spelling, e.g. with *dis-* and *un-: appoint – **dis**appoint, satisfied – **dis**satisfied, like – **un**like, necessary – **un**necessary*

Note: Before words beginning with 'r', we use *ir-: **ir**relevant;* before words beginning with 'm' or 'p', we use *im-: **im**mature, **im**patient;* before words beginning with 'l', we use *il-: **il**logical, **il**literate.*

These words are frequently misspelled by exam candidates:

 The most common spelling errors by candidates

accommodation advertisement beautiful because beginning believe between children comfortable communicate convenient country/countries course different embarrassed/embarrassing environment excellent experience government loose lose necessary nowadays opinion opportunity/opportunities prefer receive recommend restaurant society their until wealthy which

Word formation

Forming personal nouns

You can form personal nouns (nouns which describe people who do particular activities) by adding:

- -er, -or, -ant, -ee to a verb, e.g. entertain – entertainer, operate – operator, inhabit – inhabitant, refer – referee
- -ist, -ian, -man/-woman/-person to a noun, e.g. motor – motorist, electricity – electrician, post – postman

Adding prefixes

Prefixes to give negative meanings

You can give some words the negative meaning by adding a prefix (e.g. dis- + like = dislike) to the beginning of a word. Here are some common prefixes which give a negative meaning:

- dis-: discourage
- in-: inexperienced
- un-: unbelievable

Before many words beginning with:

- 'l' we add the prefix il-: illegal
- 'm' and 'p' we add the prefix im-: impatient
- 'r' we add the prefix ir-: irresponsible

Other prefixes and their meanings:

- mis- usually means 'wrongly' or 'badly': misunderstand (= understand wrongly or badly)
- re- usually means 'do again' and is often added to verbs: rewrite (= write again)
- inter- means 'between or among': interact

Note: When you add a prefix to a word, the spelling of the original word does not change: dis + satisfied = dissatisfied

Adding suffixes

You can form verbs, nouns, adjectives and adverbs from other related or base words by adding a suffix (e.g. appear + -ance = appearance) to the end of the word. There are no clear rules – each word and the words which can be formed from it must be learned individually.

See also page 176: Spelling – spelling changes when adding prefixes and other suffixes

Some of the most common suffixes are listed below.

EP verb → noun

suffix	verb	noun
-ment	adjust	adjustment
-ation/-ition/-tion/-sion	combine define create divide	combination definition creation division
-er/-or	publish survive	publisher survivor
-ance/-ence	guide exist	guidance existence
-ant	inhabit	inhabitant
-al	approve	approval
-ee	employ	employee

EP adjective → noun

suffix	adjective	noun
-ance/-ence	relevant patient	relevance patience
-ness	friendly	friendliness
-ity	popular available	popularity availability

EP noun → adjective

suffix	noun	adjective
-y	boss	bossy
-ful	meaning	meaningful
-ous	fury	furious
-less	hope	hopeless
-al	emotion	emotional
-ic	optimist	optimistic
-ish	child	childish

EP noun → noun

suffix	noun	noun
-ism	critic	criticism
-ist	motor	motorist
-ship	partner	partnership

EP adjective/noun → adjective/noun

suffix	adjective / noun	verb
-ify	simple	simplify
	class	classify
-ise/-ize	special	specialise/specialize
	critic	criticise/criticize

EP verb → adjective

suffix	verb	adjective
-ed	educate	educated
-ing	mislead	misleading
-able/-ible	rely	reliable
	respond	responsible
-ent	confide	confident
-ive	compete	competitive

EP adjective → adverb

Adverbs are almost always formed by adding -ly. If the adjective ends in -ic, you change it to an adverb by adding -ally.

suffix	adjective	adverb
-ly / -ally	simple	simply
	organic	organically

Words which are often confused

👁 These words are often confused by candidates at Cambridge English: First.

Unit 4, Vocabulary, Exercise 1 (page 42)

food *noun* [U] something that people and animals eat, or plants absorb, to keep them alive: *baby food. There was lots of food and drink at the party.*

dish FOOD *noun* [C] food prepared in a particular way as part of a meal: *a chicken/vegetarian dish*

meal FOOD *noun* [C] an occasion when food is eaten, or the food which is eaten on such an occasion: *I have my main meal at midday. You must come round for a meal sometime.*

Unit 6, Vocabulary, Exercise 1 (page 63)

fun or **funny**?

If something is **fun**, you enjoy doing it.
I really liked the skating – it was such fun.

1 If something is **funny**, it makes you laugh.
It's a very funny film.

2 If something is **funny**, it is strange, surprising, unexpected or difficult to explain or understand.
The washing machine is making a funny noise again.

possibility, occasion or **opportunity**?

A **possibility** is a chance that something may happen or be true. **Possibility** cannot be followed by an infinitive.
Is there a possibility of getting a job in your organisation?

An **occasion** is an event, or a time when something happens. Occasion does not mean 'chance' or 'opportunity'.
Birthdays are always special occasions.

An **opportunity** is a possibility of doing something, or a situation which gives you the possibility of doing something.
The trip to Paris gave me an opportunity to speak French.
I have more opportunity to travel than my parents did.

work or **job**?

Work is something you do to earn money. This noun is uncountable.
She enjoys her work in the hospital.

Job is used to talk about the particular type of work activity which you do. This noun is countable.
He's looking for a job in computer programming.

Unit 5, Vocabulary, Exercise 3 (page 54)

assist *verb* [I or T] *formal*: to help: *You will be expected to assist the editor with the selection of illustrations for the book.*

attend BE PRESENT *verb* [I or T] *slightly formal*: to go to an event, place, etc.: *The meeting is on the fifth and we're hoping everyone will attend.*

get to know sb/sth: to spend time with somebody or something so that you gradually learn more about them: *The first couple of meetings are for the doctor and patient to get to know each other.*

join BECOME A MEMBER *verb* [I or T]: to become a member of an organisation: *I felt so unfit after Christmas that I decided to join a gym.*

take part: to be involved in an activity with other people: *She doesn't usually take part in any of the class activities.*

know or **find out**?

If you **know** something, you already have the information.
Andy knows what time the train leaves.

If you **find** something **out**, you learn new information for the first time.
I'll ring the station to find out what time the train leaves.

learn, teach or **study**?

To **learn** is to get new knowledge or skills.
I want to learn how to drive.

When you **teach** someone, you give them new knowledge or skills.
My dad taught me how to drive.

When you **study**, you go to classes, read books, etc. to try to understand new ideas and facts.
He is studying biology at university.

Unit 7, Vocabulary, Exercise 2 (page 80)

look, see or **watch**?

See means to notice people and things with your eyes.
She saw a big spider and screamed.

Look (**at**) is used when you are trying to see something or someone. If **look** is followed by an object, you must use a preposition. The usual preposition is **at**.
I've looked everywhere, but can't find my keys.
I looked at the map to find the road.

Watch means to look at something for a period of time, usually something which moves or changes.
He watched television all evening.

listen, listen to or **hear**?
Use **hear** when you want to say that sounds, music, etc. come to your ears. You can hear something without wanting to.
I could hear his music through the wall.

Use **listen** to say that you pay attention to sounds or try to hear something.
The audience listened carefully.

Use **listen to** when you want to say what it is that you are trying to hear.
The audience listened to the speaker.

Unit 8, Vocabulary, Exercise 6 (page 87)

acting *noun* [U] the job of performing in films or plays:
He wants to get into acting.

audience *group noun* [C] the group of people gathered in one place to watch or listen to a play, film, someone speaking, etc., or the (number of) people watching or listening to a particular television or radio programme, or reading a particular book

performance *noun* [C] the action of entertaining other people by dancing, singing, acting or playing music

play *noun* [C] a piece of writing that is intended to be acted in a theatre or on radio or television

(the) public *noun* [U + singular or plural verb] all ordinary people

scene *noun* [C] a part of a play or film in which the action stays in one place for a continuous period of time

spectator *noun* [C] a person who watches an activity, especially a sports event, without taking part

stage *noun* [C] the area in a theatre which is often raised above ground level and on which actors or entertainers perform

Unit 9, Vocabulary, Exercise 1 (page 98)

stay *verb* to continue doing something, or to continue to be in a particular state:
He's decided not to stay in teaching.
The shops stay open until nine o'clock.

spend *verb* to use time doing something or being somewhere:
My sister always spends ages in the bathroom.

pass *verb* If you **pass** time, you do something to stop yourself being bored during that period:
The visitors pass their days swimming, windsurfing and playing volleyball.

make *verb* (+ noun/adjective) to cause to be, to become or to appear as:
It's the good weather that makes Spain such a popular tourist destination.
Don't stand over me all the time – it makes me nervous.

cause *verb* to make something happen, especially something bad:
The difficult driving conditions caused several accidents.

Some common collocations with **cause**: *cause trouble, cause problems, cause damage, cause traffic jams, cause stress, cause pollution.*

Note, however, these collocations:
have an effect (on): *The good weather has had a beneficial effect on his health and happiness.*
have/make an impact (on): *The anti-smoking campaign had/made quite an impact on young people.*

Unit 10, Vocabulary, Exercise 1 (page 110)

arrive (+ **at**) *verb* to reach a place, especially at the end of a journey:
It was dark by the time we arrived at the station.
You **arrive at** a building or part of a building:
We arrived at the theatre just as the play was starting.
You **arrive in** a town, city or country:
When did you arrive in London?
You **arrive home/here/there**: *We arrived home yesterday.*

get (+ **to**) *verb* to reach or arrive at a place:
If you get to the hotel before us, just wait at reception.
You **get home/here/there**:
What time does he normally get home?

reach *verb* to arrive at a place, especially after spending a long time or a lot of effort travelling:
We finally reached the hotel just after midnight.
It is not normally followed by a preposition. It is not normally used with *here* or *there*.

Unit 12, Vocabulary, Exercise 2 (page 129)

prevent *verb* to stop something from happening or someone from doing something:
Label your suitcases to prevent confusion.

avoid *verb* to stay away from someone or something:
We left early to avoid the traffic.

protect *verb* to keep someone or something safe from injury, damage or loss:
It's important to protect your skin from the harmful effects of the sun.

check *verb* to make certain that something or someone is correct, safe or suitable by examining it or them quickly:
You should always check your oil, water and tyres before taking your car on a long trip. After I'd finished the exam, I checked my answers for mistakes.

supervise *verb* to watch a person or activity to make certain that everything is done correctly, safely, etc.:
The UN is supervising the distribution of aid by local agencies in the disaster area.

control *verb* to order, limit, instruct or rule something, or someone's actions or behaviour:
If you can't control your dog, put it on a lead!
The temperature is controlled by a thermostat.

keep an eye on to watch or look after something or someone:
Will you keep your eye on my suitcase while I go to get the tickets?

Unit 13, Vocabulary, Exercise 2 (page 142)

space EMPTY PLACE *noun* [C or U] an empty area which is available to be used:
Is there any space for my clothes in that cupboard?

place AREA *noun* [C] an area, town, building, etc.:
Her garden was a cool, pleasant place to sit.

[U] a suitable area, building, situation or occasion:
University is a great place for making new friends.

room SPACE *noun* [C or U] the amount of space that someone or something needs:
That sofa would take up too much room in the flat.

area PLACE *noun* [C or U] a particular part of a place, piece of land or country:
All areas of the country will have some rain tonight.

location POSITION *noun* [C or U] SLIGHTLY FORMAL a place or position:
The hotel is in a lovely location overlooking the lake.
A map showing the location of the property will be sent to you.

square SHAPE *noun* [C] an area of approximately square-shaped land in a city or a town, often including the buildings that surround it:
A band were playing in the town square.

Writing reference

What to expect in the exam

The Writing paper is Paper 2. It lasts 1 hour and 20 minutes. You do two tasks.

- In Part 1, there is one task (an essay) which you must do.
- In Part 2, you choose one of three tasks.

Part 1: Essays

You write an essay. The purpose of an essay is for you to discuss a subject, express your opinion and give reasons for your opinion.

You are given an essay title and some notes.

- You must write an essay answering the essay question and using all the notes. The task will tell you: *In your English class, you have been talking about / discussing … Now your English teacher has asked you to write an essay.*

The notes outline three areas you must cover. The final note will always be your own idea.

- Your essay must be between 140 and 190 words.

The title will ask you to write one of **two** types of essay:

1 An essay in which you are asked to discuss a statement and give your opinion, e.g. *Private cars should be banned from city centres. Do you agree?*
2 An essay in which you are asked to discuss which of two things is better, e.g. *Is it better for students to study something they really enjoy when they leave school, or something which will give them a good job?*

You should:

- cover the two points you are given in the notes as well as your own idea in the third point
- organise your answer in a logical way using paragraphs and linking sentences and paragraphs appropriately
- express your opinion clearly on the subject of the essay
- give reasons and examples to support your ideas
- use a style appropriate for the situation (this should be quite formal, as it is an essay for your teacher)
- write grammatically correct sentences
- use accurate spelling and punctuation.

You have 40 minutes to do this part (the Writing paper lasts 1 hour 20 minutes, so if you spend more time on this part, you will have less time for the other part).

You studied and practised writing essays for Part 1 in Units 1, 5, 8, 11 and 14.

How to do Part 1

1 Read the instructions, i.e. the task (what you have talked about in class, the essay title and the notes) carefully.
2 Underline the areas you must deal with in the essay title and in the notes. You'll lose marks if you don't deal with them all.
3 Think and decide what your opinion or position is on the subject of the essay and why you have this opinion.
4 Think and make notes about how you can cover the points listed in the notes.
5 Organise your notes into a plan. When writing your plan, decide how many paragraphs you need and what each paragraph will cover. Your plan should include short introductory and concluding paragraphs (see Units 5 and 11).
6 Before writing your essay, check that your plan covers the three areas.
7 Write your essay following your plan.
8 Make sure you express your opinion clearly in your answer and that the arguments you express support your opinion.
9 When you have finished, read your answer carefully. Check you have written between 140 and 190 words and correct any mistakes you find.

Note: If you write fewer than 140 words, you probably haven't answered the question/task completely and you will lose marks. If you write more than 190 words in the time, you may make too many mistakes and risk being irrelevant. Also, if you write too much, the examiner will stop reading after about 200 words and you will lose marks for an incomplete answer.

Exercise 1

1 Read this writing task, which asks you to discuss an opinion, and <u>underline</u> the areas you must deal with.
2 Decide what your position or opinion is and why.
3 Think how you can cover notes 1 and 2 to support your position/opinion.
4 Think what your own idea is and how you can use this to support your position/opinion.

In your English class, you have been talking about how long young people should stay in education.

Now your English teacher has asked you to write an essay.

Write an essay using **all** the notes and give reasons for your point of view.

Essay question
All young people should continue at school or college until at least the age of 18. Do you agree?

Notes
Write about:

1. *qualifications for jobs*
2. *students who don't like school*
3. .... *(your own idea)*

Write your **essay**.

Exercise 2

Read the essay in the next column and complete this plan for it.

Para. 1: Introduction: the situation now + ...
Para. 2: Why stay at school:
   1st reason ....
   2nd reason ....
Para. 3: Why leave school:
   1st reason ....
   2nd reason ....
Para. 4: My own idea: .... + solution: ....
Para. 5: My opinion .... + reason(s) ....

Write a brief introductory paragraph where you:
• explain the present situation
• outline your position/opinion.

An essay for your teacher has quite a formal style, so don't use contractions.

Use linking words and phrases to help your readers follow the ideas.

Although in my country compulsory education finishes at the age of 16, I believe that young people should continue in education at least till they are 18.

There are two good reasons for encouraging young people to stay at school. Firstly, because jobs are becoming more and more specialised and technical, it is almost impossible for 16-year-olds to find work. Secondly, if they stay at school, they will receive the education and training which will create more opportunities for them in the future.

On the other hand, many students would like to leave school at 16. This is because they find school difficult or they do not enjoy studying. They would prefer to be working and earning money.

A further point is that unmotivated students disrupt lessons, and this causes problems for students who do want to study. Therefore, after 16 they should only study technical or practical subjects that interest them.

In conclusion, I believe it is a mistake for people to leave school too soon, because they will miss opportunities which may arise in the future.

Exercise 3

Read this writing task and <u>underline</u> the areas you must deal with.

In your English class, you have been talking about the advantages and disadvantages of travelling abroad on holiday.

Now your English teacher has asked you to write an essay.

Write an essay using **all** the notes and give reasons for your point of view.

Essay question
Is it better to visit places in your own country or a foreign country when you go on holiday?

Notes
Write about:

1. *which is more interesting*
2. *which is cheaper*
3. .... *(your own idea)*

Write your **essay**.

Exercise 4

Read this essay. It shows a different way of organising an essay from the sample answer in Exercise 2. How is this essay organised differently?

There are strong arguments in favour of both staying in your own country and travelling abroad. I personally think that people should do both.

There are several reasons for staying in your own country. Firstly, I think it's important to know, enjoy and feel proud of your country and there is usually a lot which is fascinating about its history and culture, which is important to learn and experience. Secondly, you may be able to save money by finding cheaper accommodation. Finally, because you speak the language, you will avoid many of the problems you might have when travelling abroad.

On the other hand, when you go abroad, you can learn from the way other people live. Also, if you choose the right destination, it may be just as cheap as travelling in your own country, especially if you use youth hostels. Finally, it gives you an opportunity to learn and practise other languages, which is good for your education.

For these reasons, I think that people should travel abroad from time to time, but also spend time visiting their own country to appreciate what is good and interesting in both.

> You don't have to choose one option or the other if you think both have advantages.

> It helps the reader if you have a short sentence or phrase at the beginning of the paragraph stating the topic.

> Use a variety of grammatical structures, e.g. conditionals and relative clauses.

Giving reasons for your point of view
- … because / since …
- Because of this, …
- For this reason, …
- That is why …
- One of the main reasons is that …

Expressing results
- As a result/consequence, …

Expressing consequences
- In consequence, …
- Consequently, …
- … which means that …

Introducing your conclusion
- In conclusion, …
- To conclude, / sum up, / summarise, …

Ways of expressing contrasts
- However, …
- On the one hand, … On the other hand, …

➜ page 168 Language reference: Linking words for contrast

Introducing a personal opinion
- In my opinion, …
- I think …
- I feel …
- I believe …
- From my point of view, …

Introducing other people's opinions (often ones you don't agree with)
- Some people think/say …
- Many people argue that …
- It is sometimes/often argued/suggested/said that …

Putting your ideas in order
- There are two good reasons for …
- On the other hand, there are a number of reasons against …
- Firstly … / Secondly … / Finally …
- Also … / Furthermore … / What is more …

Part 2

In Part 2, you must choose from one of three writing tasks.

- The tasks you choose from will be three of these four possibilities: an article, an email/letter, a report or a review. It is important to know how to write all of these possibilities so you can make the best choice in the exam.
- You must answer the task with your own ideas. In most tasks, there are two things you must deal with.
- You must write between 140 and 190 words.

This part tests your ability to:
- deal with the type of task you have chosen
- use an appropriate style for the task you have chosen
- organise and structure your writing
- express opinions, describe, explain, make recommendations, make suggestions, etc.
- use an appropriate range of vocabulary and grammatical structures.

How to do Part 2

1 Quickly read the questions and choose the task you think you can do best.
2 Read the task you choose carefully and underline:
   - who will read what you write
   - the points you must deal with
   - anything else you think is important.
3 Decide if you need a formal or informal style.
4 Think of ideas you can use to deal with the question and note them down while you're thinking.
5 Decide which ideas are the most useful and write a plan. When writing your plan, decide how many paragraphs you need and what to say in each paragraph.
6 Think of useful vocabulary you can include in your answer and note it down in your plan.
7 Write your answer following your plan.
8 When you have finished, read your answer carefully. Check you have written between 140 and 190 words and correct any mistakes you find.

Emails and letters

You studied and practised writing an email/letter in Units 6 and 12.

Exercise 1

Read the writing task below and <u>underline</u>:
1 who the reader(s) will be
2 what points you must deal with
3 anything else you think is important.

> You have received this letter from an English friend, Pat. Read this part of the letter.
>
> > I'm doing a project on family life in different countries and I wonder if you could tell me a bit about family life in your country. I'd like to know what a typical family in your country is like and how family life is changing.
>
> Write your **letter**.

Exercise 2

Read Teresa's answer below.
1 What details does she give of a typical family in Spain?
2 How is family life changing?

Dear Pat,

Thanks for your letter asking for information about family life in Spain. Families in Spain are still very close, and family members take a lot of trouble to spend time together and help each other. Families often get together at weekends, and young people normally live with their parents until they are 25 or 30. People tend to get married in their 30s, which means that they start to have children quite late. As a result, families usually have just one or two children.

However, family life is changing. One of the main reasons is that most women now work. As a consequence, men have to take more responsibility in the home.

Another change is that, because both partners work, people are richer, so more and more families are now moving out of the cities to larger houses in the suburbs.

I hope that answers your questions. Please write to me if you need any more information. I'd love to see your finished project and read what you say about family life in other countries too.

Love,
Teresa

> Write a natural introduction and conclusion.

> Use linking words and phrases, e.g. *As a result, However, As a consequence ...*

Starting and finishing emails and letters

You know the person well

	emails	letters
start with	*Dear/Hello/Hi* + name: **Hi** *Magda,* **Hello** *Francesco*	*Dear Barbara,*
finish with	*Best wishes, / All the best,*	*Best wishes, / Love, / With love,*

You don't know the person well

	emails	letters
start with	*Dear* + first name: **Dear** *Barbara* (if you would use their first name when you speak to them) *Dear* + surname: **Dear** *Mr Hatton* (if you don't feel comfortable using their first name)	*Dear Mr Hatton,* (if you know the person's name) *Dear Sir or Madam,* (if you don't know the person's name)
finish with	*Best wishes, / Kind regards,*	*Yours sincerely, or Yours,* (if you know the person's name) *Yours faithfully,* (if you don't know the person's name)

Starting the first paragraph of a letter or email
- Thanks for your email …
- Thank you for your letter about …
- I am writing to request information about / complain about / apologise for / explain, etc.

Referring to something in a letter or email which you're replying to
- Your short film sounds an excellent idea and …
- As for the audience, …
- With reference to the audience, …
- You mentioned/asked about the audience in your letter and …

Making suggestions
- How about + verb + -*ing*:
  How about holding the meeting on the 5th?
- What about + verb + -*ing*:
  What about having a meal in a restaurant afterwards?
- It might also be a good idea to …:
  It might also be a good idea to visit the museum.
- Can I suggest that …?:
  Can I suggest that you give your talk on 5th May?
- I suggest + verb + -*ing*:
  I suggest holding the meeting on 4th November.

Asking for information
- Could you tell me …
- I would / I'd like to know if …
- I would / I'd like information on …
- Do you know if/whether/when/what, etc.

Complaining
- I'm not very happy about + noun/verb + -*ing*:
  I'm not very happy about the price. I'm not very happy about paying so much.
- I would like to complain about + noun/verb + -*ing*:
  I would like to complain about traffic noise in our street.
  I would like to complain about children playing football in our street.
- I am writing to complain about + noun/verb + -*ing*:
  I am writing to complain about the service I received at your hotel recently.

Apologising
- Sorry about + noun / verb + -*ing* (informal):
  Sorry about being late for the concert last Saturday.
- I would like to apologise for + noun / verb + -*ing*:
  I would like to apologise for arriving late for the concert on Saturday.

Inviting
- How about …?:
  How about coming windsurfing with me next weekend?
- Would you like to …?: **Would you like to** travel together?
- I would like to invite you to … + noun/infinitive:
  I would like to invite you to visit our town next summer.
  I would like to invite you to my house next weekend.

Giving advice
- You should …
- If I were you, I would / I'd …
- It would be a good idea to … + infinitive

Reports

You studied and practised writing reports in Units 3 and 9.

Exercise 1

Read this task and answer the questions below.

> Your teacher has asked you to write a report on things for young people to do in their free time in the area where you live. In your report, you should mention what free-time facilities there are and recommend improvements.
>
> Write your **report**.

1 Do you think you should use a formal or informal style for this report?

2 Read Christine's report on the right.
  • Is the style formal or informal?
  • Does it answer the question completely?

Report on free-time facilities in my area

Introduction

The aim of this report is to outline what young people do in my area in their free time, what facilities exist for them and how these could be made better.

Free-time activities

My town, Beauvoir, is quite small, so it does not have a cinema or theatre and there is only one club for young people. As a result, young people have to take the train or bus to Nantes, which is about 30 kilometres away if they want these things. On the other hand, it is situated by the sea, so many young people spend their free time on the beach or doing water sports.

Other facilities

Beauvoir has a sports centre with tennis courts, a football pitch and a swimming pool. There are also a number of cafés where young people normally go to meet each other and spend their free time.

Recommendations

I recommend that the town council should set up a youth club where young people could meet, do other activities and also see films. This would encourage young people to stay in the town at weekends and improve their social life.

> Notice the layout. The report has:
> • a title
> • is divided into sections
> • each section has a heading.

> Normally, we state the aim or purpose of the report at the beginning.

> Avoid repeating exactly the words of the question, e.g. the question says *recommend improvements*, but the report says *how these could be made better*.

> Give reasons for your recommendations.

Starting a report
• The aim of this report is + infinitive: *The aim of this report is to outline* …
• The purpose of this report is + infinitive: *The purpose of this report is to describe* …

Making recommendations and suggestions
• I recommend that: *I recommend that the town council should set up a youth club* …
• I (would) recommend + verb + -ing: *I would recommend setting up a youth club* …
• I suggest + verb + -ing: *I suggest buying more equipment for the sports centre.*
• I suggest that … : *I suggest that the council should provide cheap transport for young people and students.*
• It would be a good idea (for somebody) + infinitive: *It would be a good idea for the council to provide cheap transport for young people and students.*

Reviews

You studied and practised writing reviews in Units 4 and 10.

Exercise 1

Read the writing task below.

1 Underline the points you must deal with.
2 Underline anything else you think is important.
3 Who will the reader(s) be, and where will your answer appear?

You see this announcement in your school's English-language magazine.

Have you seen a film or read a book recently that you think everyone would enjoy? We want to know about it! Write a review of the film or book saying what it's about and why we would all enjoy it.

Write your **review**.

Exercise 2

Read Franz's review below. Which paragraphs say:
1 what the book is about?
2 why we would all enjoy it?

Give your review a title.

'The Time Traveler's Wife' by Audrey Niffenegger

This is an original and moving love story told from the point of view of the two main characters, Henry and Clare. Henry is a librarian who has a genetic problem which causes him to move backwards and forwards in time. Without warning, he disappears leaving everything behind and arrives at another time in his life. He can't control when or where he's going.

When he travels, he often meets the same girl, Clare, at different times in her life. Eventually they fall in love even though sometimes when they meet he is much older than her and at other times they are the same age.

I think everyone will enjoy this unusual story because it combines a little science fiction with a wonderful romantic story. Henry's problem causes situations which are funny, sometimes frightening, usually awkward and often very strange. The novel is fascinating because it makes you think about the nature of time. At the same time, you see how the characters and their relationships change during their lives but how their love grows stronger.

Mention:
- the type of book/film
- the characters
- some of the story
- what makes the book/film different.

Use plenty of adjectives to describe:
- the book/film
- how you feel about it.

Ways of praising

- I think everyone will enjoy this ... (book/film/restaurant, etc.) because ... The ... (book/film/restaurant, etc.) is fascinating/wonderful/marvellous because ...
- This ... (book/film/restaurant, etc.) is really worth (reading/seeing/visiting, etc.) because ...

Part 3

In Part 3, you work with the other candidate.

This part of the Speaking paper is divided into two parts.

In the first part, which takes two minutes:
- The examiner gives you a page with a question and five prompts.
- You have 15 seconds to consider the options before you start speaking.
- You should discuss each of the options in turn.

In the second part, the examiner asks you to summarise your thoughts, for example by choosing the option that is best and saying why. You have one minute for this.

You studied and practised Part 3 in Units 3, 7, 12 and 14.

How to do Part 3

For the first part:

1 Listen carefully to the question, which is also printed next to the options to help you. It will be in a mind map with the question in the middle of the page and the prompts around it.
2 You have 15 seconds to think about the task before you start speaking:

   Think about:
   - the options and how you can express them in your own words and discuss their relative merits in relation to the question
   - how you can start the discussion, perhaps with a suggestion and a reason for your idea.

3 To start the conversation, you can give a brief opinion about one of the options or make a suggestion and ask your partner what he/she thinks.
4 When you discuss, deal with each option in turn.
5 When your partner says something, react to his/her ideas. Listen carefully to what he/she is saying. Try to make the discussion like a natural conversation. Don't try to dominate the conversation.
6 Keep the discussion moving by saying things like *What about this option? What do you think?* or *Shall we move on to the next option?*.
7 Don't spend too long talking about one particular option.
8 Continue your discussion until the examiner says 'Thank you'.

For the second part:

1 Don't discuss each option again, but discuss the options which seem most reasonable to you.
2 Try to reach a decision, but remember that it's not essential to agree.
3 Remember you should discuss the question for a minute, so if you agree with your partner's first idea, say so, but suggest discussing other options (see Unit 3).
4 Continue your discussion until the examiner says 'Thank you'.

Example task: First part

 I'd like you to imagine that a town wants to attract more visitors and tourists. Here are some of the ideas they are considering. Talk to each other about how effective these different ideas might be. You now have some time to look at the task. Then decide which two would attract the most tourists.

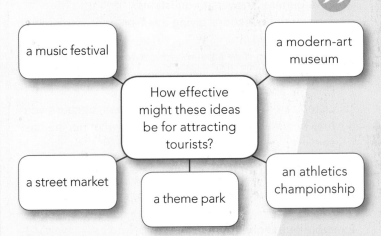

a music festival

a modern-art museum

How effective might these ideas be for attracting tourists?

a street market

a theme park

an athletics championship

Example task : Second part

 Now you have a minute to decide which two ideas would be best for attracting tourists.

Involving your partner
- What do you think?
- Do you agree?
- What about (a music festival)?
- I think … What about you?

Keeping the discussion moving
- What about (a theme park)? What do you think?
- Let's move on to the next option.
- Shall we move on to the next option?

Part 4

> **In Part 4, you continue to work together.**
> - The examiner asks both of you questions about your opinions connected with the topic you discussed in Part 3.
> - You may be asked the same question as your partner, if you agree with your partner's answer, or a completely different question.
>
> Part 4 lasts about four minutes.
>
> You studied and practised Part 4 in Units 4, 8, 12 and 14.

How to do Part 4

> 1 Listen carefully to the questions. If you don't understand a question, don't feel afraid to ask the examiner to repeat (*Sorry could you say that again, please?*). You won't lose any marks asking them to repeat.
> 2 Give general answers to questions.
> 3 Answer the questions giving a reason or an explanation or an example.
> 4 You can try to give a balanced answer, i.e. express two points of view and say which one you agree with (see Units 12 and 14).
> 5 Listen carefully to what your partner says, because you may be asked to give your opinion on what he/she has said.
> 6 If you don't know the answer to a question, don't just say *I don't know*. Say *I don't know a lot about this subject, but I think …* and then give some ideas.

Example questions
- Some places attract large numbers of tourists. What problems are caused by having too many tourists?
- What can people learn by going as tourists to other places?
- Do you think it's better for people to spend their holidays in their own country or travel to other countries? Why?
- What are the advantages of living in another country instead of just going as a tourist? What's the main advantage?

- What things should people try to find out before visiting a country? (Why?)
- How important is it for tourists to respect the culture of the country they are visiting?

> **Introducing an opinion and giving a reason**
> - I think …
> - Well, in my opinion, … because …
> - I feel …
> - I'm not sure. I think …
> - No, I don't think so …

> **Introducing an explanation**
> - I mean …
> - You see …

> **Giving an example**
> - For example …
> - For instance …
> - … such as …

> **Speaking in general**
> - In general, …
> - Generally, …
> - As a rule, …
> - … tend to …

Grammar
Making comparisons

1 **1** a bit more   **2** much safer, far more   **3** most
4 better   **5** much harder   **6** most   **7** biggest
8 so much

2 **1** ~~the healthier~~ the healthiest   **2** ~~more cheaper~~
cheaper   **3** ~~that~~ than   **4** ~~more hardly~~ harder   **5** ~~as~~
~~often than~~ as often as   **6** ~~the more risky~~ the riskiest
/ the most risky   **7** ~~the less interesting~~ the least
interesting / less interesting   **8** ~~more good~~ better

3 *Suggested answers*
1 difficult to park in the city.   **2** difficult as it looks.
3 important thing is to participate, not to win.
4 skiing than skating.   **5** nicer than I am.
6 as bad for you as some people say.

Reading and Use of English | Part 5

2 *Suggested answer*
His girlfriend left him for someone with a motorbike;
he had enjoyed riding a motorbike when he was six;
it would allow him to get to places.

3 *Suggested underlining*
1 Such trivialities   **2** did not buy   **3** adults,
frightened, because   **4** main reason for buying
5 desire, meant   **6** result / accident

4 **1** D   **2** B   **3** C   **4** D   **5** A   **6** C

Vocabulary
Phrasal verbs and expressions

1 **1** d   **2** a   **3** h   **4** f   **5** g   **6** c   **7** b   **8** e

2 **1** taking risks   **2** sum up   **3** have a go   **4** make up
5 didn't have / hadn't got a clue   **6** keep a promise /
keep promises   **7** taking up   **8** get hold of

Grammar
Adjectives with -ed and -ing

1 **1** thrilled, elated   **2** exciting

2 **1** amusing   **2** irritating   **3** bored   **4** confused
5 embarrassing   **6** excited

3 **1** astonishing   **2** puzzled   **3** motivating   **4** worried
5 amusing   **6** exhausted

4 g

 CD 1 Track 06

Young woman: The whole experience was amazing
actually. I mean, I'd been working really hard,
studying, and so I was feeling pretty tired and
nervous already, so when my boyfriend suggested
I went along with him, I was like shocked, like 'No
way!' – I mean the thought of breaking a bone or
something even worse just before an exam was
terrifying. But you know, he just kept on at me,
so for the sake of a bit of peace, in the end I said
yes. When we were up there in the sky, I was just
so scared I can't tell you. I just wanted to get out
of the plane. I felt trapped, but the only way to do
that was to jump, and in fact, the jump itself was
really thrilling. I'd love to do it again. And I didn't
break a thing!

---

5 **2** tired and nervous   **3** shocked   **4** terrifying
5 scared and trapped   **6** thrilling

Reading and Use of English | Part 4

1 **1** one of the easiest   **2** not as/so interesting as
3 play tennis so/as well as   **4** is the noisiest person
in   **5** not as/so cheap as   **6** more quickly than

Speaking | Part 2

2 *Suggested answers*
Football: getting exercise, good for you, good for
health, helps you relax, having fun, laughing, builds
up social relationships and friendships, breaks
down social boundaries between boys and girls
Chatting in a café: communicating, sharing ideas
and experiences, talk about problems, relax, enjoy
friendship

▶ **CD 1 Track 07**

Examiner: In this part of the test, I'm going to give each of you two photographs. I'd like you to talk about your photographs on your own for about a minute, and also to answer a short question about your partner's photographs. Martyna, it's your turn first. Here are your photographs. They show people doing different activities in their free time. I'd like you to compare the photographs, and say how you think the people can benefit from spending their free time doing these different activities. All right?

Martyna: Well, in the first photo, there's a group of children, both boys and girls, playing football together in the park. They don't seem to be taking the game too seriously and they seem to be enjoying themselves. I think they benefit from this in several ways. Firstly, they're getting some exercise, which is always good for you because it's great for your health and helps you to relax. At the same time, they're having fun together, which is important because it builds up their social relationships and their friendships. Also, it's good to see boys and girls doing a bit of sport together instead of separately, because I think it helps break down social boundaries between boys and girls.

In the second photo, there are four girls chatting together in a café and laughing. They aren't so active as the children in the first photo because they're not doing a sport, but they are probably communicating more and sharing their ideas and experiences. I think they also benefit because they can talk about their problems, relax and also enjoy their friendship. Mm, all in all, I think they get a lot fr–

Examiner: Thank you.

Martyna: –om both activities.

3 ✓ 3, 4, 5, 7

4 ▶ See recording script for Track 07 above.

5 a 1 **b** 2 **c** 3, 4, 5

6 b First of all, To start with
   c Besides, In addition, What is more

Pronunciation: sentence stress (1)

7.1 See underlining in recording script for Track 08.

▶ **CD 1 Track 08**

1 <u>Firstly</u>, they're getting some <u>exercise</u>, which is always <u>good</u> for you.
2 It's <u>great</u> for your <u>health</u> and helps you to <u>relax</u>.
3 At the <u>same</u> time, they're having <u>fun</u> together …
4 … which is important because it <u>builds</u> up their social <u>relationships</u> and their <u>friendships</u>.
5 Also, it's good to see <u>boys</u> and <u>girls</u> doing a bit of sport <u>together</u> instead of <u>separately</u>.
6 I think it helps <u>break</u> down social <u>boundaries</u> between boys and <u>girls</u>.

Writing | Part 2 An article

1 *Suggested underlining*
magazine for teenagers, leisure-time activity, How did you get started?, Why do you enjoy it so much?

3 1 Para. 1: I first got interested … simple dishes at first   Para. 2: I found I really enjoyed cooking … usually ate the food quite happily   Para. 3: When I went back to school … enjoying a meal I've cooked   Para. 4: I'd recommend … that anyone can do.
   2 *Suggested answers:* Para. 1: how I started
   Para. 2: how I continued   Para. 3: why I enjoy it
   Para. 4: why I'd recommend it

4 *Suggested answers*

   1 I found I really enjoyed cooking; I was soon doing things which were more complicated.
   2 My younger brother and sister complained about some of my dishes; they usually ate the food quite happily.
   3 When friends come round to my house I often cook them something; I find it really satisfying and relaxing.
   4 I'd recommend it as a hobby; for me, it's one of the most creative and useful free-time activities that anyone can do.
   5 When I went back to school after the summer, I decided to do cookery lessons; now I think I'm quite a competent cook.

5 *Suggested answers*

   2 I got interested in flying when I was about 14 and my father took me to an airshow.
   3 My parents don't want me to fly because they think it is / it's dangerous.
   4 One of my friends is learning to fly and he's asked me to come with him because he thinks I'd like it.

6 *Suggested answers*

  2 I was staying with my aunt. My aunt is a keen cook.

  3 I was soon doing things. They / The things were more complicated.

  4 I went back to school after the summer. I decided to do cookery lessons.

  5 Friends come round to my house. I often cook my friends / them something.

  6 For me, cooking is one of the most creative and useful free-time activities. Anyone can cook / do it.

7 *Suggested answers*

  1 I was 13 when I started running seriously. / I started running seriously when I was 13.

  2 My aunt, who is a keen athlete, encouraged me.

  3 I go running most days when/after I've finished school and done my homework.

  4 Running is a sport which/that gets you really fit.

8 *Suggested answers*

  1 I started windsurfing when I was 13 and I was staying with friends by the sea.

  2 One of my friends, who is a keen windsurfer, encouraged me to start because she thought I would enjoy it.

  3 I kept falling into the sea to start with because it was a fairly windy day and there were a lot of waves.

  4 I didn't enjoy it at first because I had to concentrate quite hard, but I carried on trying.

  5 I started to windsurf quite fast, which was exciting, and I started to find it quite enjoyable.

9 **1** satisfying, relaxing, fascinating, wonderful
  2 creative, useful **3** competent

10

feelings about an activity	the type of activity
astonishing, delightful, depressing, dreadful, entertaining, exhausting, incredible, irritating, superb, tremendous, unbelievable	competitive, demanding, economical, popular, time-consuming

Vocabulary and grammar review
Unit 1

1 **2** bad-tempered **3** hardworking / hard-working
  4 unreliable **5** anxious **6** sensitive **7** mature
  8 concerned/anxious

2 **1** clear; up **2** pick; up **3** get on with **4** worn; out
  5 do up **6** went on

3 **1** do **2** make **3** do **4** doing **5** do **6** made
  7 made **8** making

4 **1** won **2** have arrived; have been expecting
  3 have spent; has turned up **4** have been having / have had; has been telling / has told; has not told; has seen **5** has lost / has been losing; has been getting **6** has finished; have been waiting
  7 has eaten; has not left **8** has been looking; has been studying

Vocabulary and grammar review
Unit 2

1 **1** keep a promise / promises **2** to take / taking risks
  3 taking up **4** make up **5** sum up **6** haven't / haven't got / don't have a clue; have a go

2 *Suggested answers*

  1 Katya took up karate when she was seven years old because she was interested in it.

  2 Her father, who is a professional karate instructor, taught her, so she progressed quickly and soon became junior regional champion.

  3 She did karate with other children who were the same age as her, but none of them was as good as her, so she felt dissatisfied.

  4 Last year, she participated in the national championship, but she did not win because she was injured during one of the matches.

  5 She hopes to become a professional karate instructor and work in the same sports centre as her father because he has too many students.

  6 Some of her father's students have been studying karate for several years, and her father thinks they would benefit from a different teacher because they are too familiar with his style of karate.

3 **1** motorbike made more noise than **2** are not as/so dangerous **3** is the best player **4** as/so stressed as
  5 much more clearly than **6** more comfortable than any of

4 **1** amazing **2** exhausting **3** puzzling
  4 disappointed **5** motivated **6** astonished

3 Happy holidays?

Starting off

1

types of holiday	holiday locations and places to stay	holiday activities
a camping holiday a beach holiday a sightseeing tour a cruise backpacking	at a campsite at a luxury hotel on a cruise ship at a youth hostel in the city centre at the seaside	walking and climbing meeting new people sunbathing relaxing visiting monuments seeing new places

2 *Suggested answers*

  1 Photo 1: a camping holiday; Photo 2: a sightseeing holiday; Photo 3: backpacking; Photo 4: a beach holiday; Photo 5: a cruise

  2 On camping holidays, people walk, climb, relax and see new places; on sightseeing holidays, they see new places and visit monuments; when backpacking, they meet new people, walk, go sightseeing and see new places; on beach holidays, people relax and sunbathe; on a cruise, they meet new people, see new places, visit monuments, sunbathe and relax.

Listening | Part 3

1 *Suggested underlining*
  B didn't mind, discomfort   **C** know, people
  D similar before   **E** low-cost holiday   **F** didn't do much during the day   **G** (not) in as much danger as, imagined   **H** a break from my parents

2 **1** G   **2** F   **3** D   **4** A   **5** C

 **CD 1 Track 09**

Presenter: One. Francesca.

Francesca: I went on one of those journeys overland to Kenya. It was awesome to be able to go off with a group of people my own age. I mean, really, on family holidays we always used to go to the same campsite and lie on the same beach and things. This was a whole new thing – seeing completely different places and doing lots of things I'd never done before. We did have a driver and a guide to keep an eye on

things, so I don't think there was anything particularly risky about it, even though my mum and gran worried from the moment I left to the moment I got back!

Presenter: Two. Mike.

Mike: It was the nightlife we went for really. I went with a couple of my mates, you know, we got up late in the morning or even in the afternoon and we usually hung around by the pool till sunset chilling out or we made a trip to the beach, which was only about 20 minutes away by bus. Except of course on days when it was cloudy. But at night, we were down at the clubs partying to the small hours, getting back to the hotel at two or three in the morning. And surprise, surprise, we managed to get through all our cash!

Presenter: Three. Sally.

Sally: I went off with a couple of my friends in March. We were out in the open air in these amazing mountain landscapes and doing some awesome climbing. We all complained about what we cooked, though, and the weather caused a few problems. We were on our way back down the mountain when we got caught in this really big storm, so that was a bit scary. But I'd done that sort of thing quite a lot with my dad when I was a kid – um, my dad used to be a climber when he was younger – so I knew what I was doing.

Presenter: Four. Paul.

Paul: Well, it wasn't really my idea of a good time at all. The meals were good, if you don't mind sitting around with a lot of middle-aged adults in smart hotels. It was just really dull. And Mum and Dad dragged me round looking at paintings and sculptures, which was just so boring! Still, there was an upside, because while we were going round yet another museum, I got to meet this Polish girl called Jolanta. She was about as fed up as I was, so we just dumped our parents and went off for the day together. We had a really great time and, actually, we're still in touch.

Presenter: Five. Katie.

Katie: It was one of my first non-family holidays too, except for a couple of summer camps when I was younger. I went backpacking with some mates round Europe, using the trains mainly, and we stayed in youth hostels, which saved us a bit of money. There were hundreds of other people like us from all over the world who were doing the same sort of thing. It was good fun, a great atmosphere. I really like that sort of mixing of cultures – it's one of the best things about foreign travel, so I'm hoping we'll do it again next year.

Grammar
Past simple, past continuous and *used to*

1 **1** used to go   **2** used to be   **3** was   **4** were going
5 got   **6** dumped   **7** went   **8** had   **9** stayed
10 were doing

2 **1** was walking   **2** used to do   **3** got; jumped; rode
4 used to spend   **5** were walking; began   **6** used to
visit; was

3 developed, enjoyed, happened, mentioned, occurred,
opened, planned, preferred, stopped, studied,
travelled (BrE) / traveled (AmE), tried

Vocabulary
travel, journey, trip and *way*

1 **1** trip   **2** Way   **3** travel   **4** journey

2 **1** trip   **2** way   **3** trip   **4** trip   **5** travel   **6** journey
7 trip   **8** journey   **9** way

3 **1** pleasant/safe/successful   **2** overnight   **3** outward
4 shopping   **5** forthcoming   **6** safe/pleasant

Reading and Use of English | Part 3

1 **2** adventurous   **3** friendly   **4** memorable
5 mysterious   **6** risky   **7** crowded   **8** thrilled/
thrilling   **9** doubtful   **10** successful   **11** remarkable
12 accessible

2 artist – artistic; caution – cautious; colour – colourful,
colourless; educate – educational, educated; emotion
– emotional; energy – energetic; mass – massive;
predict – predictable; reason – reasonable; respond
– responsible; storm – stormy; thought – thoughtful,
thoughtless; wealth – wealthy

3 **1** uncomfortable   **2** thoughtful   **3** colourful
4 unforgettable   **5** optimistic   **6** considerable
7 anxious   **8** sympathetic

Grammar
at, in or *on* in time phrases

1 **1** in, in   **2** on   **3** at, at   **4** in

2 **1** ~~on July~~ in July   **2** ~~In the weekends~~ At the weekends*,
~~on the afternoon~~ in the afternoon   **3** ~~in 11.00~~ at 11.00
4 correct   **5** ~~at 2008~~ in 2008   **6** correct   **7** ~~in certain
times~~ at certain times   **8** ~~at the morning in a normal
day~~ in the morning on a normal day

***Note:** *on the weekends* is correct in American English.

Reading and Use of English | Part 7

2 *Suggested underlining*
1 hide from danger   **2** employee intimidating
3 not pleased, spend so long   **4** visited, previous
occasion   **5** worried, strong   **6** missed speaking,
people   **7** painful experience   **8** travelled with, ex-
criminal   **9** unaware, danger   **10** holiday, mistake,
before arriving

3 **1** B   **2** C   **3** C   **4** D   **5** B   **6** D   **7** A   **8** C   **9** A   **10** D

Grammar
Past perfect simple and continuous

1 **1** A   **2** had organised (past perfect)   **3** In the first
sentence, her father organised the trip before they
arrived; in the second sentence, he organised it when
they were already in the country.

2 **A** Pauline Vernon: *until that point, no one **had
bothered** to mention the sea-snakes – The sting, on
both legs, was agony, …*
B Sandy Henderson: *we'**d passed** a small cabin a little
way back on the trail – we made a dash for that*
C Cat O'Donovan: *what I **had let** myself in for –
Twenty-three hours into an epic bus trip across the
States, I began to wonder; I **had been filled** with
romantic ideas – Before boarding the first bus in LA;
After the guy next to me **had finished** talking about
his time in jail – I realised my expectations were
a bit off; she **had eaten** several passengers – One
unfriendly staff member was so large I feared*

3 **1** had eaten   **2** had never been   **3** organised /
had organised   **4** arrived; had lost   **5** recognised;
had never spoken **6** had damaged

4 **1** A
2 **A** past perfect continuous   **B** past perfect simple

5 **1** had been living   **2** had been walking; began   **3** had already finished; offered   **4** had only been speaking   **5** got; had been walking

6 **1** ~~have done~~ had done   **2** ~~didn't have~~ hadn't had   **3** ~~didn't go~~ hadn't been   **4** ~~had bought~~ bought; ~~always wanted~~ had always wanted   **5** ~~she just finished~~ she had just finished   **6** ~~I have been cleaning~~ I had been cleaning

Speaking | Part 3

2 A city sightseeing tour: you learn about architecture and history, other cultures and visit somewhere different. A weekend camping trip in the mountains: you have exciting experiences and adventures, and learn to be independent, learn to work together to solve problems, learn teamwork, educational. A beach activity day: learn something from doing different sports and activities.

▶ **CD 1 Track 10**

Miguel: Shall we start with this one?

Antonia: OK.

Miguel: How do you think doing a sightseeing tour of a city might be good for students?

Antonia: I think you can learn a lot about architecture and history and things like that.

Miguel: Yes, and also you can visit somewhere very different and learn about other cultures.

Antonia: Right. What about this sort of activity holiday in the mountains? I think it can give young people exciting experiences and adventures, things they don't get in their everyday lives.

Miguel: Yes, and they learn to be more independent because they're away from home and their families, don't you think?

Antonia: I think that's right. Also, they learn to work together to solve problems, so it's good for learning teamwork.

Miguel: That's an important point, because if the school's organising the trip, it should be educational, shouldn't it? I mean, students have got to be learning something. And the beach activity day: what about that?

Antonia: It sounds great, doesn't it? And I think just by doing sports and activities they don't normally do at school, students learn something.

Miguel: I agree.

3 **1** Shall; this one   **2** think   **3** What about   **4** don't you   **5** about that

Pronunciation: intonation (1)

4.1 **1** good for students ↘
  2 architecture ↗, history ↗, things like that ↘
  3 different ↘, cultures ↘
  4 activity ↗, mountains ↘
  5 experiences ↗, adventures ↗, lives ↘

▶ **CD 1 Track 11** See page 38.

6 *Suggested answers*
  1 N, there isn't time – you need to reach a decision in one minute.
  2 Y, it gets the discussion started and your partner involved.
  3 N, it prevents further discussion.
  4 Y, this is a possible way of creating more discussion
  5 Y, it creates further discussion.
  6 N, you only have a minute and you'll get higher marks if you can have a natural conversation.

7 Miguel does 2; Antonia does 4; Irene and Nikolai both do 5

▶ **CD 1 Track 12**

Miguel and Antonia

Miguel: Well, Antonia, in my opinion, the best choice for the trip is the camping and walking activity in the mountains, because it'll be an adventure for everyone, and if it goes well, everyone will enjoy it. What do you think?

Antonia: Hmm, I think your suggestion would be fine if the weather is good, but no one will enjoy it if it rains all the time, and it's a lot of responsibility for the teachers who're supervising the trip. I think the beach-activities trip is a better option because at least the kids'll be staying in a hostel if the weather turns bad.

Irene and Nikolai

Irene: OK, I think we should choose the theme park because all teenagers enjoy the thrill of a theme park, and it gives everyone plenty to talk about and discuss before and after they go.

Nikolai: Yes, I think you're right, but I think we should also consider the visit to the museum because that might be more popular with the teachers, and we have to take their preferences into consideration as well.

Irene: Hmm, you might be right, but I think we should put the students' tastes first because it is their trip.

Nikolai: Maybe, but they can go to a theme park in their own time.

Irene: Yes, of course they can, but sometimes it's important to do these activities as a school group.

8 1 a **2** a **3** b **4** e **5** e **6** d **7** c

Writing | Part 2
A report

1 *Suggested underlining*
one-day excursion, local place of interest, what you did, why, the day, a success

3 1 took **2** went **3** was **4** had been **5** rode
6 were **7** took **8** had operated **9** was **10** were
11 enjoyed **12** learned **13** had **14** found

4 1 yes, *Excursion to London*
2 three, each has a heading: *Purpose of trip, What we did, Comments*
3 three: a break from normal lessons, to see the London Eye and do a tour of the Globe Theatre
4 The activities were interesting, different, everyone enjoyed something, plenty of opportunities to practise English, motivating.

4 Food, glorious food

Starting off

1 See page 42.

2 1 Photo 5 **2** Photo 1 **3** Photo 2 **4** Photo 3 **5** Photo 4

Reading and Use of English | Part 6

2 *Suggested answers*
Para. 2: the campaign and the reasons for it; Para. 3: the food and where it comes from; Para. 4: classroom activities in the garden; Para. 5: classroom activities in the kitchen; Para. 6: Teo's opinion; Para. 7: The general aim of the garden

3 *Suggested underlining*
C One lesson **D** The problem, these projects
E These two projects **F** We, in this small space
G Lessons like this one

4 1 G **2** E **3** F **4** B **5** C **6** A

Vocabulary
food, dish and meal

1 1 food, meals **2** food, dishes **3** meal

2 2 ~~meals~~ dishes **3** ~~food~~ dish **4** ~~meal~~ food
5 ~~meals~~ food **6** ~~food~~ dish **7** ~~dishes~~ meals

3 1 food **2** food **3** meal; dish **4** meal

4 2 food shortages **3** heavy/filling meal
4 food source **5** convenience food **6** balanced meals **7** food supply **8** organic food

Grammar
so and such

1 1 such a; So **2** such a; so **3** such

2 1 such **2** so **3** such a **4** so **5** so **6** such a

3 1 ~~such~~ so **2** ~~a so much~~ such **3** correct **4** ~~so~~ such
5 ~~so~~ such a **6** ~~such~~ so **7** correct **8** ~~so~~ such

4 1 never eaten such a good **2** so quickly that we
3 answered the question so well/excellently **4** with so little food **5** had so much fun at **6** make so much noise

Listening | Part 4

2 *Suggested underlining*
1 started, because
2 most important, chose the site **3** décor **4** How, behave with, customers **5** purpose, back room
6 food, should be **7** What, parents like

3 1 B **2** C **3** C **4** A **5** B **6** B **7** A

> ▶ **CD 1 Track 13**
>
> **Interviewer:** Hi! Today I'm talking to Cherry Smith, owner of Cherry's Café, a well-known spot for youngsters in our town. Cherry – can you tell us a little bit about your café and why you started it?
>
> **Cherry:** Sure. I was working in one of the local supermarkets – it was always my ambition from when I was quite little to be working with people and I noticed that there were lots of secondary school kids coming in to buy snacks and soft drinks and things and just hanging around and I thought, 'Poor things,

they've got too much free time and they're not eating well enough and they need somewhere they can hang out.' So I came up with this idea of a café where kids could just spend their free time and I could make a living out of it as well.

Interviewer: Great! So did you choose this site for your café because it's between the two local schools?

Cherry: Well, that was one consideration, but I thought it was essential to have a place which was just that bit bigger than the other cafés in the area and I found this place with an extra room at the back where customers can go and not be seen from the street by passers-by and you know everyone from the two schools does go past.

Interviewer: And, Cherry, did you need to put much thought into the interior decoration?

Cherry: Yeah, lots. I was really wanting a place where kids can come at lunchtime or after school and feel comfortable, so comfy chairs, warm colours, things that make them feel at home. Nothing fragile because we don't want to be replacing furniture every five minutes. I get them to help out a bit too, so, you know, they help wipe tables and sweep up from time to time, otherwise we wouldn't manage.

Interviewer: So, your customers are mainly young people from the local schools. Do they give you any problems?

Cherry: They're almost all from the local schools and not really. They behave quite well really, and I say 'quite' because they are young, so they're going to be noisy and want to play around a bit, but they're never rude to me or rough. I just like people and young people especially. I think everyone's interesting so I try to find out things about them and I pull their legs sometimes – we have a good laugh – like they're friends. And they react to that. I don't impose discipline or anything 'cos it's not like lessons. And that doesn't mean I'm always going to look happy – I have my 'off' days, just like anyone else.

Interviewer: You mentioned a room at the back as being important. Why's that?

Cherry: Well, I want kids to come here and feel that it's like another home. Somewhere they can just be themselves, so the back room is the sort of quiet room where they can just sit down and read, or do their internet stuff, or finish their homework, or have a quiet chat. You know, young people need these sorts of places where they can be quiet if they want to be, but have company if they want it too.

Interviewer: Fantastic. How about food? Do you just give your customers whatever they want?

Cherry: Well, I think it's important to offer young people food they can afford. I mean, I don't worry about if it's good for them or not. We do serve things like, hamburgers and chips, but we also offer salads and fresh vegetables. You'd be surprised how popular they are. I don't do the cooking – Mikey does that 'cos I don't have enough time. They're all simple dishes but they can be quite filling.

Interviewer: Great! And finally, Cherry, what do parents think of your café? Do you get any comments?

Cherry: Actually, I don't see too many parents, but the odd comment comes back. I think what they really appreciate is that, you know, their kids are in a friendly place where they feel happy. Parents sometimes sort of jokingly complain when their kids tell them they don't cook as well as Mikey. And you know, in the end, this café is a cost for the parents, but I think they think it's worth it.

Interviewer: Cherry, thanks.

Cherry: Thank you.

Grammar

too and enough

1 **1** too much; enough **2** too **3** enough **4** enough **5** too many

2 **1** too many; enough **2** enough **3** too **4** too **5** enough

3 **1** ~~the food wasn't enough~~ there wasn't enough food **2** ~~not too much good~~ not very good **3** ~~money enough~~ enough money **4** ~~enough comfortable~~ comfortable enough **5** ~~too much long~~ (much) too long **6** ~~doing too hard work~~ working too hard / doing too much hard work **7** ~~too much tasty~~ very tasty **8** ~~too much expensive~~ (much) too expensive

4 **1** is too expensive for **2** enough petrol to get **3** was too astonished by **4** was not / wasn't warm enough for

Speaking | Part 4

1 **b** balanced diet **c** cut down **d** junk food **e** dairy products **f** live on **g** lifestyle

2 **1** in other words **2** because **3** On the other hand **4** then **5** but **6** which **7** what

▶ **CD 1 Track 14**

Examiner: Do you think fast food is bad for you?

Martyna: I think it depends. I think the most important thing / is to have a balanced diet, / in other words, you eat a variety of / vegetables, / meat, /cereals and so on. I'm not sure it matters so much / how long it takes to prepare, / because I think fast food is / just / food which is prepared quickly. On the other hand, / if you just live on / what's it called / junk food, / for instance hamburgers and pizzas and things like that, / then you probably need to cut down / and have a more balanced diet.

Examiner: And Miguel, what do you think?

Miguel: I agree with Martyna. / I think it's fine to eat fast food occasionally, / but you have to balance it with other things like / fresh fruit and / vegetables which are in season and / cut down on dairy products and fat. / Also I think that what you eat is only one part of a / healthy lifestyle.

Martyna: I agree.

3 **1** in other words   **2** because   **3** for instance, like
4 but, on the other hand

Pronunciation: grouping words and pausing (1)

4.1

▶ **CD 1 Track 15**

Examiner: How can families benefit from eating together?

Miguel: Well, / the important thing is not eating, / it's spending time together / so that they can talk about / what they have been doing during the day. / They get the chance to / exchange opinions / and make plans as well, / because everyone can contribute and / that's what makes a / rich, / meaningful family life. / Children learn ideas and attitudes from their parents, / while parents keep up to date with their children / and what they are thinking and doing.

Examiner: And Martyna, do you agree?

Martyna: Yes, I do. / And also I think people cook better / when they are cooking for several people / than when they are just cooking for themselves, / so that as a result, / people who eat together / eat more healthily.

4.3 See recording script for Track 15 above.

Reading and Use of English | Part 1

1 The surroundings, the service, the food, the price

2 **1** C   **2** B   **3** C   **4** B   **5** A   **6** D   **7** C   **8** A

Writing | Part 2
A review

1 *Suggested underlining*
local English-language newspaper, recommend, local restaurant, café or snack bar, review, what, place, food, like, why, family, enjoy eating there

2 **2** a, b, c, d, f, h, i

3 and **4** *Suggested answers*
the waiters / the service: rushed, welcoming, informative, cheerful, exceptional, satisfactory, superb
the interior: airy, cosy, modern, attractive, cheerful, colourful, elegant, exclusive, original, welcoming
the food and menu: delicious, fresh, satisfying, tasty, wonderful, attractive, colourful, delightful, elegant, exceptional, original, raw, satisfactory, superb, well-balanced
the price: reasonable, competitive
the restaurant in general: modern, attractive, colourful, delightful, exceptional, elegant, exclusive, original, superb, welcoming

5 *Suggested underlining*
college magazine, favourite restaurant, café or snack bar, review, 'Free Time' section, what, place, like, why, recommend it

Vocabulary and grammar review Unit 3

1 **1** journey   **2** trip   **3** travel   **4** way   **5** journey
6 way   **7** trip   **8** journey

2 **1** while I was visiting   **2** I had lost   **3** used to go to school   **4** she was still going to   **5** had never met
6 used to be more

3 **1** considerable   **2** exclusive   **3** dramatic
4 unacceptable   **5** disorganised   **6** unhelpful
7 remaining   **8** preferable

Vocabulary and grammar review
Unit 4

1 **1** meal **2** food **3** dish **4** food **5** dish **6** food/meal
7 meal **8** food

2 **1** too hot (for us) to **2** slowly enough (for us) to
3 was so full (that) **4** such delicious food that
5 cook well enough **6** such a long time / so much
time

3 **1** filling **2** convenience **3** increasingly
4 organisations **5** discourage **6** balanced
7 disappearance **8** choice

5 Study time

Listening | Part 1

1 **1** h **2** d **3** b **4** a **5** i **6** e **7** f **8** c **9** g

2 *Suggested underlining*
1 How does he feel, now **2** What, problem
3 What, like most **4** What, main benefit **5** Why,
talking **6** What surprised her, school **7** think
about, lesson **8** What, advice about

3 **1** C **2** B **3** B **4** A **5** A **6** C **7** C **8** B

> ▶ **CD 1 Track 16**
>
> **Presenter:** One. You overhear a student talking about a
> course he has been doing.
>
> **Will:** Actually, at the beginning of term, I was a bit
> lost. You know, my family has only just moved to this
> country, so I was new in this school, and I felt that
> everyone else knew more about the subject than
> I did. Listening to them, I got the impression that
> some of them felt this particular course was a bit of
> a waste of time. In my case, I was having problems
> not just with the language but also with the ideas.
> But I managed to get over all that and, in fact, the
> course has lived up to my original expectations, so I
> feel all the hard work's been worth it. I mean, we've
> got an exam next week, which I expected to feel a bit
> anxious about, but in fact I'm feeling fine about it.

Presenter: Two. You hear a student complaining about
a problem she has had.

Mike: Oh, Helena! What's up?

Helena: Do you know what just happened? I was given
an essay to write at the beginning of the month and
I spent lots of time researching it. Anyway, Valerie –
you know her – she came round to my place and while
she was there she must have copied all my notes! All
my research! I only found out in my tutorial just now
when the tutor handed my essay back to me. He said
he couldn't mark it because my essay repeated all the
same key points that Valerie had made in hers. I'm
absolutely furious, and she's going to get away with
it, too!

Presenter: Three. You hear a student at a language
school in Japan.

Boy: So, what are you doing here in Japan?

Girl: I'm learning Japanese at a language school. I go
to classes for just two hours a day, which is good
because I learn Japanese from Japanese teachers,
and then I'm free to practise it during the rest of the
day.

Boy: That sounds a good idea.

Girl: It is. You see, it's not all academic work. They also
organise lots of other things for us learners to take
part in after school. There are clubs we can join if
we're interested, and they really are the best part.
For example, I'm also doing a karate course taught in
Japanese, which is great fun. I'm learning something
completely different in the language I'm studying and
I'm getting to know lots of local people.

Boy: Fantastic!

Girl: Yes, if you speak a bit of the language, it's much
easier to make friends.

Presenter: Four. You hear an interview with a student
who is thinking of studying abroad.

Sandra: I'm not sure whether I'll study abroad. I've
been thinking of going to an Italian university and
studying international business for a year – that's if
I get through the admission process. The trouble is
partly that if I went, it might make it more difficult
for me to get a good pass in my exams back home.
On the other hand, I think the opportunity to live
abroad for a year would be extremely educational,
because I'd learn about the Italian way of life and way
of thinking. Trouble is, I'd have to leave all my friends
and probably live on my own, and I'm not sure if I'm
ready for that.

Presenter: Five. You overhear the director of a school talking to students.

Peter: Now, just a few things I need to point out to new students. First, you're expected to attend all your lessons and do the work your teachers give you. If for any reason you can't make it to a lesson, remember to let your teacher know. If your teacher has to cancel a lesson or put it off, he or she'll try to tell you in advance. Also, please remember that most of what you study here is very practical, and you have to do one big piece of project work during the year. You're allowed to do it in groups, and if you work with other students, you'll probably find it easier. Apart from that, you'll also have to sit an end-of-year exam, so it's important to study hard throughout the year.

Presenter: Six. You hear a girl leaving a message about her first day at a new school.

Carrie: Hi, Mum! I'm just calling to say I'm back and I'm still alive! You know how worried I was because I wouldn't know anyone, and you said there'd be lots of other kids in the same situation – and you were right, so we all sort of mixed in. Classes were fine – you know, the usual sort of stuff you do on the first day like course requirements and so on. One or two of the teachers might turn out to be monsters, but most seem fine. Oh, and the classrooms are nice, very bright and lots of technology like electronic screens and we're all connected up with wifi and stuff, so a lot better than I expected.

Presenter: Seven. You hear two students, a boy and a girl, talking about a lesson.

Jan: Hi, Max. So you got into trouble in maths again for staring out of the window!

Max: Yeah! I reckon Mr Drew's got it in for me! I mean, you don't have to look at the teacher to be listening to him.

Jan: So, unlike most of us, you were actually finding the lesson useful, you mean?

Max: Sure. Mr Drew knows what he's talking about, and there are some interesting concepts, but unfortunately it's all rather chaotic, and it takes him such a long time to get to the stuff we really need. His classes could do with a bit more planning in my opinion.

Jan: Hmm, perhaps that's why the rest of us all get lost, while you're staring at the kids outside – and taking it all in!

Presenter: Eight. You hear a teacher talking to a student.

Teacher: Well, it's fine to study history or archaeology if that's the area you're planning to work in when you finish, but you must remember, you'll only find the sort of job you want in research if you get a really good degree – and the job itself won't be very well paid either.

Jan: I know.

Teacher: I mean, you've got a good brain and if you applied yourself, you could study anything. I'd hate to think of you looking back in 20 years' time and thinking, I wish I'd studied IT or accountancy or something with better job prospects.

Vocabulary
Phrasal verbs

1 1 c 2 a 3 e 4 g 5 h 6 b 7 d 8 f

2 1 put off 2 gets away with 3 handed; back; gets over 4 live up to; looks back 5 turned out; point out / pointed out / have pointed out

find out, get to know, know, learn, teach and study; attend, join, take part and assist

3 1 studying 2 found out 3 learn 4 learn 5 taught 6 getting to know 7 take part 8 join 9 attend

4 1 studying 2 got to know 3 study 4 learnt/learned 5 find out 6 know 7 taught 8 assist 9 joined 10 taken part

Grammar
Zero, first and second conditionals

1 a 3, 5, 6 b 2, 4 c 1

2 1 h 2 f 3 j 4 g 5 a 6 e 7 c 8 d 9 i (or f) 10 b

3 1 ~~say~~ said 2 ~~live~~ lived 3 ~~study~~ studied OR ~~would~~ will 4 ~~we'll have~~ we have 5 ~~you'll have~~ you have 6 ~~will be~~ is 7 ~~buy~~ bought OR ~~would~~ will 8 ~~take~~ took OR ~~would~~ will; ~~could~~ can 9 ~~you'll decide~~ you decide 10 ~~travelled~~ travel OR ~~will~~ would

4 1 you assist (us) with the 2 if you join 3 would take part in 4 will have to put off 5 better unless your teacher pointed 6 I get over my cold

Reading and Use of English | Part 7

1 2 *Suggested answers*
1 unfamiliar food and a difficult/strange host family, food the student doesn't like. **2** not having friends, feeling lonely **3** not knowing their way around, feeling lost **4** difficulty understanding people / the teacher / the lessons

2 *Suggested underlining*
1 surprised, different approach to education
2 cooperating, host family **3** more adult as a result
4 equip, for the future **5** responsibility, take as much advantage as possible **6** felt differently, attending school **7** change from, normal school life **8** had not expected, do an exchange **9** mixed feelings, type of school **10** change, opinion of people

3 1 D **2** C **3** C **4** A **5** B **6** C **7** A **8** A **9** D **10** B

Reading and Use of English | Part 3

1 2 intention **3** response (responsibility)
4 adjustment **5** comparison **6** existence
7 demand **8** development **9** behaviour
10 advice/ advisor **11** appearance **12** knowledge

2 2 assess **3** feel **4** involve **5** investigate **6** confuse
7 prefer **8** approve

3 1 friendships **2** variety **3** expectations
4 comparison **5** unprepared **6** independent
7 behaviour **8** welcoming

Speaking | Part 1

1 1 because **2** if **3** when (if) **4** who **5** if **6** and

▶ **CD 1 Track 17** See page 59.

2 *Suggested answers*
1 three **2** three **3** Candidates receive marks based on their ability to manage grammar and longer units of discourse. Candidates also achieve a higher score for longer, more complex sentences. **4** It creates a good, positive impression

Pronunciation: word stress (2)

4.1 ne<u>cess</u>ary, ne<u>cess</u>ity

▶ **CD 1 Track 18** See page 59.

4.2 <u>sat</u>isfying/satis<u>fac</u>tory, <u>edu</u>cate/edu<u>ca</u>tion, ex<u>am</u>/ exami<u>na</u>tion, ex<u>plain</u>/expla<u>na</u>tion, <u>grad</u>uate/ gradu<u>a</u>tion, <u>poss</u>ible/possi<u>bil</u>ity, pre<u>fer</u>/<u>pref</u>erence, re<u>fer</u>/<u>ref</u>erence, <u>rel</u>ative/re<u>la</u>tion, <u>in</u>stitute/ insti<u>tu</u>tion

4.3 The stress is always on the syllable before the suffix (*-tion, -ity*).

▶ **CD 1 Track 19** See page 59.

Writing | Part 1

3 *Suggested answers*
1 No, because it's better to use your own words in the answer than repeat words from the task.
3 Yes, candidates will lose marks if they don't cover all the points in the task as they have not answered the question completely.

5 a 3 **b** 2 **c** 1

7 1 with the result that **2** Also **3** for example when **4** These opportunities **5** if **6** A further point is that **7** It **8** For all these reasons **9** do so

9 *Sample answer*
In the modern world, it is essential for young people to get experience of other countries and other cultures, not only to learn the language, but also to learn to live with people from other parts of the world. For this reason, I believe it is a good idea to do an international exchange.
Young people who study abroad have to study in the language of the country they visit, with the result that they gain extra language skills. They also learn to interact with people from other countries and understand their interests and way of life.
Another major advantage of studying abroad is that young people learn independence, because many of them live away from home for the first time. This allows them to return home more mature and self-confident than they were when they left.
Finally, I think it is important to build international understanding, and this can be achieved when young people form friendships across borders.
For all these reasons, I am strongly in favour of giving people the chance to study abroad when they are young.

6 My first job

Listening | Part 3

1 *Suggested answers*

B I didn't expect to have to work so hard   **C** I get a lot of new ideas from the people I meet   **D** I might get the chance to do something I've always wanted to   **E** I'm learning to do new things   **F** not all the job is fun, but some of it is   **G** I like not having to rely on my parents for money   **H** I get annoyed when there are problems I can't solve

2 **1** A   **2** E   **3** B   **4** H   **5** D

> ▶ **CD 1 Track 20**
>
> **Speaker 1:** This is my first student job and I'm a part-time hospital porter taking patients to different departments for treatment. It's hard physical work, but I think I expected that when I started. For me, the best thing's the human contact with, you know, older people who've had interesting lives – well, actually everyone's older than me, I'm only 18. I hear lots of good stories, and they have the opportunity to talk about things outside the hospital, which probably makes them feel better and brightens up their stay a bit. At least, I think it does.
>
> **Speaker 2:** I'm just 17 and I'm working as a trainee receptionist in a hotel. I'm normally quite shy really, but I'm really happy to be doing this job because it's great to be getting some work experience. Anyway, they've given me lots of responsibility quite early on, so I've learned to do all the sorts of things which you need for almost any job, really practical things like how to answer the phone correctly – you know, not just saying 'Hey' or whatever. On some occasions, I've also been left on my own in charge of the whole hotel. That's really built up my self-confidence.
>
> **Speaker 3:** Well, nobody expects babysitting to be a complete doddle, at least not when there are three small kids to look after. But, well, their mum's very nice and she did warn me – and she's paying me over the usual rate because she knows what it's like – she has to have them when I'm not around – but I really think I've let myself in for a lot more than I bargained for. I've done babysitting before, but it's never been like this. They never stop running around and shouting, and bath time – well, that's just chaos. I reckon I get wetter than they do!
>
> **Speaker 4:** It isn't a very well-paid job and it's not exactly fun, but then first jobs usually aren't. But I'm earning my own money for the first time – not enough to live on, but it's a start. I'm working in a call centre for a large computer company, answering customers' queries, complaints, um, you know, whatever. Sometimes they just want information, but often it's a real problem which I have to help them sort out. Sometimes it's quite simple and that's fine because with a few instructions they go away happy, but I don't have any training in computer skills, so often I can't help them and I hate that.
>
> **Speaker 5:** Well, I'm only making the tea and coffee and running round doing odd jobs – I'm a typical runner on a film set, basically. It sounds terribly glamorous, doesn't it? But the money's not great – actually, I reckon it costs more in train tickets than I actually earn, but what an experience! I'm getting to see exactly how films are made, and the people are really funny, so there are lots of laughs on set – though I do have to keep quiet and only speak when spoken to. There's even the possibility that I'll be given a small part, and that, well, that'd be a dream come true!

Vocabulary

work or job; possibility, occasion or opportunity; fun or funny

1 **1** job   **2** work   **3** opportunity   **4** occasions   **5** job; jobs   **6** funny   **7** possibility

2 **1** funny   **2** fun   **3** possibility   **4** occasions   **5** opportunity   **6** job   **7** work   **8** jobs

3 **2** badly paid   **4** challenging   **5** demanding   **6** tiring   **7** tough   **9** office   **11** manual   **13** holiday   **14** part-time   **15** permanent   **16** temporary   **17** weekend   **19** pleasant   **20** responsible   **21** worthwhile

Reading and Use of English | Part 5

2 1 She was a waitress.
  2 The special role her dad created for her, creating packed lunches, cakes and puddings.

3 *Suggested underlining*
  1 None of us had ever worked in a hotel before.
  2 impressive chef's hat and a terrifying ability to lose his temper and get violent
  3 I … always grabbed the dishes he set down with a forbidding expression on my face which was transformed into a charming smile in the brief space between kitchen and dining room.
  4 and I took pleasure in my ability to get on with the people at each table. It was funny how differently people behaved in the evenings, dressed up and talking with louder, colder voices, not always returning my smile.
  5 the most extraordinary collection of puddings, cakes and other desserts ever to grace a Scottish hotel. Most were things I had invented myself and I had cooked all of them. Some – Jacobite Grenades, Mocha Genghis Khan and Goat's Milk Bavarios to name a few – were undeniably strange.

4 1 C **2** B **3** D **4** B **5** D **6** B

Speaking | Part 2

2 See recording script for Track 21.

3 a B **b** B **c** B **d** 2 **e** 1 **f** 2 **g** 2 **h** 1 **i** 2

 **CD 1 Track 21**

Examiner: Here are your photographs. They show young people doing jobs. I'd like you to compare the photographs and say what you think the people are learning from doing these two types of work.

Nikolai: Well, OK, so firstly I can say that <u>both photos show</u> young people, perhaps teenagers, working. Er, <u>both the jobs in the photos involve</u> working in situations where they need good skills in dealing with people in the correct way. I'm sure <u>neither of them</u> is very well paid. <u>Anyway, the first photo shows</u> a <u>girl</u> serving <u>young people</u> in a <u>restaurant, whereas in the second photo</u> a boy is working with children and coaching them to play football. The girl's job may be full time, <u>whereas the boy's</u> is probably part time. <u>I think both can</u> learn a lot from these jobs. The girl can learn how to keep customers happy, while the boy has

---

to keep children in order. The girl has to learn to work efficiently under pressure. <u>On the other hand,</u> the boy has to learn to keep cool. He'll probably learn <u>not just</u> to deal with children, <u>but also</u> their parents.

Examiner: Thank you. Antonia, which of these jobs would you prefer to do?

Antonia: I'd prefer to coach children than work in a restaurant because really I enjoy being in the fresh air more than being indoors. And I like kids.

Examiner: Thank you.

4 b

5 See recording script for Track 21 (Nikolai does not use the phrases *While the girl in the first photo … , Another thing in the second photo is …*)

Pronunciation: sentence stress (2)

6.1 first, girl, young people, restaurant, second, boy, children

6.2 See underlining in recording script for Track 22.

 **CD 1 Track 22**

Anyway, the <u>first</u> photo shows a <u>girl</u> serving <u>young people</u> in a <u>restaurant</u>, whereas in the <u>second</u> photo, a <u>boy</u> is working with <u>children</u>.

6.3 See underlining in recording script for Track 23.

 **CD 1 Track 23**

The <u>girl's</u> job may be <u>full</u> time, whereas the <u>boy's</u> is probably <u>part</u> time.

The <u>girl</u> can learn how to keep <u>customers</u> <u>happy</u>, while the <u>boy</u> has to keep <u>children</u> in <u>order</u>.

He'll probably learn not just to deal with <u>children</u>, but also their <u>parents</u>.

I'd prefer to <u>coach children</u> than work in a <u>restaurant</u> because really I enjoy being in the fresh <u>air</u> more than being <u>indoors</u>.

Grammar
Countable and uncountable nouns

1 1 ~~informations~~ information **2** ~~an advice~~ some / a piece of / a bit of advice **3** ~~a work~~ work / a job
  4 correct **5** ~~accommodations~~ accommodation

6 correct **7** ~~furnitures~~ furniture **8** ~~many damages~~ much damage **9** ~~luggages~~ luggage **10** ~~musics~~ music

2 2 advice; information; knowledge; news **3** damage; transport **4** furniture **5** food **6** homework; work **7** equipment **8** music

3 1 piece/bit **2** number **3** piece/bit **4** piece/bit **5** deal **6** number, amount

Articles

4 2 c **3** f **4** d **5** e **6** a

5 1 the **2** an **3** the **4** – **5** a **6** a **7** – **8** the **9** the **10** – **11** the **12** a

6 1 ~~a latest news~~ the latest news **2** ~~my age~~ the age **3** town ~~the~~ next year **4** useful information on <u>the</u> Internet **5** parking in <u>the</u> city centre **6** are <u>the</u> most effective **7** ~~The money~~ Money **8** listening to ~~the~~ music **9** ~~the~~ foreign cities, ~~the~~ shopping **10** having <u>a</u> wonderful time **11** ~~a~~ plenty of spare time at ~~this~~ the moment, have ~~a~~ dinner **12** ~~an~~ accommodation

Reading and Use of English | Part 2

1 rock climbing, rafting, trekking, planning and setting up a volunteering project

2 1 get **2** If **3** the **4** every **5** So **6** away **7** such **8** just/only

Writing | Part 2 A letter or email

1 *Suggested underlining*
jobs students do, describing, in your country, problems, best way to find a good student job

4 1 *It's good* … indicates that he is answering the email + being friendly; *I hope* … rounds off the email in a friendly way. In the exam, both these sentences will make the email sound more authentic.
2 The first sentence of each paragraph tells us the subject of the paragraph.

5 ~~restaurans~~ restaurants, ~~easely~~ easily, ~~studing~~ studying, ~~wich~~ which, ~~payed~~ paid, ~~usefull~~ useful, ~~becaus~~ because, ~~corses~~ courses, ~~especialy~~ especially, ~~advertisment~~ advertisement

6 embarrassing, opportunity, comfortable, grateful, environment, necessary, beginning, communicate, excellent, forward, prefer, received, recommend, which

7 *Suggested underlining*
first jobs, describing your first job, or someone you know well, when, what, learned, any problems

8 *Sample answer*
Hi Bob,
It's nice to hear from you again.
My first job, which I did for a month during my last summer holidays, was as a part-time assistant at a shoe shop in my town. I used to work every day from 9 a.m. until lunchtime serving customers. Basically, I had to welcome them to the shop and help them to find the shoes they were looking for.
The job was a good experience because I learned how to deal with customers and help them to make up their minds when they were not sure what they wanted. On days when there weren't many customers I had to tidy the store room, which was quite boring, but I certainly also learned a lot about shoes: which are comfortable, what sort of shoes suit different types of people and so on.
I didn't have any particular difficulties except when dealing with customers who were rude or in too much of a hurry, but I managed to smile just the same.
Good luck with your project!
Louise

Vocabulary and grammar review Unit 5

1 1 get away with **2** put off; got over **3** live up to **4** look back; turned out **5** handed back; pointed out

2 1 learn **2** study **3** teaching **4** join; get to know **5** attend **6** take part

3 1 harder, he would / he'd **2** study abroad, you will become / you'll become **3** she would not / wouldn't attend **4** look after my book **5** knew the answer, I would **6** he wasn't / was not so tired

4 1 preference **2** knowledge **3** behaviour **4** comparison **5** activities **6** assistance **7** measurement **8** ability

Vocabulary and grammar review Unit 6

1 **1** occasion **2** work **3** job **4** occasion **5** fun
6 opportunity **7** funny **8** possibility

2 **1** had such / so much / a lot of fun on **2** have/get/take the/an opportunity to speak **3** have the possibility of studying **4** was much better than **5** with a good/ great deal of **6** on one occasion

3 **1** deal **2** bit/piece **3** bit/piece **4** bit/piece **5** number

4 **1** – **2** a **3** the **4** a **5** – **6** a **7** – **8** a **9** the **10** a
11 a **12** – **13** a **14** an **15** the **16** an **17** –

7 High adventure

Starting off

1 **1** mountain biking **2** rock climbing **3** snowboarding
4 windsurfing **5** canoeing/kayaking **6** parasailing

Listening | Part 2

1 *Suggested answers*
1 a person or group of people **2** a time or place
3 a type of person **4** a type of person **5** a type of
(probably natural) place **6** people, place or thing
7 a title **8** a time (duration) **9** a type of ability or
activity **10** a descriptive adjective / an opinion

3 **1** family **2** (early) 1990s **3** men and women /
women and men **4** specialists **5** mountains or
deserts / deserts or mountains **6** inhabitants
7 South Island **8** ten/10 days
9 staying awake **10** (very) motivating

▶ **CD 1 Track 24**

Gary: … so I'm going to talk to you about adventure
racing as my part of the project. Adventure racing's
a sport you do in teams, and I got interested in this
because I actually took part in one for the first time
last year in the north of England with the rest of my
family, and we were racing against lots of other teams
made up of people of different ages. Anyway, I've
done some research and what I've found out turns
out to be much more interesting than I expected.

The sport's been around for some time. There were
races as far back as a hundred years ago and some
newish ones which were started in the 1970s and
80s, but really people have been doing adventure
racing in large numbers since the early 1990s, and
it's one of the toughest sports you can imagine.
Unlike marathons or pentathlons or those sorts of
things, where the winner's the individual runner
who finishes first, in adventure races the winners are
the first team of four to six people, depending on
the race, to all get over the finishing line together,
and in many races one of the rules is that the team
must be made up of an equal number of men and
women – two or three of each depending on the size
of the team. Anyway, it's not like just going jogging or
running or something like that. These races combine
a mixture of different activities or sports – running,
swimming, kayaking, climbing and cycling to name
just some of them. I've been looking a bit at the teams
who win, and one of the things I've noticed is that the
winning teams tend to contain specialists in different
skills, such as climbing and kayaking, and that seems
to give them an advantage. The races are organised
in all sorts of different places. Occasionally, they're
organised in cities – there's a very famous one which
takes place in Chicago – you know, in North America
– but the majority are held in mountains or deserts.
This apparently heightens the sense of adventure and
actually makes the race more hazardous because the
course runs over an area which has little in the way of
roads, certainly no telephones or hotels, and probably
very few inhabitants, so competitors are really isolated
and on their own. Of course, they do carry a radio so
they can call for help if they run into real trouble. Well,
perhaps it won't surprise you, but I want to do more
of these races, and one of the goals I've set myself
is to go to New Zealand and do one of the most
spectacular races in the world, the South Island Race,
where you run, cycle and kayak for 160 miles through
mountains and down rivers. If that race sounds hard
to you, and I guess it is, remember it only takes about
24 hours to do the whole course. I say 'only' because
some of them go on for as long as ten days. Now that's
really extreme. At the moment, I'd say that two or
three days would be my absolute maximum in terms of
endurance. Competitors have to carry everything they
need with them – clothes, food and drink, the lot – and
if they run out, they just go hungry or thirsty. On long
races, my impression is that the greatest problem is
just staying awake, because there are no fixed times
for breaks, so teams tend to go on racing for as many
hours as they can. In fact, I've heard of people falling

asleep while they're riding a bike and that, as you can imagine, can be really dangerous. Just to finish off, another interesting fact: many people who are at the top of their sport in other fields are now taking part because they find that, rather than competing as individuals as they've done all their lives in sports stadiums and the like, they need to work as a team and help each other, and they find this very motivating. I think there's often quite a learning curve for other sports professionals.

Vocabulary
Verb collocations with sporting activities

1 1 do   **2** going   **3** organised   **4** held   **5** taking part; competing

2 1 organise/hold; compete / take part / enter
2 go; doing/taking   **3** play; play; go

Reading and Use of English | Part 6

2 Para. 2: type of team which is successful; Para. 3: Rebecca's first race; Para. 4: Training for Australia; Para. 5: How they started the race in Australia; Para. 6: their result in the race; Para. 7: conclusion

3 *Suggested underlining*
A Another, his feet   **B** followed them   **C** We won it even so, Eco-Challenge in Australia   **D** His, it
E That (was how much I had prepared)   **F** When I did it   **G** To achieve this

1 G   **2** F   **3** C   **4** E   **5** B   **6** A

Grammar
Infinitive and verb + -ing

1 2 f   **3** g   **4** b, i   **5** i   **6** d   **7** a   **8** c   **9** h   **10** a

2 1 starting   **2** to go   **3** to hold   **4** Training   **5** to get **6** injuring   **7** running   **8** pushing

3 1 to do   **2** to learn   **3** doing   **4** taking part in

5 1 ~~running~~ to run   **2** ~~spending~~ to spend   **3** ~~to live~~ living   **4** ~~to run~~ running   **5** correct   **6** ~~take~~ taking   **7** ~~to win~~ in winning   **8** ~~to sit and read~~ (with) sitting and reading

9 correct   **10** ~~ride~~ riding / ~~for~~ to

Reading and Use of English | Part 4

1 1 A: too many words
B: correct
C: *suggest* is not followed by the infinitive, and the option doesn't use the word given without changing it
D: doesn't use the word given
2 A: correct
B: too many words
C: changes the word given
D: doesn't use the word given

2 1 (in order / so as) to get ready   **2** could not / couldn't help laughing   **3** are not allowed to use

3 1 taking part in   **2** more expensive to hire   **3** to give her a ring/call   **4** succeeded in winning   **5** to lose his temper with   **6** had no difficulty (in) learning

Listening | Part 4

2 *Suggested underlining*
1 try paragliding   **2** choose, in France   **3** advantage of learning, sand dune   **4** spend the first morning **5** started, instructor   **6** when you land, it feels like **7** best reason

3 1 A   **2** C   **3** B   **4** A   **5** B   **6** A   **7** C

▶ **CD 1 Track 25**

Interviewer: So, Hannah, what made you want to go on a paragliding course? It sounds like an extremely risky thing to want to do, even for a journalist like yourself.

Hannah: Well, I thought it was a bit risky too. I mean, as a sports journalist, I spend my life watching people do different sports and I've done a fair number of them myself. It's one of the qualifications for the job, I suppose. Anyway, a couple of years ago, I was actually in Switzerland playing golf with friends. I was researching for an article on golf courses and, you know, golf isn't the most exciting of sports. Anyway, I was looking down the course planning my next shot or something when I saw these paragliders floating down from the heights. I thought to myself, that looks like fun. Perhaps I should have a go at it myself.

Interviewer: So you went on a course in France, I believe.

Hannah: That's right. I'd actually tried to go on a paragliding course in England a few years ago. I'd even paid the course fee – about £500 – but every time I went down to do the course, it was either too windy or it was raining, so in the end I got fed up and asked for my money back. Anyway, looking on the Internet, I found this rather wonderful place, called Dune du Pyla on the coast in south-west France. It's actually the highest sand dune in Europe – and they run courses there. The price was a bit higher with the travel, but it was a really nice place, and since sunshine was almost guaranteed, I went for it.

Interviewer: Great! And can you tell me, are there any advantages to jumping off a sand dune? I imagine it's rather less dangerous than jumping off a mountain, isn't it?

Hannah: Well, it isn't so high – only about 150 metres, in fact – but wherever you fall, it's going to hurt, so from that point of view, it doesn't necessarily make a lot of difference. But the good thing is that the beach guarantees you a relatively soft landing. Too soft if you go off the beach and into the water, because then you'll need rescuing, although there's usually a steady breeze to keep you from going into the sea.

Interviewer: And what's the main difficulty for a beginner? I imagine it's taking off and landing.

Hannah: The major problem for a complete beginner like myself is actually learning how to hold your paraglider up in the air – er, you know, so that both sides open properly. They only allow you to run off the edge and fly when you've mastered that technique, so I didn't get to fly till after lunch on my first day. Getting your paraglider open is quite tricky to start with. It makes you feel a bit silly when you see other people happily flying around below you or above you all morning!

Interviewer: And when you actually start flying, how does your teacher tell you what to do? Does he fly along beside you?

Hannah: No, it sounds a nice idea, and I'd have felt a lot safer if I'd had someone beside me. In fact, I listened to my instructor, Chantalle, through an earphone – she stayed down below and spoke into a small microphone device to tell me what to do. It was generally very quiet, calm and civilised, except when she raised her voice to shout at other flyers to keep away from me. And then you really heard her!

Interviewer: And is landing a problem?

Hannah: Surprisingly not. I was expecting something rather violent – you know, I've come off a horse in my time and that's a lot rougher, I can tell you. This was a relatively soft landing – the sand cushions you a bit – so hardly more of a bump than hopping off a park bench. And you're wearing a helmet, of course, rather like a biker's, so the danger's minimal.

Interviewer: But is it really as safe as you make out?

Hannah: They say it is. I mean, there are a couple of serious accidents every year, but the people I know who do it are very safety-conscious. Most sports, including slow earthbound ones like golf, have some element of risk – I've known a few people get hit by golf balls – some of my own even! Most of all, though, I was taken by the silence. I mean, you're not disturbing anybody in your rather strange eccentric quest for thrills and new sensations. That for me's the best thing and something I've rarely come across before.

Interviewer: Hannah, thank you.

Hannah: A pleasure.

Vocabulary
look, see, watch, listen and *hear*

1 **1** watching   **2** looking; saw   **3** listened   **4** heard

2 **1** looked at   **2** watching   **3** hear   **4** looking at   **5** see   **6** watching **7** hear   **8** listening to

Speaking | Part 3

3 Miguel and Irene did 2, 3 and 4.

 CD 1 Track 26

Examiner: I'd like you to imagine that your college is interested in getting students to do more sport. Here are some ideas they are thinking about and a question for you to discuss. First, you have some time to look at the task. Now talk to each other about why these ideas might encourage students to do more sport.

Irene: So, shall I start? How do you think a visit to the national athletics championship would encourage students to do more sport?

Miguel: Um, well, perhaps seeing elite athletes doing their sports will inspire students to take up the sport and imitate them.

Irene: Yes, and I imagine students would see how fantastic these people look and how much they enjoy the activity.

Miguel: Maybe, but it might only interest some of the students, but not others. And what about a talk by a professional footballer? I suppose that might be interesting because he'll probably describe what life's really like for a footballer and how – what's the word – how glamorous he is.

Irene: I suppose so, but I don't think it would encourage me to start playing football myself. There are lots of people like me who aren't really interested in football at all.

Miguel: Yes, I see what you mean. And what about the next one – a weekend doing adventure sports? That's just the sort of thing I'd enjoy, and I think lots of students would get interested in adventure sports if they tried them.

Irene: That's a good point, and it could be a good, fun weekend, but do you really think many people are going to get involved in adventure sports as a result? They're quite expensive, you know, and you can't do them every day, not living in a big city.

Miguel: That's true – but you can always go to one of those sports centres with a … a climbing wall, I think it's called.

Irene: Maybe, but I don't think it's the same as going to the mountains to do these things, and not everyone can afford to do that. Now, what about a school sports day? To me, that just sounds – mm, what's the word – childish. We used to do sports days at primary school.

Miguel: Well, perhaps this could be organised in a more adult way – you know, with some serious sports for people who were interested and less serious activities for other people. That way everyone could get involved.

Irene: Yes, good idea, and people could be organised into teams and it could all be made quite competitive and enjoyable at the same time. When I think about it, it could be really successful.

Miguel: You're right. And the idea of free membership of a sports club is also a great idea. Hm. Lots of students would be interested in that.

Irene: Yes, but I think that would mainly interest people who already do sports, so I'm not sure it would encourage other people to start.

Miguel: No … unless it was also a social club at the same time. I think that would be extremely effective.

Examiner: Thank you.

4 **suggesting ideas:** Well, perhaps …; I imagine students would see …; What about …?; I suppose it could be …
asking your partner's opinion: How do you think …?; Do you really think …?
agreeing: Yes, and …; Yes, I see what you mean; That's a good point, and …; That's true; Yes, good idea; You're right
disagreeing: Maybe, but …; I suppose so, but …; Yes, but …

Pronunciation: intonation (2)

5.1 ▶ **CD 1 Track 27** See page 81.

Writing | Part 2 An article

1 *Suggested underlining*
college magazine, keep fit, sporting activity, form of exercise you enjoy, how you started, why, recommend it to other people, article

3 running past opponents, scoring points, playing in a team, it's a ball game, running and keeping fit

4 **1** Para. 2   **2** Para. 1   **3** Para. 3

5 **1** Although   **2** Despite   **3** Although   **4** despite   **5** However   **6** although   **7** Despite   **8** However

6 **1** competitive   **2** rough   **3** athletic   **4** opponents   **5** coach   **6** spectators   **7** trophy

8 Dream of the stars

Reading and Use of English | Part 7

2 *Suggested underlining*
1 accept negative comments   **2** learned a lot from people already working   **3** other people's suggestions improve their acting   **4** excited, people watching   **5** planned to enter a different profession   **6** prefers, theatre   **7** *Underline the whole question.*   **8** worried about performing in front of some important people   **9** tried to train, somewhere else   **10** *Underline the whole question.*

3 **1** E   **2** D   **3** E   **4** B   **5** C   **6** C   **7** A   **8** A   **9** D   **10** B

Vocabulary

Verb collocations with *ambition*, *career*, *experience* and *job*

1 **1** pursue **2** achieve **3** offered **4** turn it down
   5 gain

2 **1** experience **2** a job **3** a career **4** an ambition

3 **1** make/pursue **2** achieve/fulfil/realise **3** gain/
   get **4** find / apply for / look for **5** build **6** offers
   7 launches

play, performance and *acting; audience, (the) public* and *spectators; scene* and *stage*

5 **1** plays **2** performance **3** acting **4** stage
   5 an audience

6 **2** play **3** acting **4** performance **5** audience
   6 scene **7** stage **8** spectators

Grammar

at, in and *on* in phrases expressing location

1 **1** in **2** in **3** on **4** at **5** at

2 **1** in **2** on **3** at **4** in **5** at; at; at **6** on **7** in; on
   8 at **9** on **10** in; in

Listening | Part 2

1 *Suggested answers*
   1 a place, noun **2** a feeling, adjective **3** means
   of transport, noun **4** something he didn't bring,
   noun **5** something you learn, noun **6** a place,
   noun **7** noun describing an occupation
   8 subject matter, noun **9** period of time, noun or
   adverb **10** a prize, noun

2 **1** shop **2** nervous **3** hired car **4** tie **5** trivial
   facts **6** Green Room **7** university lecturer
   8 general knowledge **9** two months
   10 (big) television/TV

▶ **CD 1 Track 28**

Julie: So, I'm going to tell you about my dad's ten
minutes of fame. It was when he starred on a TV show
a few years ago and it happened like this. The family
had a small shop just round the corner from where we
live, and one day my aunt was working there on her
own when a TV producer just happened to walk in
and ask her if she'd like to take part in this quiz show
called 'The Big Question'. That was a big show, you
remember, when we were small kids. I suppose he
thought she'd look good on TV, sort of photogenic.
Anyway, when she was asked, she just refused to
even consider it. She said she was afraid she'd get
so nervous that she'd be unable to say a word when
a question came to her! My elder sister, who was
only 11 at the time, told her she should go because
it was the chance of a lifetime, but no one could say
anything that'd make her change her mind. Just by
chance, at that moment, my dad walked in. Well, he
saw his opportunity and offered to go on the show
himself! Anyway, the producer agreed, and a couple
of weeks later, my father took a hired car – because
ours was very old – and he drove to the TV studios.

I don't think he trusted the trains to arrive on time,
but I reckon there must have been quite a chance
he'd get stuck in traffic. You know what it's like
round London. Well, anyway, when he got there,
he suddenly realised that he'd left his tie behind,
so he had to ask the producer if they'd got a spare
one at the studio he could borrow. Anyway, he was
told he didn't need one – or a jacket for that matter
either. Oh, and I forgot to say, he didn't really study
for the show – you know, by reading encyclopedias
and so on. In fact, I don't think we've ever had an
encyclopedia in the house, though I did suggest
buying one for the occasion. I suppose he could've
gone online, but as far as I know, he didn't. He told
me later that the only thing he'd done was what he
always did in the evening, which was read the popular
press that we hadn't sold during the day and pick up
lots of trivial facts.

Anyway, later, what he told me was that before the
show he stood around with the other participants
in somewhere called 'The Green Room', where they
chatted to each other and were given something to
eat and drink, and they got to know each other a bit.

My dad felt a bit intimidated, I think, because the other competitors seemed very confident and looked really keen. My dad was expecting them to be doctors or lawyers or something, but in fact, although one of the women really was a university lecturer, the others were a bus driver and somebody who worked in a bank, so quite a mixture. When the show started, I think my dad felt quite lucky and very surprised to be able to answer his questions, which were all about general knowledge and nothing too specialist, because he actually managed to win. Anyway, he did the show, which was recorded, and all of us were longing to see him in it, especially as we knew he'd won. We thought it'd be broadcast like the following week, so it'd be really up to date, but in fact it came on nearly two months later and we almost missed it because we'd almost forgotten about it by then. But it was good, because for weeks after, people were stopping my dad in the street and saying, 'Didn't I see you on the "The Big Question"?' Finally though, my dad didn't become a millionaire or come home in a sports car unfortunately, but he did win a big television with a wide screen – we've still got it at home, and it's great for the football – and a big fluffy elephant, which he gave to me. They were pretty impressive prizes for us then – well, for me, because I was still quite small. So, that was my dad's ten minutes of fame. I wonder what mine'll be.

Grammar
Reported speech

1 **1** a   **2** b

2 **1** previous night he had seen   **2** she would (get/come) back   **3** would arrive (on/in)
4 wasn't allowed to borrow   **5** (had) made several mistakes   **6** (had) found the play

3 **1** to even consider   **2** to go   **3** if they'd got   **4** buying

4 **1** stealing / that she had stolen   **2** lying   **3** to buy
4 breaking   **5** to visit   **6** to buy   **7** to visit
8 installing   **9** to send   **10** not to use

5 **1** advised him to see   **2** suggested going swimming that   **3** told me to switch off   **4** reminded Natasha to post   **5** of not taking any   **6** to do her best

Reading and Use of English | Part 1

2 Through advertisements

3 **1** B   **2** C   **3** A   **4** C   **5** A   **6** D   **7** D   **8** B

Speaking | Part 4

1 generally speaking, generally, on the whole

> **CD 1 Track 29**
>
> **Examiner:** Do you think schools should teach subjects such as dance, drama or music?
>
> **Antonia:** Well, / I think generally speaking / schools should teach these subjects to small children / so that they can find out / if they like them. / I think these subjects / help children to learn / how to express themselves. / But I don't think generally it's so important for older children / or teenagers to do these subjects because / they tend to have lots of other things to study. / So, / on the whole / I guess these subjects should be / voluntary, / not compulsory / as children get older.
>
> **Examiner:** Peter, do you agree with Antonia?
>
> **Peter:** Generally, yes, but / I feel it's a pity when students / don't have time / for the subjects they enjoy.

2 *Answers and suggested answers*
   1 She talks about teaching young children these subjects and then balances it with *but* and her views on older children and teenagers.
   2 Young children: to discover if they like the subjects and to learn self-expression; Older children and teenagers: so many other subjects to study.
   3 b

Pronunciation: grouping words and pausing (2)

4.2 See recording script for Track 29 above.

5 *Suggested answers*
   1 a compulsory / voluntary activity, develop musical abilities, develop artistic expression, develop their musical knowledge
   2 develop their artistic expression, work in a team
   3 interrupt a film with advertisements, when the film is released
   4 a celebrity, avoid / cause a scandal, disturb / protect someone's privacy, the media, a tabloid (newspaper)
   5 help society develop, make people aware of problems

Writing | Part 1 An essay

1 *Suggested underlining*
famous / film star / both advantages and
disadvantages / media attention / lifestyle /
your own idea

6 2 *Suggested answers*

	advantages (Para. 1)	disadvantages (Para. 2)
1	if actors are well-known, they will be offered more jobs,	film stars have little privacy or time to themselves
2	they live exciting and glamorous lives with plenty of foreign travel and luxury,	people with glamorous lifestyles meet other glamorous people and this can sometimes cause problems with, for example, their family relationships
3	fame and success go together	they have to work very hard to be successful and this may lead to considerable stress

3 The underlined sentences and phrase say what the
paragraph will contain. This helps the reader know
where the essay is going.

4 However, which, Firstly, if, and if, Also, with,
Finally, On the other hand, First, because, Next,
and this, Finally, and this, To conclude, because,
However

5 in the final paragraph

6 It is required by the writing task, which asks *Do
you agree?*

8 *Sample answer*
Many young people's ambition is to go into the music
industry or the theatre. However, careers in these
fields have both advantages and disadvantages.
There are two main advantages to these professions.
Firstly, you can earn a living from a hobby. For
example, if you enjoy playing a musical instrument,
becoming a member of a band or an orchestra
appears to be the perfect job. The second advantage
is that if you are successful, you may become famous,
and people will admire you for your professional
abilities.

However, there are also two disadvantages. Being
well known means that you may have less privacy.
Many actors, for example, are continually followed
by photographers, so they have to be very careful
what they do or say in public. Also, the majority of
actors and musicians do not earn very much money
from their work and may have to teach music or
drama in order to survive.
In my opinion, unless you are very talented, the best
thing is to pursue your music or acting interests as
free-time activities and concentrate on studying for a
safer, more conventional profession instead.

Vocabulary and grammar review
Unit 7

1 1 unpredictable   **2** patience   **3** preparations
4 inexperienced   **5** simply   **6** unwilling   **7** realistic
8 valuable

2 1 taking   **2** to get   **3** to invite   **4** changing
5 to have   **6** stealing   **7** to finish   **8** to become
9 working   **10** asking   **11** working   **12** spending

3 1 aren't allowed / are not allowed to go   **2** to avoid
getting   **3** can't bear windsurfing   **4** you mind
turning   **5** you (may) risk having   **6** no/little point
(in) going

Vocabulary and grammar review
Unit 8

1 1 C   **2** B   **3** A   **4** C   **5** A   **6** D   **7** C   **8** B

2 1 Although / Even though   **2** despite / in spite of
3 While/Whereas   **4** Despite / In spite of
5 However   **6** while/whereas   **7** although / even
though   **8** while/whereas

3 1 of the danger   **2** the tickets were expensive
3 despite not feeling (very)   **4** even though her salary
is   **5** she had slept the / she had been asleep the
6 would call at/after the

10 Spend, spend, spend?

Reading and Use of English | Part 2

2 Local shops: personal service, social relationships, more satisfying experience; Shopping online: discount prices, 24/7 shopping and deliveries

3 **1** which **2** up **3** but **4** According **5** much **6** like **7** as **8** a

Grammar

as and like

1 **1** as **2** like

2 **1** as **2** as **3** as **4** like **5** as **6** as, as **7** as **8** like **9** as, as **10** as

Reading and Use of English | Part 5

3 **1** B **2** D **3** D **4** C **5** C **6** A

4 **1** b **2** b **3** a **4** a **5** b **6** a **7** a **8** a **9** b

Vocabulary

arrive, get and reach

1 **1** get **2** arrived **3** reached

2 **1** reached **2** get **3** gets/arrives **4** get **5** arrived **6** reach

3 **1** safe and sound **2** in time **3** on time **4** shortly **5** unannounced **6** finally

Listening | Part 4

1 & 2 *Suggested answers*
Reasons the interviewees mention: access (station and motorway), good shops, good quality, caters for every taste including people who don't want to shop, family fun, safe and crime free, luxurious surroundings, reduce family conflicts.

▶ **CD 2 Track 07**

Interviewer: Hi! I'm in a new shopping centre with some guys who've been finding out a bit more about the place. Kerry?

Kerry: Yeah – first, let me tell you where it is. You know you'd expect to drive for miles out into the countryside to a place among green fields. When they build them in the country, everyone has to get there by car, but at least then the parking's easy. This new one's taken over some abandoned industrial land on the outskirts of the city and it's pulling in young people, families, everyone, so there's a really great atmosphere.

Interviewer: So why do you think they went for this particular site? Salim?

Salim: Well, apparently, they were offered a place in the country and the plans were approved, but they chose this place for its convenient access from the station and the motorway. The locals did start kicking up a fuss about traffic noise and fumes and that sort of thing, so it took quite a long time to get things started, but they managed to get permission in the end.

Interviewer: But why do you think there are such masses of people here now? What's behind its popularity?

Salim: Well, you see, people don't just come to shop. They come to spend the day. There are tons of good stores with branches here, so even though you end up spending quite a bit, in general the stuff's good quality and there's something here for everyone. It caters for every taste, including people like myself who'd rather not shop at all but would prefer to take in a film or hit the gym instead. So you see lots of families having fun here too, without having to hang around with each other the whole time. Dad goes off to look at sports equipment or electronics, while mum hunts for clothes. You know, that sort of thing.

Interviewer: From where I'm standing now I can see trees and fountains. There are cafés, music for chilling out and even a free fashion show. It's a bit of a change from your normal high street, isn't it?

Kerry: Yeah, it's incredible, isn't it? You know, these places are pretty safe – I mean, I know some rough lads come here, but with all the security staff around, there's never any trouble. But what I really like is that the place feels a bit like a palace. You know, I can spend all day here with my friends surrounded by all this expensive stuff without it costing me a penny. People treat you pretty well and you don't have to spend anything unless you want to.

Interviewer: We're always hearing about families having arguments when they go shopping. Why's that?

Salim: Apparently, it's because they're spending the day together and their tastes in how to spend their free time are different, so they get irritable with each other, and this breaks down into arguments about which shops to go to and so on.

Interviewer: And this place is organised to cater for different tastes, isn't it?

Kerry: Well, yeah, what they've done is organise the shops, cafés and other places so there's a wide range of quite different shops in each section. This means that families can still be fairly close to each other, even though they're up to different things. You know, mum can wander into the clothes shop if that's what she wants to do, while dad can pop into the computer shop next door and the kids can go to a games shop or a music shop. They're all nearby and they can find each other easily.

Interviewer: And what else have they done, Salim?

Salim: Well, they've come up with ways of making shopping less tiring. You know, a day's shopping wears people out. They thought of hiring out small electrically driven cars to shoppers to cut down the amount they walk. They came up against problems of space – there just wasn't enough room for them all – so they also thought about those moving walkways you see at airports and that would've involved redesigning everything. What they actually came up with is a new technology which sends everything you've bought to your exit point, and you just pick it up there.

Interviewer: Awesome. Thanks, Kerry and Salim.

Kerry: Cheers.

4 **1** B **2** C **3** B **4** A **5** A **6** B **7** C

Vocabulary
Phrasal verbs

1 **1** j **2** a **3** g **4** h **5** l **6** k **7** d **8** f **9** c
10 e **11** i **12** b

2 **1** came up with   **2** cut down on   **3** pop into   **4** caters for   **5** hanging around   **6** wore us out   **7** pulling in   **8** taken over   **9** come up against   **10** pick up   **11** been up to   **12** chill out

Grammar
Modals expressing ability

1 **1** d; f   **2** c; g   **3** a; e   **4** b; h

2 **1** were able to   **2** couldn't sleep   **3** could   **4** Can you   **5** could have bought   **6** were able to

3 **1** able to cut down   **2** you could have had   **3** you able to pick up   **4** cannot/can't cater for such

4 **1** ~~can't~~ couldn't   **2** ~~could~~ was able to OR ~~that I could~~ to be able to   **3** ~~can~~ could   **4** ~~could~~ can   **5** ~~can~~ could   **6** ~~could~~ were able to   **7** correct   **8** ~~could~~ can

Speaking | Part 1

2 **1** P   **2** B   **3** P   **4** I

 CD 2 Track 08

Examiner: Peter, what things do you enjoy spending money on?

Peter: Well, like many young people in my country, I'm a big football fan. I support Bayern Munich and I try to go to all their home matches and a few away matches when I don't have too much school work. So that's what I really like spending money on: my season ticket to Bayern.

Examiner: And Irene, what do teenagers in your country typically spend their money on?

Irene: I think it really depends, because girls_and boys typically spend their money a bit differently. I guess girls spend more money on clothes_and magazines, while boys spend more money_on music_and things like football matches. In general though, I think both boys_and girls spend_a lot_of money just going_out to places_and having_a good time.

Examiner: Peter, do you have a favourite shop?

Peter: Hmm, I'd have to think, because I'm not too keen on shopping, actually. Um, there is one shop I really enjoy going to. It's one of a chain of sports shops and what I really like about it is just to wander round and see all the clothes and equipment they sell. I see things for sports I don't do but I'd like to try, and that gives me the idea that one day I could try the sport, when I can afford the clothes and equipment, I mean.

Examiner: Irene. Is there anything you'd like to buy that you can't afford?

Irene: Of course! Lots of things! I mean, I don't have a lot of money. My parents give me an allowance, and other people in my family give me money for my birthday and at other times. At the moment, I'm saving up for a better computer – I'd like to study IT when I go to university.

Pronunciation: linking (1)

4.1 ▶ **CD 2 Track 09** See page 113.

4.2 ▶ **CD 2 Track 10** See page 113.

4.3 1 We don't pronounce final 't's and 'd's when the word which follows begins with a consonant.
    2 We link the word to the following word when the word ends with a consonant and the following word begins with a vowel.

4.5 See recording script for Track 11.

▶ **CD 2 Track 11**

Peter: Hmm, I'd have to think because I'm not too keen on shopping actually. Um, there is one shop I really enjoy going to. It's one of a chain of sports shops and what I really like about it is just to wander round and see all the clothes and equipment they sell. I see things for sports I don't do but I'd like to try, and that gives me the idea that one day I could try the sport, when I can afford the clothes and equipment, I mean.

---

5 1 Peter uses strategy 1; Irene uses strategy 3.

▶ **CD 2 Track 12**

Examiner: Peter, what's shopping like in the area where you live?

Peter: I'm not sure, because I don't do a lot of shopping, at least not where I live. There's a place where they sell snacks and takeaways that I quite like and I've been there a a few times with my mates and I guess the shopping must be pretty good, because my mum and dad do all the shopping locally and they never complain!

Examiner: And Irene, what's shopping like in the area where you live?

Irene: I think it's really good. My dad and I love cooking together at weekends and doing these really exotic dishes, and there are plenty of shops in the area which sell good vegetables, food from different parts of the world, and spices and things, so we can find

---

all our ingredients locally. My dad's a great cook. I'm learning a lot from him and we have a great time together!

Writing | Part 2 A review

1 *Suggested underlining*
website for visitors, visitors to our town, enjoy, place in or near our town, people your age, meeting up, having a good time, review, type of place, what do there, how to find, why recommend

4 *Suggested answers*
Para. 1: Place – Cinecity – activities available
Para. 2: Most popular activities – (mention karaoke)
Para. 3: Location + using the underground
Para. 4: Why I recommend it

5 *Suggested answers*
  2 Apart from three roller coasters, there is a tunnel of horrors, a terror swing and many other rides.
  3 Although the theme park is quite expensive, it's well worth the entrance fee, which includes all the attractions.
  4 If you bring your swimsuit, one of the best attractions is a waterslide, where you slide more than 100 metres into a bubbling pool.
  5 Funtime is about ten kilometres from the town centre, but if you don't have a car don't worry because you can get there by bus.
  6 In fact, taking the bus is probably the best way to avoid parking problems.
  7 I would recommend Funtime because there is such a huge variety of attractions that everyone who goes there will be entertained.
  8 What is more, you can get a weekend pass, which is an entrance ticket for the whole weekend, so you will have time to visit every attraction.

Vocabulary and grammar review Unit 9

1 1 spent **2** have **3** causes **4** pass **5** had
  6 made **7** spent

2 1 may be **2** could just **3** might be doing it **4** very different **5** look **6** appear to **7** look as if
  8 perhaps **9** both

3 1 must have switched **2** can't have turned
3 may not have heard **4** could have left **5** might
answer **6** might have forgotten **7** can't have
forgotten

Vocabulary and grammar review Unit 10

1 1 C **2** B **3** D **4** A **5** C **6** B **7** B **8** A

2 1 was not / wasn't able to finish **2** down (on) the
amount of **3** was/felt so worn out by **4** could not /
couldn't come up with **5** able to pick Paz up
6 get to the cinema until

3 1 as **2** as **3** as **4** as **5** like **6** as **7** as **8** Like
9 like **10** like

11 Medical matters

Starting off

1 1 active **2** workout **3** catch; infection; get over
4 check-up; treatment **5** illness **6** balanced diet;
putting on

2 A 2 **B** 4 **C** 6 **D** 1 **E** 5 **F** 3

3

> ▶ **CD 2 Tracks 13 and 14**
>
> **Speaker A:** I really do believe in a healthy mind in a
> healthy body, so I get up pretty early, about 6.30. /
> I do an hour's workout in the morning before going to
> college, and in the evening, I usually have time for a
> couple of hours' sport, so I really think I'm very fit.
>
> **Speaker B:** I take my health pretty seriously. I think you
> have to. / I visit the doctor regularly once a year for
> a check-up. Once or twice I've needed treatment for
> something she's found, but it's never been anything
> very serious.
>
> **Speaker C:** I think I'm healthy, but then I take good
> care of myself because I believe that old saying:
> 'Everything in moderation'. So / I'm very careful to
> eat a balanced diet – only a little meat and plenty of
> fresh fruit and vegetables – and I'm careful about not
> putting on weight, so I do a reasonable amount of
> exercise as well.

> **Speaker D:** I think I'm pretty healthy. I mean, I have a
> lovely life. I've been retired now for nearly 20 years
> on a nice pension, so no financial problems, and /
> here I am, in my 80s, still quite active – I mean, I go
> shopping, visit my friends and go to the cinema when
> I want to. What more can you ask for?
>
> **Speaker E:** I'm just a naturally happy, relaxed person
> and I think that's a large part of the secret of good
> health. / I never go to the doctor and in fact, I don't
> even know my doctor's name. I'm lucky: I've never
> had a day's illness in my life.
>
> **Speaker F:** Me, healthy? I should think so. I've never
> been stopped from doing anything I want to do
> because of an illness. Of course, / I do catch the
> occasional cold or other infection. I'm a doctor, so
> I can't really avoid them, but I get over them pretty
> quickly and they don't usually stop me going to work.

Listening | Part 3

1 1 five, eight **2** read and think about the meaning of
each option **3** express the same idea

2 1 g **2** d **3** f **4** h **5** c **6** b **7** i **8** e **9** a

3 Speaker 1: surgery, prescribe, treat
Speaker 2: cure(d), diagnose
Speaker 3: examination, vaccination, sick note
Speaker 4: examination
Speaker 5: heal

> ▶ **CD 2 Track 15**
>
> **Speaker 1:** Well, I got to the surgery at a quarter past
> eight for an appointment at eight-thirty, but in fact
> I had to hang around there till nearly half past nine
> to see him, so I was feeling pretty uptight, because
> there were only a couple of other people ahead of
> me. I mean, I only had a sore throat – so I was with
> the doctor for about a couple of minutes. Anyway,
> he said I'd just got a slight infection, which is what I
> was expecting, and he prescribed some antibiotics to
> treat it. But I did find it a bit annoying to have to wait
> so long, especially as I was missing my favourite class
> of the week!
>
> **Speaker 2:** I've been feeling a bit off-colour for some
> time now and I've been to the doctor several times
> to try to get to the bottom of it. Anyway, this time my
> doctor was so sympathetic. She asked me all sorts of
> questions about my medical history and my family

background and she took lots of notes. She spent a really long time and sounded so interested that when I left, I felt almost cured! Not that she was able to diagnose my problem straight away, but she did send me off for tests.

Speaker 3: My mum sent me to see the doctor the other day because I thought I'd got the flu and needed a few days off school. Anyway, the doctor gave me quite a thorough examination and then she told me I was hardly ill at all and that I should've had a vaccination and she refused to give me a sick note. Frankly, I was amazed and pretty annoyed, because I'd been coughing and sneezing all week and feeling very under the weather. Anyway, there was nothing I could do to change her mind, so it was back to school the same morning, worse luck!

Speaker 4: When I went in, my doctor just asked me a few questions but she didn't examine me. Then she prescribed me some pills and said that if the symptoms persisted, I should come back the following week. I told her I wanted a proper examination straight away and I stayed there sitting in my chair. I must say she looked a bit taken aback, but then she got up from her desk and came and gave me a really thorough check-up. In the end, she apologised and said she'd been up all night on duty in the local hospital.

Speaker 5: I went to my doctor complaining of neck pains and I was there for what seemed like hours. She gave me a very complete check-up and took ages over it. She looked at my neck, asked about my medical history and my daily routine. Then she told me that the problem was probably caused by too much sitting in front of the computer studying, and with a good rest, my neck would heal itself. She suggested that I should take time off to unwind and then the pain would just go away on its own.

4 1 G   2 E   3 C   4 A   5 B

Reading and Use of English | Part 6

2 *Suggested answers*
Para. 2: tutorials; Para. 3: extra degree + academic research; Para. 4: being a clinical student; Para. 5: clinical training, part of a team; Para. 6: conclusion

3 *Suggested underlining (and reference)*
B opportunity to do many things (what things?)
C the different specialties (what specialties?), the

three years (which three years?)   **D** the team (what team?)   **E** I was expected to work extremely hard (by whom? where?)   **F** These well-known people (who are they?)   **G** This usually consisted of (what does *this* refer to?)

4 1 G   2 A   3 F   4 C   5 B   6 D

Vocabulary
Idiomatic expressions

1 c   **2** a   **3** d   **4** b   **5** e   **6** f   **7** g

Grammar
Relative pronouns and relative clauses

1 **1** who   **2** whose   **3** which   **4** where   **5** that/which

2 **1** D   **2** ND   **3** D   **4** D   **5** ND   **6** D

3 3, 4 and 6

4 3 and 4, because they are the object of the clause.

5 **1** ~~it's~~ which is   **2** ~~his~~ whose   **3** ~~that~~ which   **4** ~~you wrote it last week~~ you wrote last week   **5** ~~who you met them this morning~~ who you met this morning   **6** ~~that~~ what   **7** ~~which it has a view~~ which has a view   **8** ~~which it won~~ which won

6 **2** He studied hard for his maths exam, which he found quite easy. / He found the maths exam, which he studied hard for, quite easy.
3 The man (who/that) they sold the car to is a taxi driver. / They sold the car to a man who is a taxi driver.
4 Could you give me the newspaper (which/that) you were reading earlier?
5 That white house over there is the house where he was born.
6 Where's the envelope (which/that) I put the money in?
7 Every morning I go running in the park with Patricia, whose brother you know.
8 Karen and Teresa, whose dog we're looking after, are on holiday in the Caribbean at the moment.

Reading and Use of English | Part 3

1 **1** a

2 **1** b   **2** a

3 *mis-*: it means 'to do something wrongly'

4 **1** undo   **2** disappoint   **3** misuse   **4** untie   **5** misspell
6 disappeared   **7** undressed   **8** misinformed

5 inability/disability, disagreement, disappear,
unaware, uncertain, inexperienced, informal,
unhappiness, unhelpful, dishonest, dislike/unlike,
impatient, unpredictable, unreliable, dissatisfied/
unsatisfied, misunderstand

6 **1** unexpected   **2** security   **3** occasionally   **4** medical
5 height   **6** calculation   **7** assistance   **8** uneasy

Speaking | Part 2

1 *Suggested answers*
When you need time to think: Let me think …
When you can't think of the word: I can't think of
the word, but it's a type of …; I'm not sure how to say
it, but it's used for …; What's the word?
When you've made a mistake: I'm sorry, what I
meant was …; No, I mean …; What I want to say is
that …; Sorry, I mean …

2   Antonia did all the things on the checklist.

> ▶ **CD 2 Track 16**
>
> **Examiner:** In this part of the test, I'm going to give each
> of you two photographs. I'd like you to talk about
> your photographs on your own for about a minute,
> and also to answer a question about your partner's
> photographs. Antonia, it's your turn first. Here are
> your photographs. They show people doing healthy
> activities. I'd like you to compare the photographs
> and say how important you think each activity is for
> staying healthy. All right?
>
> **Antonia:** OK, so <u>both</u> photographs show people
> doing things which might be good for their <u>sanity</u>,
> sorry, I mean their <u>health</u>. In the <u>first</u> photo, I can see
> someone who looks as if he's, <u>what's</u> the <u>word</u>, he's
> <u>commuting</u> by <u>bicycle</u> in busy <u>traffic</u>. So, he's getting
> some exercise, which must be good for his general
> fitness. In the second photo, there are some young
> people who are doing some cooking – well,

> not exactly cooking because what they're doing is
> preparing a salad. What I want to say is, they're going
> to eat something quite healthy. I mean, it's not like
> eating pizza or hamburgers. So both photos show
> people doing something healthy – getting exercise
> and eating a good deeat, sorry, I mean diet. I'd say
> there are some <u>problems</u> with the idea of <u>health</u> in
> the <u>first</u> photo because of the <u>danger</u> from the <u>traffic</u>,
> especially because he's cycling in the <u>night</u>, I mean
> in the <u>dark</u>, and the, I can't think of the <u>word</u>, but it's
> a type of <u>smoke</u> which comes from the <u>cars</u>. On the
> other hand, if you live in the <u>city</u>, it's a good way of
> getting <u>exercise.</u> In the <u>second</u> photo, the kids should
> <u>remember</u> that they need to eat a <u>mixed</u>, um, sorry, a
> <u>balanced</u> diet, not just <u>salad</u> and <u>fruit</u>.
>
> **Examiner:** Thank you.

3 **2 a** Nikolai   **b** Miguel   **c** Peter

Pronunciation: intonation (3)

4.1 Underline on: both, sanity, health, first, what's,
word, commuting, bicycle, traffic

> ▶ **CD 2 Track 17** See page 125.

4.2 The speaker is more confident in a). Her voice falls
on the final stressed words. In b), her voice rises
on the final stressed words, making her sound
uncertain.

> ▶ **CD 2 Track 18** See page 125.

4.4 Stressed words: a) problems, health, first, danger,
traffic, night, dark, word, smoke, cars
b) city, exercise, second, remember, mixed,
balanced, salad, fruit

> ▶ **CD 2 Track 18** See page 125.

4.5 b Her voice falls at the end of phrases.

5

> ▶ **CD 2 Track 20**
>
> **Examiner:** In this part of the test, I'm going to give each
> of you two photographs. I'd like you to talk about
> your photographs on your own for about a minute,
> and also to answer a question about your partner's
> photographs. Student A, here are your photographs.
> They show people doing healthy activities. I'd like you
> to compare the photographs and say how important
> you think each activity is for staying healthy. All right?

6

 CD 2 Track 21

Examiner: Student B, which activity would you prefer to do to keep healthy, and why?

7

 CD 2 Track 22

Examiner: Now, Student B, here are your photographs. They show two people with minor health problems. I'd like you to compare the photographs and say why it is important for these people to deal with their problems. All right?

8

 CD 2 Track 23

Examiner: Student A, which problem do you think is more serious, and why?

Writing | Part 1 An essay

2 *Suggested underlining*
Modern lifestyles, endanger, health, food, physical activity

3 *Suggested answers*
Strong points: it's clearly written in paragraphs, covers the notes in the task and is well linked together.
Weak points: the writer's opinion is not clear; there is no concluding paragraph.

5 **1** c **2** a **3** b

6 **1 a** an explanation of healthy aspects of our lifestyles
b things which stop people living healthily
2 *However* (contrasts information and ideas with the paragraph before)

7 *Suggested answers*
1 There are three main advantages to living in the country.
2 On the other hand, there are several disadvantages to a country life.
3 Exercise is important for the following reasons.
4 However, there are some dangers attached to taking too much exercise.

9 *Sample answer*
Everyone knows that a healthy lifestyle when you are young is essential for staying well as you grow older. However, many young people could do more to look after their health.
Like everyone else, teenagers should take regular exercise. In my town, perhaps half of the young people I know go running or play football or do some other form of sport, but I have many friends who only do sporting activities occasionally, so they are not really fit. This may be because of the amount of time they have to spend studying.
On the other hand, it is becoming increasingly common for young people to have a healthy balanced diet, so few people become overweight, which is very important.
Finally, perhaps because cigarettes are very expensive, few of my friends smoke and this is becoming less fashionable. As a result, I think my generation is healthier than my parents were at my age.
In conclusion, I believe young people take a reasonable amount of care of themselves although many would benefit from following a regular exercise routine.

12 Animal kingdom

Listening | Part 1

1 **1** eight; different subjects **2** twice **3** read but don't hear **4** in the question only **5** after you have heard the whole of each piece

2 **1** C **2** B **3** C **4** B **5** C **6** B **7** A **8** A

CD 2 Track 24

Presenter: One. You overhear a conversation between two women about animals.

Woman 1: My husband is always saying he wishes he had a dog to go for walks with.

Woman 2: So do you think you'll get one?

Woman 1: I don't know. It's such a commitment. I mean, we'd have to take him with us on holiday, that sort of thing, so I'd rule that out. Then my daughter, Patsy, would really like to have a horse.

Woman 2: But that's even more of a commitment!

Woman 1: I know, which is why I hesitate. I mean, we'd have to supervise her quite closely to start with to make sure she was safe. At least until we know she can control it.

Woman 2: What about a cat?

Woman 1: Well, they're definitely the easiest to look after – not that they interest any of us. In the end, we'll probably let Patsy have her choice – it's a mistake to deny your kids the things they really want.

Presenter: Two. You hear part of a television programme about zebras.

Man: To us, every zebra looks alike. During their migration, all the stripes form a confusing pattern which helps to protect them from lions and other predators. But while to the untrained eye they appear identical, each individual's pattern is unique, helping others to identify them. While male zebras have wider, darker, shinier stripes than females, at a distance and in a mass they may all look the same. Even so, young zebras who go off to play can always pick out their mums from thousands of others.

Presenter: Three. You overhear a conversation between a boy and a girl about birds in the girl's garden.

Boy: Hi, Trish. What've you been up to this weekend?

Girl: Oh, I've been helping my mum in the garden a lot of the time.

Boy: So working hard.

Girl: You're telling me! But my mum loves the garden, especially the birds which go there to feed – you know, on insects and berries and things.

Boy: Uh-huh.

Girl: Yeah, and when she's not in the garden, she's watching the birds from the window and keeping an eye out to make sure the cats don't get them. There are tons of cats in our neighbourhood, and she hates the idea of them catching birds And she's right: dead birds are gross!

Presenter: Four. You overhear part of a conversation in which a girl and a boy are talking about dogs.

Girl: Have you still got that lovely dog of yours?

Boy: We sure have!

Girl: Lucky you! I wish I had a dog.

Boy: Well, he is nice to look at, but we really got him to protect us from burglars. Probably, if we lived in a safer area, we wouldn't have bought one. In fact, he barks at everything, which doesn't make us very popular in the neighbourhood.

Girl: Well, all that barking might prevent a burglary. And I bet he's good fun to play with, isn't he?

Boy: Sure, he's great for that, but I'd be happier if my parents had bought a house in the country. Then we wouldn't worry about neighbours or burglars.

Presenter: Five. You hear a woman giving part of a lecture about animal rights.

Woman: It would, I think, be ignorant to suggest that zoos no longer serve a useful purpose. Many of them do quite valuable work conserving rare species. What I do think, and I'm sure you'd agree with me here, is that those old-fashioned zoos which were designed and built in the 19th century just don't give animals enough space. There's no feeling that animals are in a natural habitat. Those zoos should all be closed and banned, while the more modern zoos need to be strictly inspected to make sure that the animals are kept in the best conditions possible. That way diseases and other problems can be avoided.

Presenter: Six. You hear a girl talking about some animals she worked with.

Girl: Last summer, you see, I went as a volunteer on a wildlife conservation project in Africa and I was asked to look after these young lions which had been orphaned – you know, they'd lost their mother. It's curious, because I'd expected to feel quite anxious – I mean, they're dangerous animals, aren't they? In fact, after I'd spent a few days feeding the lion cubs and playing with them, we had a very easy, comfortable relationship. I had to keep an eye on them as well, because they could be quite rough when playing with each other, and we didn't want them to harm each other, but I never felt they were going to attack me.

Presenter: Seven. You hear a boy talking about hippos.

Boy: I always thought hippos spent their day hiding in the water, but then I saw this awesome video on YouTube of a guy on holiday in South Africa. It shows him walking along a river bank – he's being filmed by a friend – when suddenly there's this crashing noise in the grass and a hippo rushes out. Wow! Anyway, the guy just manages to leap to one side and run while his mate screams and drops the camera. If he hadn't reacted quickly, the hippo would've killed him, for sure, trampled him underfoot!

Anyway, I got sort of interested in this and Googled 'hippos'. Apparently, they get nervous if someone walks between them and the river, which is their natural habitat, and more people are killed by hippos in Africa every year than by any other animal just because they get between the hippo and the water.

6 *Suggested answers*
Para. 1: Type of flat and location; my present accommodation; advantages of ideal flat
Para. 2: Characteristics of flat
Para. 3: Conclusion: room for my things

7 1 from 2 where 3 own 4 what/whatever/anything 5 have 6 few 7 long 8 If

8 1 T 2 T 3 F 4 T (She would like to live alone and make her own decisions, she enjoys art and reading, she wants an active social life.) 5 T 6 F (She lives in a suburban house.)

14 Fiesta!

Starting off

1 1 celebrate 2 dress up; perform 3 march; commemorate 4 hold 5 play/perform 6 gather round 7 let off 8 wearing

2 1 traditional costumes, parade 2 fireworks
3 traditional costumes, traditional dances
4 street parties 5 parade, bands, traditional costumes 6 disguises, traditional costumes
7 street performers

Listening | Part 4

1 *Suggested answers*
fire-eating, sword-swallowing, acrobatics, clowning and comedy, singing and dancing, etc.

2 1 an interview 2 seven 3 underline; different words 4 general ideas

3 1 C 2 A 3 B 4 A 5 B 6 A 7 C

 **CD 2 Track 36**

Interviewer: Today, *South Live* visits the Winchester Hat Fair, an extravaganza of processions, fireworks and street theatre with performers from as far away as Australia and Brazil. And we're talking to a veteran performer at the Hat Fair, Mighty Max, who's come all the way from Canada once again. Max, why's the festival called the Hat Fair?

Max: Well, I've been told the fair was only started in 1974, as a way of encouraging street performers like myself. It's not like there was one of those great old

English traditions like hat-making here in the 18th century or anything. Lots of people come to the fair wearing funny hats because of the name, but that wasn't its origins. It was always supposed to be about street theatre, and during the act, a hat's passed around so that the performers can earn a living. And that, in fact's where the name comes from.

Interviewer: Now, you've been coming here for a number of years. Why do you keep coming back?

Max: Oh, I just love performing here. There are artists like myself from all over the world who come here year after year and we get to know each other and stuff. But what makes the fair unique is the people who come to watch. You know, you jump around and do your act and they really let their hair down and love it when they're being made a fool of by other people in the crowd, and that's really what makes it such fun.

Interviewer: So, how did you get involved in street theatre in the first place?

Max: Well, you know, my big ambition was to be a circus performer. I actually went to quite a famous circus school in Canada as a teenager where I was taught juggling and acrobatics. My dad was dead against it, but he paid for the classes on the condition that I went to university and got myself what he called 'a proper education' as well. It was ironic, really, because if I hadn't gone to university, I might never have got into street theatre. You see, every vacation I had time to travel and I found I could pay for my trips by performing in the street and making a collection.

Interviewer: Fantastic! Your act's been attracting tremendous crowds here in Winchester. How do you explain your popularity?

Max: Well, it's a combination of high-class acrobatics, which are performed without any safety equipment at all, and some quite risky stunts. So it gives the audience a thrill – you know, there are plenty of oohs and aahs, but what I think really gets them into it is that I make them laugh. There's a lot of clowning in my act, which builds a sort of two-way communication with the audience, and they love it.

Interviewer: The acts I've seen around town today have been pretty high quality. Why do you think that is?

Max: Well, there's plenty of money around this town, which certainly attracts the best people from around the world, but you know none of that money's going to go in the hat unless your act's a good one, and so you've gotta make sure people have a really great time watching you work.

Interviewer: And what difficulties do street performers come up against?

Max: Good question. In a place like Winchester, not many. We're each given a place and a time to perform. As you've seen, I attract pretty large crowds and I need plenty of space, so narrow streets are no good. Here, we're given the main shopping street, which is fine. In other places, if you haven't got permission, you'll get moved on by the police, so I always make sure that I've got the right permits. Actually, what's most likely to stop things happening the way you'd like is usually the rain or even just a bit of drizzle. I mean, where's the fun in standing around getting cold and wet?

Interviewer: None at all. But what about Winchester? Has the Hat Fair put the town on the map? I mean, does it attract a lot of visitors from outside?

Max: I'm not the best person to answer that question. I get the impression that the people who come here tend to be from the surrounding area rather than tourists. What Winchester gets is an amusing party – something they can do which is just plain fun. They gather in the streets and parks and unwind and forget about the other stuff in their lives.

Interviewer Mighty Max, thank you, and I hope the rest of the fair goes well for you.

Max: Thank you.

4 *Suggested answers*
Some residents may find it annoying or noisy, it interrupts traffic, it may encourage pickpockets and crime, it may be dangerous, etc.

Grammar

The passive

1 **a** I've been told; was only started   **b** 's passed around
c they're being made a fool of   **d** was taught
e we're given; you'll get moved on

2 *Suggested answers*
2 a   **3** b, d, first passive in e
4 a, b, c, d, first passive in e

3 **1** was founded in 1904   **2** has been stolen   **3** is being repaired   **4** 've been given a place on the course   **5** would have been told off (by the teacher)

4 **2** ~~going to replace~~ going to be replaced
3 ~~that is going to be read on the radio a short story by Agatha Christie~~ that a short story by Agatha Christie is going to be read on the radio
4 ~~if the computer weren't invented~~ if the computer hadn't been invented
5 ~~which has already published~~ which has already been published
6 ~~had been using~~ have been used
7 ~~nobody wants to be revealed their private life in public~~ nobody wants their private life to be revealed in public

5 People go out in the open air in the early morning; they eat traditional foods; young men swim in the Nile.

6 **1** are   **2** as   **3** been   **4** to   **5** is   **6** being   **7** by   **8** have   **9** doing   **10** were (**Note:** *fish* can be singular or plural, depending on the context.)

7 **1** a
2 A large number of contemporary Egyptian traditions are said to have their origins in very ancient times.
For example, offerings of fish are believed to have been made to the ancient gods …
3 It is said that a large number of contemporary Egyptian traditions have their origins in very ancient times.
For example, it is believed that offerings of fish were made to the ancient gods.

8 **1** It is thought that Sham el Nessím marked the start of the spring festival in ancient Egypt.
2 It is known that eating salted fish was a custom of the ancient Egyptians.
3 Five thousand people are reported to have joined in the festivities.
4 Our festival is said to have the best fireworks in the world.

9 **1** is believed to have originated   **2** expected to be chosen   **3** said that the festival is   **4** is thought to be   **5** is considered to be   **6** to go/date back more than

Reading and Use of English | Part 6

1 **1** F, there are six questions and no example.   **2** T
3 T   **4** T   **5** F, read the completed text again to check
it reads logically.

3 *Suggested answers*
Para. 2: people who attend festival; Para. 3: where
the festival happens; Para. 4: the writer's arrival;
Para. 5: the market; Para. 6: festival activities

4 & 5
1 F   **2** C   **3** E   **4** G   **5** B   **6** A

Reading and Use of English | Part 3

1 **1** tourists   **2** dancers

2 **1** designer   **2** novelist   **3** researcher   **4** collector
5 survivor   **6** consultant   **7** motorist   **8** comedian
9 salesman/saleswoman/salesperson   **10** specialist
11 refugee

3 **1** eight   **2** Read the whole text quickly before
answering the questions   **3** think what type of word
you need   **4** Make sure you have spelled the word
correctly   **5** read the completed text again

4 **1** organisers   **2** arrangements   **3** activities
4 participants   **5** surrounding   **6** energetic
7 unusually   **8** impressive

Speaking | Parts 3 and 4

1 **1** T   **2** T   **3** T   **4** F (You should try to reach a
decision, but if you don't succeed, don't worry.)   **5** F
(It's the same subject.)   **6** T   **7** T   **8** T

2

 CD 2 Track 37

Examiner: I'd like you to imagine that you are going to
do a class project on festivals around the world. Here
are some aspects of festivals that you could investigate
and a question for you to discuss. First, you have some
time to look at the task. Now talk to each other about
what you can learn about different places by studying
these aspects of their festivals.

3

 CD 2 Track 38

Examiner: Now you have about a minute to decide
which two aspects you and your partner should work
on together.

4

 CD 2 Track 39

Antonia: OK, let's see. What can we learn from studying
their clothes and costumes?

Nikolai: Well, I think it shows how people carried things
in the past.

Antonia: You mean, how they dressed in the past?

Nikolai: Yes, thank you, how they dressed in the past,
which perhaps shows the sorts of activities they did
and the materials which were available.

Antonia: That's a very good point. I think we can learn
how they looked in the past, um …

Nikolai: Good, and let's move on to the food. What do
you think we can learn from that?

Antonia: Um, well, I, um …

Nikolai: I mean, do you think it might show us what
food was available on special occasions in the past?

Antonia: Yes, it probably does, so we learn about their
past eating habits and perhaps also what they think is
still important in the present.

Nikolai: Yes, that's a good idea, because of course
festivals change–

Antonia: You mean they evolve.

Nikolai: Exactly, they evolve. I mean I think of festivals
in my country, and the customs and traditions have
changed over the years.

Antonia: An interesting point. You must have studied
this a bit.

Nikolai: Yes, I have a bit. What about dances and
music?

Antonia: Well, I think this is very interesting because I'm
a musician myself–

Nikolai: Oh great!

Antonia: –and I think by playing and listening to
traditional festival music we learn about what is
beautiful, what was lovely in the past can still be
lovely for us today.

Nikolai: I think that's a very interesting general idea
about all these things: that festivals really, what's the

word, join the best things from the past with the best things in the present–

Antonia: In other words, combine the best things!

Nikolai: Exactly, combine the best things, so that, so that, um …

Antonia: So that, well, that's evolution, isn't it? Where the best aspects of the past and present take us on to the future.

Nikolai: Well, we're getting philosophical. I think what you're trying to explain is how we can learn about progress by looking at how festivals change, um, but what about these special activities …

5 1 *Suggested answer:* They help each other with vocabulary and expressing ideas, they react to what the other person says, they invite the other person to speak and express ideas. This is important because they should try to have a normal conversation.

   2 a That's a very good point; Yes, that's a good idea; An interesting point; I think that's a very interesting general idea …

     b You mean … ; In other words

     c I mean … ; So that (i.e. Antonia continues where Nikolai dries up)

6

▶ **CD 2 Track 40**

Examiner: I'd like you to imagine that you are doing a class project on celebrations. Here are some things people often celebrate and a question for you to discuss. First, you have some time to look at the task. Now talk to each other about how you think we should celebrate each of these occasions.

7

▶ **CD 2 Track 41**

Examiner: Now you have about a minute to decide which two occasions it would be most enjoyable to celebrate.

8

▶ **CD 2 Track 42**

Examiner: Antonia, how do towns and cities benefit from having festivals and other celebrations?

Antonia: Hmm, that's a good question. Some people say that it's good for, what's it called, community spirit, but I think the main benefit is for local businesses because tourists and visitors are attracted to the town to spend their money in shops and restaurants.

Examiner: Nikolai, do you agree with Antonia?

Nikolai: Yes, I partly agree with her. I think in many places, people spend a lot of time during the year preparing for their festival and I think it really encourages a feeling of cooperation and a community feeling.

Examiner: And, Nikolai, do you think festivals should be organised more for tourists or more for local people?

Pronunciation: improving fluency

9.1–9.3 See underlining, pause marks and intonation arrows in recording script for Track 43.

▶ **CD 2 Track 43**

Hmm, ↗ that's a good question. ↘ / Some ↗ people say that it's good for, / what's it called, / community spirit ↘ , / but ↗ I think the main benefit is for local businesses ↘ / because tourists and visitors are attracted ↗ to the town ↗ / to spend their money in shops and restaurants ↘ .

9.4 See underlining, pause marks and intonation arrows in recording script for Track 44.

▶ **CD 2 Track 44**

Yes, I partly ↗ agree with her./ I think in many ↗ places / people spend a lot of time during the year preparing ↗ for their festival / and I think it really encourages a feeling of cooperation ↘ /and a community ↘ feeling.

Writing | Part 1 An essay

1 1 140—190 words; 40   2 you must deal with three points, one of which is your own idea   3 write a plan first   4 you should check your answer carefully when you finish

2 *Suggested underlining*
better, live, recorded music, quality, convenience, own idea

5 *Suggested answers*
Although people can listen to recorded music on their music players when they are travelling, working or studying, music festivals and concerts are becoming more and more popular. This is because, I believe, they offer two main advantages.

The first advantage is that the quality of the sound is much better at live concerts, where the music and voices come directly from the performers. This makes it a much more emotional experience because you have direct contact with the musicians and you react to them and they react to you.

The second advantage is the atmosphere. Instead of listening to a recording alone on your personal music player, you are listening with a huge crowd of people and enjoying the music together. This means it is a social as well as an artistic experience.

The main disadvantage is that you cannot listen to live music whenever you want, like you can on a personal device. Apart from that, the noise from the audience sometimes spoils the quality of the sound. In my opinion, however, the best way to enjoy music is the spontaneous atmosphere of a live concert. It is more exciting because you are surrounded by other enthusiastic fans, who are dancing with you.

6 2 music festivals and concerts are becoming more and more popular
   3 music festivals and concerts
   4 the music and voices come directly from the performers
   5 listening to music at live concerts
   6 the musicians
   7 you are listening with a huge crowd of people and enjoying the music together
   8 The main disadvantage is that you cannot listen to live music whenever you want
   9 a live concert

7 1 It/This   2 it   3 they   4 they; that   5 that
   6 This   7 that/this   8 that/this

8 *Sample answer*
   Films are now as popular as they were when my grandparents were young. However, now with the Internet and DVDs we have much more choice about when and where we can watch them.
   There's no doubt that for the quality of the experience the best place to watch a new film is in the cinema on a wide screen with excellent sound. What is more, you can see films which everybody is talking about because they have recently been released.
   The drawback of the cinema is the price of the tickets. If they were cheaper, people would go more often. This means that if, like me, you are a cinema fanatic, you have little choice but to download films

off the Internet if you want to see them frequently. I also believe that it is worth seeing a good film several times. The best way of doing this is to see them first in the cinema, then later at home, when you can appreciate other aspects of the film.
For me, however, going to the cinema is a far better experience because it is a special location.

Vocabulary and grammar review Unit 13

1 1 space   2 room   3 place   4 location   5 area
   6 place   7 space   8 square   9 room   10 place

2 1 since   2 made   3 out   4 than   5 enough   6 there
   7 one   8 What

3 1 have a tennis court built   2 you have the car checked   3 to clear up   4 have to do   5 are supposed to pay   6 are not allowed to speak

Vocabulary and grammar review Unit 14

1 1 lawyer   2 possibilities   3 especially   4 suitably
   5 responsibility   6 appropriately   7 demanding
   8 representative

2 1 reputation   2 safety   3 amazement
   4 dissatisfaction   5 existence   6 truth   7 width
   8 addition   9 difference   10 obligations

3 1 is expected to arrive   2 was broken into by
   3 are reported to have   4 has not / hasn't been serviced for   5 is said to be living   6 cake was / had been eaten

Writing reference

Part 1

1 **1** All young people, continue at school or college until, 18, qualifications for jobs, don't like school, own idea

2 Para. 1: should continue (my opinion)
Para. 2: jobs more specialised; more training gives more opportunities
Para. 3: many students don't enjoy school; prefer to earn money
Para. 4: uninterested students cause problems; should only study things they like after 16
Para. 5: shouldn't leave school at 16; miss opportunities

3 visit, your own country, foreign country, holiday, more interesting, cheaper, own idea

4 *Suggested answer:* The sample answer in Exercise 2 deals with each of the notes in order in separate paragraphs. This essay deals with each of the three notes in paragraph 2 with reasons for staying in your own country, and then each of the notes again in paragraph 3 with reasons for travelling abroad.

Part 2

Emails and letters

1 **1** An English friend, Pat
2 What a typical family in your country is like, and how family life is changing
3 Pat's project, different countries

2 **1** families close, spend time together, help each other, get together at weekends, young people live with parents until 25 or 30, get married in 30s, have children quite late, just one or two children
2 women now work, men take more responsibility in home, people richer, more families moving to larger houses in suburbs

Reports

1 **1** formal (It's for your teacher.)
2 The style is formal; Yes, it answers the question.

Reviews

1 **1** what it's about, why we would all enjoy it
2 everyone would enjoy, film or book
3 readers of your school's English-language magazine, i.e. other students; in the magazine

2 **1** first and second paragraphs
2 third paragraph

Articles

1 **1** g **2** d **3** e **4** h **5** c **6** b **7** a **8** i **9** f

2 Para. 1: c Para. 2: b Para. 3: a Para. 4: d

Speaking reference

2 e **3** c **4** h **5** f **6** g **7** d **8** i **9** a

Acknowledgements

I would like to thank everyone who has worked on this book and with particular thanks to Brigit Viney, Nicholas White, Catriona Watson-Brown and Lynn Townsend for their enthusiasm, expertise, eye for detail and sheer dedication. Thanks also to Elizabeth Knowelden and Linda Matthews (production controllers), Hilary Fletcher and Kevin Brown (picture researchers), Michelle Simpson (permissions clearance controller), Leon Chambers (audio producer), Mark Oliver (sound engineer) and Lucy Mordini (proofreader). Special thanks to the design team at Wild Apple Design. Thanks also to David Castillo, Academic Co-ordinator at the Asociación Cultural Peruano Británica, el Británico, for his feedback and advice on text on pages 154 and 155.

My warmest thanks also to Paz for her enthusiasm, encouragement, support together with constant feedback from using the First Edition. This book is for her, with love.

Guy Brook-Hart, Valencia, January 2014

The author and publishers are grateful to the following for reviewing the material:
Kathryn Alevizos (UK), Petrina Cliff (UK), Allan Dalcher (Switzerland), Lyubov Figurovskaya (Russia), Robert Islam (Italy), Fiona Mulcahy (Spain), Peter Sunderland (UK).

This product is informed by the English Vocabulary Profile, built as part of English Profile, a collaborative programme designed to enhance the learning, teaching and assessment of English worldwide. Its main funding partners are Cambridge University Press and Cambridge English Language Assessment and its aim is to create a 'profile' for English linked to the Common European Framework of Reference for Languages (CEF). English Profile outcomes, such as the English Vocabulary Profile, will provide detailed information about the language that learners can be expected to demonstrate at each CEF level, offering a clear benchmark for learners' proficiency. For more information, please visit www.englishprofile.org

Development of this publication has made use of the Cambridge English Corpus (CEC). The CEC is a computer database of contemporary spoken and written English, which currently stands at over one billion words. It includes British English, American English and other varieties of English. It also includes the Cambridge Learner Corpus, developed in collaboration with the University of Cambridge ESOL Examinations. Cambridge University Press has built up the CEC to provide evidence about language use that helps to produce better language-teaching materials.

The *Cambridge Advanced Learner's Dictionary* is the world's most widely used dictionary for learners of English. Including all the words and phrases that learners are likely to come across, it also has easy-to-understand definitions and example sentences to show how the word is used in context. The *Cambridge Advanced Learner's Dictionary* is available online at dictionary.cambridge.org. © Cambridge University Press. Reproduced with permission.

The author and publishers acknowledge the following sources of copyright material and are grateful for the permissions granted. While every effort has been made, it has not always been possible to identify the sources of all the material used, or to trace all copyright holders. If any omissions are brought to our notice, we will be happy to include the appropriate acknowledgements on reprinting.

pp. 10–11: Telegraph Media Group Limited for the adapted article 'Can teenagers ever be tamed' by Rachel Carlyle, *The Daily Telegraph* 27 July 2005; p. 41: adapted article 'Food Glorious food' by Rose Prince, *The Daily Telegraph* 16 September 2006; p. 132: adapted article 'Circus life, Neil and Toti Gifford run the show' *The Daily Telegraph* 6 July 2005. Copyright © Telegraph Media Group Limited 2013.
p. 20: Little, Brown Book Group Limited and United Agents for the adapted text 'My first bike' from *Long Way Round* by Ewan McGregor and Charley Boorman. Copyright © Long Way Round Limited 2004. Used by permission of Little, Brown Book Group Limited and United Agents.
p. 35: Guardian News & Media Limited for the adapted article (a) 'My crap holiday, so that's why the beach was deserted' by Pauline Vernon *The Observer* 22 November 2009; p. 35: adapted article (c) 'My crap holiday, then I woke up and smelt the coffee' by Cat Donovan *The Observer* 26 April 2009; p. 35: adapted article (d) 'My crap holiday, nightmare trek with sudden movements' by Graham Whitely *The Observer* 15 April 2007; p. 144: adapted article 'My kitchen' by Tamsin Blanchard *The Observer* 10 June 2001. Copyright © Guardian News & Media Limited 2009, 2007, 2001.
p. 35: Ninemsn Pty Ltd for the adapted text (b) 'Reader story: attacked by a bear' by Sandy Henderson, 18 June 2009. © 1997–2013 Ninemsn Pty Ltd – All rights reserved.
p. 47: Manchester Evening News for the adapted article 'Moso Moso' by Kyla *Manchester Evening News* 17 August 2005. Used by permission of Manchester Evening News.
p. 64: Lucy Irvine for the heavily adapted text 'Lucy's first job' from *Runaway*. Copyright © Lucy Irvine 1987. Used by kind permission of Lucy Irvine.
p. 69: The Independent for the adapted article 'The teenagers who may yet bring big society to life' by Oliver Wright *The Independent* 28 August 2012; p. 120: for the adapted article 'What's it like to study medicine?' by Fred Clough *The Independent* 14 September 2012. Copyright © The Independent.
p. 76: Adventure Sports Journal for the adapted text 'Are you ready for an adventure race?' by Rebecca Rusch *Adventure Sports Journal 2006*. Used by permission of Adventure Sports Journal.
p. 85: The Scotsman Publications Limited for the adapted text 'City's Student actors reach a crucial stage' by Adrian Mather, *The Evening News* 29 March 2006. Used by permission of The Scotsman Publications Limited.
p. 90: The Daily Mail for the adapted article 'You Tube "geek" one day, millionaire celeb the next' from *This is Money online* 10 December 2010. Copyright © Associated Newspapers Limited.
pp. 96–97: Mihaly Csikzentmihalyi for the adapted text 'The secrets of happiness' *The Times* 19 September 2005. Used by kind permission of Mihaly Csikzentmihalyi.
p. 108: Teen Ink for the text 'My greatest influence' by Rachel S., Colleyville, Texas. Reproduced with permission of Teen Ink.
pp. 134–135: News Syndication for the adapted article 'Surviving an animal attack' *The Sunday Times* 23 April 2006. Copyright © News Syndication.

p. 141: Darley and Anderson Literary Agency for the adapted text 'My new home in Venice' from *The Cemetery of Secrets* by David Hewson, published by Pan Macmillan 2009. Reproduced with permission.

The authors and publishers acknowledge the following sources of copyright material and are grateful for the permissions granted. While every effort has been made, it has not always been possible to identify the sources of all the material used, or to trace all copyright holders. If any omissions are brought to our notice, we will be happy to include the appropriate acknowledgements on reprinting.

The publisher has used its best endeavours to ensure that the URLs for external websites referred to in this book are correct and active at the time of going to press. However, the publisher has no responsibility for the websites and can make no guarantee that a site will remain live or that the content is or will remain appropriate.

Photo acknowledgements:
p. 8 (t): Altrendo/Juice Images/Corbis; p. 8 (c): PhotoAlto sas/Alamy; p. 8 (bl): CREATISTA/Shutterstock; p. 8 (br): Simon Dack/Alamy; p. 9 Muskopf Photography LLC/Alamy; p. 10: Denkou Images/Alamy; p. 11 (bl): Jon Feingersh/Blend Images/Getty Images; p. 11 (bc): aberCPC/Alamy; p. 11 (tc): Beyond Fotomedia GmbH/Alamy; p. 11 (bl): Jon Feingersh/Blend Images/Getty Images; p. 11(br): Piti Tan/Shutterstock; p. 12: Catchlight Visual Services/Alamy; p. 13 (l): Kiselev Andrey Valerevich/Shutterstock; p. 13 (c): Yellow Dog Productions/Getty Images; p. 13 (r): Beyond Fotomedia GmbH/Alamy; p. 15 (bl): Brian Kinney/Shutterstock; p. 15 (tl): vario images GmbH & Co.KG/Alamy; p. 15(br): JOHN KELLERMAN/Alamy; p. 16: Pressmaster/Shutterstock; p. 17: Ocean/Corbis; p. 18 (tl): Kevin Dodge/Corbis; p. 18 (tr): Corbis; p. 18 (c): sainthorant daniel/Shutterstock; p. 18 (bl): carlo dapino/Shutterstock; p. 18 (bc): Oliver Furrer/Alamy; p. 18 (br): Blue Jean Images/Alamy; p. 19: Horizons WWP/Alamy; p. 20 (tl): Sven Arnstein/Bravo/NBCUniversal Photo Bank/Getty Images; p. 20 (background): Athanasia Nomikou/Shutterstock; p. 22: iStockphoto/Thinkstock; p. 23: Erin Patrice O'Brien/Getty Images; p. 24 (t): Lifesize/Thinkstock; p. 24 (b): Kathrin Ziegler/Taxi/Getty Images; p. 25 (t): KidStock/Blend Images/Corbis; p.25 (b): Outdoor-Archiv/Alamy; p. 27: Design Pics/Superstock; p. 30 (1): Bananastock/Jupiterimages/Thinkstock; p. 30 (2): Justin Kase zsixz/Alamy; p. 30 John Henshall/Alamy (3): p. 30 (4): Ableimages/Superstock; p. 30 (5): NAN728/Shutterstock; p. 32: Marka/Superstock; p. 33: Ben Pipe/Robert Harding World Imagery/Corbis; p. 34: iStockphoto/Thinkstock; p. 35 (tl): Atlantide Phototravel/Corbis; p. 35 (bl): David Lobos/Shutterstock; p. 35 (tr): Tips Images/Superstock; p. 35 (br): Ed Darack/Science Faction/Corbis; p. 37 (t, b): Británico Language School, Peru;; p. 39: AKP Photos/Alamy; p. 40 (1): Topic Photo Agency/Corbis; p. 40 (2): Maximilian Weinzierl/Alamy; p. 40 (3): nexus 7/Shutterstock; p. 40 (4): MARGRIT HIRSCH/Shutterstock; p. 40 (5): Mauro Fermariello/Science Photo Library; p. 41: Photo by www.katiestandke.com; p. 42: H. Mark Weidman Photography/Alamy; p. 44 (l): Paul Simcock/Corbis; p. 44 (br): Lee Foster/Getty Images; p. 45 (l): photopalace/Alamy;p. 46 (l): Eyecandy Images/Alamy; p. 46 (r): Británico Language School, Peru; p. 47: Sakarin Sawasdinaka/Shutterstock; p. 48 (l): Ilpo Musto/Rex Features; p. 48/49 (t): Andersen Ross/Cultura/Getty Images; p. 48/49 (b): blickwinkel/Alamy; p. 52 (tl): wavebreakmedia/Shutterstock; p. 52 (tc): Martin Shields/Alamy; p. 52(tr): Ocean/Corbis; p. 52 (cl): Fuse/Getty Images; p. 52 (bl): Corbis/Superstock; p. 55 (l): Lou Linwei/Alamy; p. 55 (br): Peter Lopeman/Alamy; p. 57 (t): VanHart/Shutterstock; p. 57 (A): Samuel Borges Photography/Shutterstock; p. 57 (B): iStockphoto/Thinkstock; p. 57 (C): Blend Images/Alamy; p. 57 (D): Big Cheese Photo/Superstock; p. 58: Golden Pixels LLC/Alamy; p. 61: Hugh Sitton/Corbis; p. 62 (tl): Radius Images/Corbis; p. 62 (tr): SHOUT/Alamy; p. 62 (c): Radius Images/Alamy; p. 62 (bl): Jaimie Duplass/Shutterstock; p. 62 (br): Merijn van der Vliet/E+/Getty Images; p. 64: iStockphoto/Thinkstock; p. 65: Courtesy of Summer Isles Hotel, Achiltibuie; p. 66 (t): Juan Silva/Getty Images; p. 66 (b): Carlos Davila/Alamy; p. 67 (t): wavebreakmedia/Shutterstock; p. 67 (b): Big Cheese Photo/Superstock; p. 68 (l): Frank Perry/AFP/Getty Images; p. 68/69 (background): Radoman Durkovic/Shutterstock; p. 69 (br): Siegfried Kuttig - RF -2/Alamy; p. 70 (l): Photofusion Picture Library/Alamy; p. 70 (r): Monkey Business Images/Shutterstock; p. 74 (1): Cultura Limited/Superstock; p. 74 (2): LumiImages/Mauritius/Superstock; p. 74 (3): Konstantin Shishkin/Shutterstock; p. 74 (4): Giles Bracher/Robert Harding World Imagery/Corbis; p. 74 (5): photofriday/Shutterstock; p. 74 (6): SFL Travel/Alamy; p. 75: Arnd Hemmersbach/NordicFocus/Getty Images; p. 76/77 (t): imago/Actionplus; p. 77 (insert): Hyoung Chang/The Denver Post via Getty Images; p. 80 (t): Nicolas Thibaut/Photononstop/Getty Images; p. 80 (background): Protasov

AN/Shutterstock; p. 81: Nick Hanna/Alamy; p. 82: John Powell/Rex Features; p. 84 (t): Cris Bouroncle/AFP/Getty Images; p. 84 (cl): Gabriel Bouys/AFP/Getty Images; p. 84 (cr): Kevin Winter/Getty Images; p. 84 (b): PictureGroup/Rex Features; p. 85: Dean Conger/Corbis; p. 87 (t): John Eder/Getty Images; p. 87 (c): Jung Yeon-Je/AFP/Getty Images; p. 87 (b): Nathan King/Alamy; p. 88 (t): ITV/Rex Features; p. 88 (b): Olga Martynenko/Shutterstock; p. 90: William Perugini/Shutterstock; p. 91 (tl): Ariel Skelley/Blend Images/Corbis; p. 91 (bl): Multi-bits/Getty Images; p. 91 (tr): MBI/Alamy; p. 91 (br): Helene Rogers/Art Directors & TRIP; p. 92: Johannes Eisele/AFP/Getty Images; p. 96 (tl): Corbis; p. 96 (tr): Edith Held/Corbis; p. 96 (bl): Ocean/Corbis; p. 96 (br): Daniel Koebe/Corbis; p. 97: plearn/Shutterstock; p. 98: Tim McPherson/Cultura/Image Source; p. 102 (tl): picturegarden/The Image Bank/Getty Images; p. 102 (bl): Juice Images/Alamy; p. 102 (tr): Cusp/Superstock; p. 102 (br): Pegaz/Alamy; p. 103: Rechitan Sorin/Shutterstock; p. 104 (tl): Blend Images/Superstock; p. 104 (bl): jay goebel/Alamy; p. 104 (tr): Peter Dazeley/Getty Images; p. 104 (br): Sharie Kennedy/LWA/Corbis; p. 106 (tl): B.O'Kane/Alamy; p. 106 (bl): vnlit/Shutterstock; p. 106 (tc): NetPhotos/Alamy; p. 106 (bc): Maxx-Studio/Shutterstock; p. 106 (tr): Andrey Armyagov/Shutterstock; p. 106 (br): Ken Welsh/Alamy; p. 109: Konstantin Yolshin/Alamy; p. 111: Photononstop/Superstock; p. 112: Peter Cade/Getty Images; p. 114 (t): John Giustina/Getty Images; p. 114 (c): BrandX Pictures/Jupiterimages/Thinkstock; p. 114 (b): Flirt/Superstock; p. 115: VikaSuh/Shutterstock; p. 116 (t): iStockphoto/Thinkstock; p. 116 (b): Erik Isakson/Corbis; p. 118 (tl): Blend Images/Superstock; p. 118 (tc): Denkou Images/Alamy; p. 118 (tr): michaeljung/Shutterstock; p. 118 (bl): F1online/Getty Images; p. 118 (bc): IgorGolovniov/Shutterstock; p. 118 (br): Chris Rout/Alamy; p. 119: LWA/Dann Tardif/Getty Images; p. 120/121 (t): T. Mayer/Corbis; p. 120/121 (background): iStockphoto/Thinkstock; p. 121 (tc): iStockphoto/Thinkstock; p. 124 (t): Peter Cade/Iconica/Getty Images; p. 124 (b): Tim Hall/cultura/Corbis; p. 125 (t): Image Source/Getty Images; p. 125 (b): ColsTravel/Alamy; p. 126 (tl): Tim Graham/Getty Images; p. 126 (tr): wavebreakmedia/Shutterstock; p. 126 (bl): YanLev/Shutterstock; p. 126 (br): Jacek Chabraszewski/Shutterstock; p. 127: Jacek Chabraszewski/Shutterstock; p. 128 (tl): Peter Llewellyn/Alamy; p. 128 (tc): Markus Altmann/Corbis; p. 128 (tr): Stock Connection/Rex Features; p. 128 (cl): Images of Africa Photobank/Alamy; p. 128 (bl): imagebroker/Alamy; p. 128 (br): Ulrich Doering/Alamy; p. 130 (l): Jason Prince/Shutterstock; p. 130 (r): Thomas Dressler/Gallo Images/Getty Images; p. 132: Mary Evans/Retrograph Collection; p. 133 (l): Corey Hochachka/Design Pics/Rex Features; p. 133 (r): Ryouchin/The Image Bank/Getty Images; p. 134 (t): Karine Aigner/National Geographic/Getty Images; p. 134 (b): Michael Redmer/Visuals Unlimited/Corbis; p. 135 (tl): Steven Kazlowski/Science Faction/Superstock; p. 135 (bl): Jenny Zhang/Shutterstock; p. 135 (tc, tl): Británico Language School, Peru; p. 136: imagebroker/Alamy; p. 137: F. J. Fdez. Bordonada/age fotostock/Superstock; p. 140 (1): Tupungato/Shutterstock; p. 140 (2): blickwinkel/Alamy; p. 140 (3): Derek Meijer/Alamy; p. 140 (4): iStockphoto/Thinkstock; p. 140 (5): picturesbyrob/Alamy; p. 140 (6): Greg Balfour Evans/Alamy; p. 141 (tl): Bridge of Sighs, Venice (La Riva degli Schiavoni) c.1740 (oil on canvas), Canaletto, (Giovanni Antonio Canal) (1697-1768) / Toledo Museum of Art, Ohio, USA /Giraudon / The Bridgeman Art Library; p. 141 (r): Honza Hruby/Shutterstock; p. 142: Patrick Lane/Blend Images/Getty Images; p. 144: Peter Horree/Alamy; p. 145 (t): moodboard/Alamy; p. 145 (b): OJO Images Ltd/Alamy; p. 146 (t): Blend Images/Superstock; p. 146 (b): frans lemmens/Alamy; p. 147 (t): Christine Webb/Alamy; p. 147 (b): Sandra Baker/Alamy; p. 148: Image Source/Corbis; p. 149: Steven Miric/Getty Images; p. 150 (t, 2): KIKE CALVO/VWPICS/Alamy; p. 150 (1): Kirsty McLaren/Alamy; p. 150 (3): Richard Wayman/Alamy; p. 150 (4): Peter Titmuss/Alamy; p. 150 (5): Geoff Burke/Getty Images; p. 150 (6): Curt Wiler/Alamy; p. 151: Gregory Davies/Alamy; p. 153: Megapress/Alamy; p. 154: Bjorn Svensson/Alamy; p. 155: Bjorn Svensson/Alamy; p. 156: Alfredo Maiquez/age fotostock/Superstock; p. 157: Blend Images/Image Source; p. 158 (l): Jilly Wendell/Getty Images; p. 158 (r): Erik Isakson/Corbis; p. 159 (t): Norbert Schaefer/Corbis; p. 159 (b): Stockbroker/Superstock; p. 196 (t): Pablo Paul/Alamy; p. 196 (b): Norbert Schaefer/Alamy.

Cover image by biletskiy/Shutterstock.

Illustration acknowledgements
Jeff Anderson (Graham-Cameron Illustration) pp. 23, 63, 122(b), 147. John Batten (Beehive Illustration) pp. 21, 89, 107. Moreno Chiacchiera (Beehive Illustration) p. 56. Fay Dalton (Pickled Ink) p. 108. Elisabeth Eudes-Pascal (Graham-Cameron Illustration) pp. 43, 101. Roger Harris (NB Illustration) p. 86. Dusan Paulic (Beehive Illustration) pp. 17, 22, 36, 99, 122(t). David Shephard (The Bright Agency) pp. 9, 45, 78, 79, 100. Sue Woollatt (Graham-Cameron Illustration) p. 26.

Installing the CD-ROM on your hard disk

- Insert the Complete First Second Edition CD-ROM into your CD/DVD drive. The CD-ROM will automatically start to install. Follow the installation instructions on your screen.
- On a Windows PC, if the CD-ROM does not automatically start to install, open My Computer, locate your CD/DVD drive and open it to view the content of the CD-ROM. Double-click on the CompleteFirstApplication file. Follow the installation instructions on your screen.
- On a Mac, if the CD-ROM does not automatically start to install, double-click on the CompleteFirst CD icon on your desktop. Double-click on the CompleteFirstApplication file. Follow the instructions on your screen.

System requirements

Windows

- Intel Pentium 4 2GHz or faster
- Microsoft® Windows® XP (SP3), Vista® (SP2), Windows 7®, Windows 8®
- Minimum 1GB RAM
- Minimum 750MB of hard drive space
- Adobe® Flash® Player 10.3.183.7 or later

Mac OS

- Intel CoreTM Duo 1.83GHz or faster
- Mac OSX 10.5 or later
- Minimum 1GB RAM
- Minimum 750 of hard drive space
- Adobe® Flash® Player 10.3.183.7 or later